XML For Dummies, 3rd Edition

D0472793

Basic Schema Declarations

An XML Schema document is built of a series of declarations that provide very detailed information about your data structure.

Declaration Name	Purpose	Syntax
Schema	Identifies the language the schema uses	`<xsd:schema xmlns:xsd="http://www.w3.org/2001/XMLSchema">`
Element	Defines an element	`<xsd:element name="name">`
Attribute	Defines an attribute	`<xsd:attribute name="name" type="type">`
Complex type	Defines an element with a required attribute	`<xsd:complexType>`
Simple type	Creates a constrained datatype	`<xsd:simpleType>`
Sequence compositor	Specifies that attributes within a complex type must be listed in order	`<xsd:sequence>`
Choice compositor	Specifies that any one of the attributes within a complex type can be used	`<xsd:choice>`
All compositor	Specifies that any or all attributes within a complex type can be used	`<xsd:all>`
Annotation	Provides additional information about the schema	`<xsd:annotation>`
Documentation	Provides human-readable information within an annotation	`<xsd:documentation>`
Application information	Provides computer-readable information within an annotation	`<xsd:appInfo>`

Browser Support for XML and Style Sheets

The support across Web browsers for XML and style sheets — CSS, XSL, and XSL-FO — is varied and less-than dependable. Knowing which browsers support which specifications can help you decide how to use XML and Web browsers in your XML solution.

Browser	XML?	CSS1?	CSS2?	XSLT 1.0?	XSL-FO?
Amaya 5.3	Yes	Yes	No	No	No
Internet Explorer 5.5	Yes	Yes	Yes	Yes	No
Internet Explorer 6.0	Yes	Yes	Yes	Yes	Yes
Mozilla 0.9.9	Yes	Yes	Yes	No	No
Netscape Navigator 6.2	Yes	Yes	Yes	Yes	No
Opera 6.1	Yes	Yes	Yes	No	No

Common Reserved Characters

There are reserved characters that can't appear in an XML document unless they're part of a CDATA section. Replace them with the character references in your content.

Character	Reference
<	`&lt;`
>	`&gt;`
&	`&amp;`
'	`&apos;`
"	`&quot;`

XML For Dummies®, 3rd Edition

Cheat Sheet

The First (and Last) Word on Valid versus Well-Formed

A **valid document** must conform to the rules in its DTD or schema, which define what elements can appear in the document and how elements may nest within one another. A **well-formed** document must have these characteristics:

- ✔ All beginning and ending tags match up. In other words, opening and closing parts must always contain the same name in the same case: `<tag>` . . . `</tag>` or `<TAG>` . . . `</TAG>`, but not `<tag>` . . . `</TAG>`.
- ✔ Empty elements follow special XML syntax, for example, `<empty_element/>`.
- ✔ All attribute values occur within single or double quotation marks: `<element id="value">` or `<element id='value'>`.
- ✔ All entities (DTDs) or fixed values for datatypes sets (schemas) are declared.

Rules for Creating DTD Elements

You may create many rules in your DTD that govern how elements can be used in an XML document.

Symbol	Meaning	Example
`#PCDATA`	Contains parsed character data or text	`<element (#PCDATA)>`
`#PCDATA, element-name`	Contains text and another element; `#PCDATA` is always listed first in a rule	`<element (#PCDATA, child)*>`
`, (comma)`	Must use in this order	`<element (child1, child2, child3)>`
`| (pipe bar)`	Use only one element of the choices provided	`<element (child1 | child2 | child3)>`
`element-name (by itself)`	Use one time only	`<element (child)>`
`element-name?`	Use either once or not at all	`<element (child1, child2?, child3?)>`
`element-name+`	Use either once or many times	`<element (child1+, child2?, child3)>`
`element-name*`	Use once, many times, or not at all	`<element (child1*, child2+, child3)>`
`( )`	Indicates groups; may be nested	`<element (#PCDATA | child)*>` or `<element ((child1*, child2+, child3)*	child4)>`

Hungry Minds, the Hungry Minds logo, For Dummies, the For Dummies Bestselling Book Series logo and all related trade dress are trademarks or registered trademarks of Hungry Minds, Inc. All other trademarks are the property of their respective owners.

Hungry Minds™

Copyright © 2002 Hungry Minds, Inc.
All rights reserved.

Item 1657-4.

For more information about Hungry Minds, call 1-800-762-2974.

For Dummies: Bestselling Book Series for Beginners

TM

BESTSELLING BOOK SERIES

References for the Rest of Us! ®

Are you intimidated and confused by computers? Do you find that traditional manuals are overloaded with technical details you'll never use? Do your friends and family always call you to fix simple problems on their PCs? Then the For Dummies® computer book series from Hungry Minds, Inc. is for you.

For Dummies books are written for those frustrated computer users who know they aren't really dumb but find that PC hardware, software, and indeed the unique vocabulary of computing make them feel helpless. For Dummies books use a lighthearted approach, a down-to-earth style, and even cartoons and humorous icons to dispel computer novices' fears and build their confidence. Lighthearted but not lightweight, these books are a perfect survival guide for anyone forced to use a computer.

"I like my copy so much I told friends; now they bought copies."

— *Irene C., Orwell, Ohio*

"Quick, concise, nontechnical, and humorous."

— *Jay A., Elburn, Illinois*

"Thanks, I needed this book. Now I can sleep at night."

— *Robin F., British Columbia, Canada*

Already, millions of satisfied readers agree. They have made For Dummies books the #1 introductory level computer book series and have written asking for more. So, if you're looking for the most fun and easy way to learn about computers, look to For Dummies books to give you a helping hand.

Hungry Minds™

1/01

by Ed Tittel, Natanya Pitts, and Frank Boumphrey

Hungry Minds™

Best-Selling Books • Digital Downloads • e-Books • Answer Networks • e-Newsletters • Branded Web Sites • e-Learning

New York, NY ◆ Cleveland, OH ◆ Indianapolis, IN

XML For Dummies,® 3rd Edition

Published by
Hungry Minds, Inc.
909 Third Avenue
New York, NY 10022
www.hungryminds.com
www.dummies.com

Copyright © 2002 Hungry Minds, Inc. All rights reserved. No part of this book, including interior design, cover design, and icons, may be reproduced or transmitted in any form, by any means (electronic, photocopying, recording, or otherwise) without the prior written permission of the publisher.

Library of Congress Control Number: 2002100344

ISBN: 0-7645-1657-4

Printed in the United States of America

10 9 8 7 6 5 4 3 2 1

3O/SS/QV/QS/IN

Distributed in the United States by Hungry Minds, Inc.

Distributed by CDG Books Canada Inc. for Canada; by Transworld Publishers Limited in the United Kingdom; by IDG Norge Books for Norway; by IDG Sweden Books for Sweden; by IDG Books Australia Publishing Corporation Pty. Ltd. for Australia and New Zealand; by TransQuest Publishers Pte Ltd. for Singapore, Malaysia, Thailand, Indonesia, and Hong Kong; by Gotop Information Inc. for Taiwan; by ICG Muse, Inc. for Japan; by Intersoft for South Africa; by Eyrolles for France; by International Thomson Publishing for Germany, Austria and Switzerland; by Distribuidora Cuspide for Argentina; by LR International for Brazil; by Galileo Libros for Chile; by Ediciones ZETA S.C.R. Ltda. for Peru; by WS Computer Publishing Corporation, Inc., for the Philippines; by Contemporanea de Ediciones for Venezuela; by Express Computer Distributors for the Caribbean and West Indies; by Micronesia Media Distributor, Inc. for Micronesia; by Chips Computadoras S.A. de C.V. for Mexico; by Editorial Norma de Panama S.A. for Panama; by American Bookshops for Finland.

For general information on Hungry Minds' products and services please contact our Customer Care Department within the U.S. at 800-762-2974, outside the U.S. at 317-572-3993 or fax 317-572-4002.

For sales inquiries and reseller information, including discounts, premium and bulk quantity sales, and foreign-language translations, please contact our Customer Care Department at 800-434-3422, fax 317-572-4002, or write to Hungry Minds, Inc., Attn: Customer Care Department, 10475 Crosspoint Boulevard, Indianapolis, IN 46256.

For information on licensing foreign or domestic rights, please contact our Sub-Rights Customer Care Department at 212-884-5000.

For information on using Hungry Minds' products and services in the classroom or for ordering examination copies, please contact our Educational Sales Department at 800-434-2086 or fax 317-572-4005.

For press review copies, author interviews, or other publicity information, please contact our Public Relations Department at 317-572-3168 or fax 317-572-4168.

For authorization to photocopy items for corporate, personal, or educational use, please contact Copyright Clearance Center, 222 Rosewood Drive, Danvers, MA 01923, or fax 978-750-4470.

LIMIT OF LIABILITY/DISCLAIMER OF WARRANTY: THE PUBLISHER AND AUTHOR HAVE USED THEIR BEST EFFORTS IN PREPARING THIS BOOK. THE PUBLISHER AND AUTHOR MAKE NO REPRESENTATIONS OR WARRANTIES WITH RESPECT TO THE ACCURACY OR COMPLETENESS OF THE CONTENTS OF THIS BOOK AND SPECIFICALLY DISCLAIM ANY IMPLIED WARRANTIES OF MERCHANTABILITY OR FITNESS FOR A PARTICULAR PURPOSE. THERE ARE NO WARRANTIES THAT EXTEND BEYOND THE DESCRIPTIONS CONTAINED IN THIS PARAGRAPH. NO WARRANTY MAY BE CREATED OR EXTENDED BY SALES REPRESENTATIVES OR WRITTEN SALES MATERIALS. THE ACCURACY AND COMPLETENESS OF THE INFORMATION PROVIDED HEREIN AND THE OPINIONS STATED HEREIN ARE NOT GUARANTEED OR WARRANTED TO PRODUCE ANY PARTICULAR RESULTS, AND THE ADVICE AND STRATEGIES CONTAINED HEREIN MAY NOT BE SUITABLE FOR EVERY INDIVIDUAL. NEITHER THE PUBLISHER NOR AUTHOR SHALL BE LIABLE FOR ANY LOSS OF PROFIT OR ANY OTHER COMMERCIAL DAMAGES, INCLUDING BUT NOT LIMITED TO SPECIAL, INCIDENTAL, CONSEQUENTIAL, OR OTHER DAMAGES. FULFILLMENT OF EACH COUPON OFFER IS THE SOLE RESPONSIBILITY OF THE OFFEROR.

Trademarks: For Dummies, Dummies Man, A Reference for the Rest of Us!, The Dummies Way, Dummies Daily, and related trade dress are registered trademarks or trademarks of Hungry Minds, Inc. in the United States and other countries, and may not be used without written permission. All other trademarks are the property of their respective owners. Hungry Minds, Inc. is not associated with any product or vendor mentioned in this book.

Hungry Minds™ is a trademark of Hungry Minds, Inc.

About the Authors

Ed Tittel is a 20-year veteran of the computing industry. After spending his first seven years in harness writing code, Ed switched to the softer side of the business as a trainer and talking head. A freelance writer since 1986, Ed has written many hundreds of magazine and Web articles and worked on more than 100 computer books, including numerous *For Dummies* titles on topics that include several Windows versions, NetWare, HTML, XHTML, and XML.

Ed still teaches on computer topics for the NetWorld + Interop trade show, and speaks at various conferences on markup languages, IT certification, and security topics. In his spare time, Ed likes to shoot pool, cook, and spend time with his trusty Labrador retriever, Blackie. Contact Ed at etittel@lanw.com.

Natanya Pitts is a writer, trainer, and Web guru in Austin, Texas. She has extensive experience in technical training and writing, including overseeing the development of the materials for live and Web-based training environments.

Natanya has authored, co-authored, or contributed to more than a dozen Web and Internet related titles; the most recent include *XML in Record Time*, *HTML 4 For Dummies*, 2nd Edition, *The XML Black Book*, 2nd Edition, *CIW Site Designer Certification Bible*, and *The Internet for iMacs For Dummies*. She also played an instrumental role in the development and launch of Austin Community College's Webmaster Certification program, where she led both in-class and online courses for over two years.

Natanya has taught classes on HTML, Dynamic HTML, and XML at several national conferences, including Macworld Expo, Networld + Interop, and HPWorld, as well as at the NASA Ames Research Center.

Frank Boumphrey is relatively new to the *For Dummies* team but not new to XML. His rather disreputable career has included punch-card programming, jumping out of airplanes and hoping he didn't get shot on the way down (or when he landed), and spells as a Doctor of Medicine and, more recently, as a medical document consultant.

He is a past member of several W3 working groups, and a past-president of the HTML Writers Guild. He is currently CEO of Netforce Inc., a Cleveland-based Internet company that survived the dot-bomb fallout!

Dedication

To the heroes at the W3C and OASIS, sung and unsung, especially members of the many XML working groups who have made the world (or the Web, at least) a better place through their tireless efforts.

Acknowledgments

Ed Tittel: Writing a book is like staging a play — there's a lot more going on behind the scenes that you might ever guess. That's why the names on the cover of a book represent just the barest suggestion of all the people who actually lay hands on such a project. There are so many people involved, in fact, that it's far too easy to fail to thank all parties responsible by name, which is my goal here. If I do fail to give credit where credit is due, please forgive me; the fault is entirely mine, and reflects only ignorance and not ingratitude on my part!

To begin with, I'd like to thank my colleagues and co-workers who contributed so much to this and previous editions of the book. Frank Boumphrey's chapters stood the tests of time and intense scrutiny better than any others in this book; thanks again for an excellent job! Thanks also to Mary Burmeister, who revised much of the book's contents in addition to managing the whole revision process for LANWrights. You continue to amaze me with your interest, enthusiasm, and ever-growing knowledge base. And finally, thanks to Lucinda Dykes, Natanya Pitts, and Chelsea Valentine for their contributions to this book, past and present.

Next, my thanks to the team at Hungry Minds. Starting with Mary Bednarek and Andy Cummings, thanks for fitting us into your most recent pub plan so early. Next, thanks to Bob Woerner and Nicole Haims for working out the details involved in squeezing a 15 week project into a paltry 9 weeks.

Thanks also to Don Jones, for tech editing our sometimes recondite work. And finally, thanks yet again to my agent extraordinaire, Carole McClendon from Waterside Productions, for making this and so many other worthwhile books possible.

On a personal note, I'd like to extend 83rd birthday greetings to my Mom, Cecilia Katherine Kociolek Tittel, and to thank her again for instilling the life-long interest in language and learning that's made it possible for me to practice my chosen livelihood. Thanks also to my sister, Kat, her husband Mike, and offspring Helen and Colin for reminding me that family is indeed the center of the universe. Thanks to my best friend and partner in crime, Dr. Robert R. Wiggins, for showing me that there's more to life than work, and more to work than life! And finally, to Leah and Chloe — the brightest stars in the sky where I live — I hope we have many more years of shared love and laughter ahead of us.

Natanya Pitts: Once again, I have to give many thanks to Ed Tittel for giving me the opportunity to collaborate with him on this book. We've been doing this for quite a while now, and we're only getting better with time. A huge thanks also goes to Mary Burmeister for keeping me in line and on deadline. Special thanks to my beloved husband Robby. All things are easier because you are part of my life. And finally, thanks to my baby girl Alanna for reminding me every day of what's really important in this world.

Frank Boumphrey: First, I would like to thank my wife, Rona, who reminds me from time to time that there is a life other than the virtual one; second, my 21-year-old cat, Hergie, who likes to sleep on my keyboard but who deigned to get off a sufficient number of occasions to allow me to complete this project; and last but not least, Mary Burmeister, who made working on this project a positive pleasure. I would also like to take this opportunity to pay my respects to Michael Hart, the founder and inspiration behind Project Gutenberg. Michael, what you have done is a gift to the future generations that will resound down the centuries.

Publisher's Acknowledgments

We're proud of this book; please send us your comments through our Hungry Minds Online Registration Form located at www.dummies.com.

Some of the people who helped bring this book to market include the following:

Acquisitions, Editorial, and Media Development

Senior Project Editor: Nicole Haims

Acquisitions Editor: Bob Woerner

Copy Editor: Jean Rogers

Technical Editor: Don Jones

Editorial Manager: Leah P. Cameron

Permissions Editor: Laura Moss

Media Development Specialist: Travis Silvers

Media Development Manager: Laura VanWinkle

Media Development Supervisor: Richard Graves

Editorial Assistant: Amanda Foxworth

Production

Project Coordinator: Jennifer Bingham

Layout and Graphics: Sean Decker, Stephanie Jumper, Tiffany Muth, Jackie Nicholas, Barry Offringa, Laurie Petrone, Brent Savage, Betty Schulte, Julie Trippetti, Jeremey Unger, Mary J. Virgin, Erin Zeltner

Proofreaders: John Bitter, John Greenough, Andy Hollandbeck, Susan Moritz, Carl Pierce

Indexer: TECHBOOKS Production Services, Inc.

Special Help: Teresa Artman

General and Administrative

Hungry Minds Technology Publishing Group: Richard Swadley, Vice President and Executive Group Publisher; Bob Ipsen, Vice President and Group Publisher; Joseph Wikert, Vice President and Publisher; Barry Pruett, Vice President and Publisher; Mary Bednarek, Editorial Director; Mary C. Corder, Editorial Director; Andy Cummings, Editorial Director

Hungry Minds Manufacturing: Ivor Parker, Vice President, Manufacturing

Hungry Minds Marketing: John Helmus, Assistant Vice President, Director of Marketing

Hungry Minds Production for Branded Press: Debbie Stailey, Production Director

Hungry Minds Sales: Michael Violano, Vice President, International Sales and Sub Rights

Cartoons at a Glance

By Rich Tennant

page 245

page 53

page 139

page 327

page 291

page 11

page 189

Cartoon Information:
Fax: 978-546-7747
E-Mail: richtennant@the5thwave.com
World Wide Web: www.the5thwave.com

Table of Contents

Introduction

● ●

*W*elcome to the latest frontier of Web technology. In *XML For Dummies,*
3rd Edition, we introduce you to the mysteries of eXtensible Markup
Language (XML). XML is helping developers capture, manipulate, and
exchange all kinds of documents and data, ranging from family trees to electronic commerce transactions. In fact, there are many experts who believe
that XML represents a kind of "lingua franca" that can represent information
of most kinds imaginable, in a way that makes that information more accessible not only to human readers, but also to all kinds of computer applications
and services.

We take a straightforward approach to telling you about XML and what it can
do for your data and document capture, management, and exchange efforts.
We try to keep the amount of technobabble to a minimum and stick to plain
English as much as possible. Besides plain talk about hypertext, XML, and
the many special-purpose applications that XML supports for document
designers and authors, graphics developers, and many other communities of
technical and business interests, we include lots of sample markup to help
you put XML to work in your organization, business, or personal life.

We also include a peachy CD that contains all the XML examples in usable
form and a number of other interesting widgets for your own documents. The
XML For Dummies CD has numerous XML authoring tools, parsers, development kits, and other goodies that we hope you find helpful for your own
projects!

About This Book

Think of this book as your friendly, approachable guide to using XML for all
kinds of interesting purposes. Using XML is a bit more challenging than using
HTML, so this book is organized to make it easier to grapple with XML's fun-
damentals and then use them well. We also document voluminous additional
sources of information, both online and offline. Here are some of the topics
we include:

 ✔ An overview of XML's capabilities, terminology, and technologies

 ✔ A comparison of XML to its junior partner XHTML and its senior partner
   SGML

✔ Information on designing, creating, and using XML's extensible characteristics

✔ Reviews of a slew of XML applications — special-purpose markup definitions that support managing document presentation, simple graphics, complex linking, XML document navigation, XML-based multimedia, and more specialized applications than you might have ever dreamed were possible

Because XML is essentially a markup language used to create other XML-based markup languages — or what we also called XML applications — it's not exactly accurate to call a document based on one particular XML application or another an XML document. It really makes more sense to call it an XML-based document because the document itself contains markup defined using XML. But for brevity's sake, we call such documents XML documents in this book (and indeed they must adhere to the rules of XML syntax and structure if they are to work properly) rather than always referring to them more correctly as "XML-based documents" or "documents based on such-and-such XML application."

Although you might think that using XML requires years of training and advanced technical wizardry, we don't think that's true. If you can tell someone how to drive across town, you can certainly use XML to build documents that do what you want them to. The purpose of this book isn't to turn you into a true-blue geek, complete with a pocket protector. Rather, *XML For Dummies,* 3rd Edition shows you which design and technical elements you need so that you can understand what XML is and how it works. We also provide numerous examples and case studies to illustrate how XML behaves, so you can gain the know-how and confidence to use XML to good effect!

Conventions Used in This Book

Throughout this book, you see lots and lots of markup. All XML markup appears in monospace type, like this:

```
<Greeting>Hello, world!</Greeting>. . .
```

If part of the markup is a placeholder, we italicize it. For example, if we mean for you to put your own element name between the brackets, and your own text between the opening and closing tags, it would look something like this:

```
<element_name>text</element_name>
```

When you type XML tags or other related information, be sure to copy the information exactly as you see it between the angle brackets (< and >) because that's part of the magic that makes XML work. Other than that, we tell you how to marshal and manage the content that makes your pages special, and we tell you exactly what you need to do to mix the elements of XML with your own work.

Because of the margins in this book, some long lines of XML markup, designations for Web sites (called URLs, for Uniform Resource Locators), or special XML identifiers for namespaces and other information objects (called URIs, or Uniform Resource Identifiers), and also just really long lines of markup wrap to the next line. On your computer, though, these wrapped lines would appear as a single line of XML or as a single URL or URI — so don't insert a hard return when you see any such lines wrap in the book. Here are some examples of wrapped lines:

```
www.infomagic.austin.com/nexus/plexus/lexus/praxis/
    this_is_deliberately_long.html
```

and

```
<Sinst>Stuff the green chiles with equal amounts of pinto beans and
    shredded jack cheese.</Sinst>
```

XML is sensitive to how element text is entered. If you're following our examples from the comfort of your living room, keep in mind that you have to use uppercase, lowercase, or other characters, exactly as they appear in the book (or more importantly, as they're defined in the document description that governs any well-formed, valid XML document — be it a Document Type Definition, or DTD, or an XML Schema). To make your work look like ours as much as possible, enter all element text exactly as it appears in this book. Better yet, copy it from the CD!

Foolish Assumptions

Someone once said that making assumptions makes a fool out of the person who makes them and the person who is their subject. Even so, we're going to make a few assumptions about you, our gentle reader:

- ✔ You're already familiar with text files, and know how to use a text editor.
- ✔ You have a working connection to the Internet.
- ✔ You understand the difference between a Web browser and a Web server.

> ✔ You know what a plug-in is and why plug-ins are needed for so much Web-related work.
>
> ✔ You want to build your own XML documents for fun, for profit, or because it's part of your job.

Also, we assume that you have a modern Web browser — one that can support XML directly. As we write this, Internet Explorer 5.5 (and higher), Netscape Navigator 6.2, Opera, and Amaya all have decent XML parsing and rendering capabilities. Don't worry, though, if you don't have such a browser. Part of what you find in these pages (and on the CD) is a collection of pointers to help you obtain the tools you need to work directly with XML on your own computer. You don't need to be a master logician or a programming whiz to work with XML; all you need is the time required to discover its ins and outs and the determination to understand its intricacies and capabilities.

If you can write a sentence and you know the difference between a heading and a paragraph, you can build and publish your own XML documents. If you have an imagination and the ability to communicate what's important to you in an organized manner, you've already mastered the ingredients necessary to build useful, information-rich XML documents and data collections. The rest is details, and we help you with those!

How This Book Is Organized

This book contains seven major parts and each part contains two or more chapters. Anytime you need help or information, pick up the book and start anywhere you like, or use the Table of Contents and Index to locate specific topics or keywords. This section gives a breakdown of the seven parts and what you find in each one.

Part 1: Why XML Is "eXtreMely cooL"

Part I sets the stage. It begins with an overview of XML's special capabilities and discusses the design goals and motivations that led to its creation and specification. We motivate your interest in XML (hopefully) by exploring the many uses for and applications to which XML is so well-suited. We also discuss the relationships between and among SGML, XML, XHTML, and HTML. We also cover what's involved in converting HTML to its XML-based equivalent, XHTML, as a way of introducing XML's syntax and structure. We conclude Part I with a review of XML examples, along with a discussion of how XML documents and data can be made subject to formal descriptions (a great way to define a set of rules that humans and computers can follow with equal facility).

Part II: XML Basics

In Part II, you find out about how XML documents gain their structure and content — from a thorough analysis of requirements and examples. We take a simple, innocent-looking bean burrito recipe and show you all the elements it contains, how those elements relate to one another, and how they can be described in formal terms. Chapter 5 picks up that thread, and jumps into the magic of metadata (data that describes other data, dontchya know?) and why document descriptions can be useful when designing XML markup to capture documents or data.

Next, we jump into a couple of chapters that explain the purpose and functions that Document Type Definitions (DTDs) can play in describing XML documents. We also guide you toward understanding, using, and building DTDs to govern your XML documents, too.

After that, we look at an "all-XML, all the time" alternative to DTDs called XML Schema that provides similar capabilities to describe, use, and control XML documents. XML Schema's appeal derives from its basis in XML itself. In simpler terms, because XML Schema is just another XML application (albeit one that allows you to describe other XML applications), a working knowledge of XML permits you to apply that knowledge to describing XML applications without having to learn yet another markup language. Because DTDs are based on SGML, not XML, the same is not true when using, customizing, or creating DTDs that describe XML applications.

Part III: Putting XML to Work

In Part III, we use a DTD to teach you about the XML markup that it enables. To begin, we explain how to read a DTD to recognize the elements, attributes, and content models it contains. Next, we explain how to put a DTD to work. After that, we explain how you can combine DTDs or even build modular DTDs to give yourself a mix-and-match set of building blocks for document markup.

Because XML Schema provides an alternative way to describe XML markup, document structure, and to assign data types to document content elements, we follow the DTD discussion with an XML Schema discussion that covers more or less the same ground in XML Schema's terms. That is, we explain how to create elements, attributes, datatypes, and content models to work in XML Schemas. Then we explain how to combine XML Schemas, and how to mix and match XML Schema contents or components to maximize this technology.

We conclude Part III by exploring the character sets and related entities that XML depends on to represent content and explain how to use them in your documents. The three chapters in this part represent some of the most important nuts and bolts in the entire book.

Part IV: Using and Delivering XML Content

In Part IV, we begin by explaining what you can do with XML when you've got some to work with. Be it some kind of human-readable document or a well-organized, well-described collection of data, using XML makes it possible to do all kinds of interesting things. From data exchange, to transforming XML into other formats, to interacting with databases, we show you many possible ways to get things done with a little help from XML.

Next, we jump into the ins and outs of the eXtensible Stylesheet Language (XSL) that may be used to turn XML-based data or documents into just about any form or format imaginable. After that, we explore the details involved in transforming an XML document into different formats, and explore the mysteries involved in putting XSL to work changing things around. Our next stop is inside the machinery that makes XML usable, as we explore what's involved when a computer reads and absorbs an XML document, and what kinds of capabilities the necessary software — usually called an XML processor — can deliver.

To conclude Part IV, we explain what's involved in bringing XML documents to the Web, and talk about the best ways to use styles to make their contents more presentable. To that end, we explore ways to use Cascading Style Sheets (CSS) and XSL to make native XML documents (or XML content transformed into HTML) easier to read and appreciate online.

Part V: XML's Lovely Linking Languages

XML supports some serious enhancements to the simple unidirectional hyperlinks you might know from HTML. In Part V, we explore XML Linking Language (XLink), which you can use to create many kinds of complex hyperlinks. We also investigate XML Path Language (XPath), which is so helpful when pointing from one location on the Web to another, be it within a site or from one site to another. This part concludes with an exploration of XML Pointer Language (XPointer), which you may use to refer to anchors and targets in XML documents.

Part VI: XML in the Real World

Part VI takes all the elements covered in prior parts of the book and puts them together to show you how XML works in organizations and companies today. We begin this part with a brief survey of popular, widely used XML tools and technologies. These include special-purpose XML editors and authoring tools, XML-based management tools, XML-capable browsers, parsers and engines, and conversion tools.

Next, we take a tour of an exciting set of XML-based applications designed to advertise, locate, and use so-called "Web Services." Championed by companies like IBM, Microsoft, and Sun Microsystems, among others, this software and messaging architecture makes it possible for service providers to advertise their services on the Web and for users to locate and use such services on the Web. These services can involve anything from access to proprietary databases, remote storage or processing, or even access to basic productivity applications (word-processing, spreadsheets, e-mail, and so forth) that users may be more used to seeing on their own desktops instead of running elsewhere on the Internet. There's plenty of hype and hope for the future of Web services, and you explore the reasons why this is the case.

Part VI concludes with a more general survey of how XML is revolutionizing the Web, along with a description of how certain very large corporations are using XML to streamline and simplify their own internal operations. You also learn more about the kinds of applications and uses to which XML is particularly well suited, and survey an annotated list of numerous popular XML applications already in wide use.

Part VII: The Part of Tens

In Part VII, you have a chance to observe some of the best and brightest uses of XML, and to understand why a certain set of XML applications are of such great interest to so many content designers and developers. Finally, in Chapter 24, you can read about some of the most appealing and useful sources of information about XML and related applications known to man (and woman).

Appendix: About the CD

The materials on the *XML For Dummies* CD are organized into separate modules that reflect the layout of the book itself. The CD is designed to help you match up the markup and examples that appear within the pages of the book to their electronic counterparts on the CD itself. Given the option, we thought you'd want to take advantage of our research and let your fingers do the walking, so to speak; therefore, you can find numerous examples and elements that might plug nicely into your own XML documents on the CD.

The remainder of the CD is devoted to as comprehensive a collection of tools and programs for XML as we were able to gather for your delectation and use.

Glossary

In the glossary, you can find definitions for all those terms that make you go "Huh?" We did our best to choose the ones that really need an explanation and defined them in a way that's easy to understand.

Icons Used in This Book

This icon signals technical details that are informative and interesting but not critical to writing XML. Skip these if you want (but please, come back and read them later).

This icon flags useful information that makes XML markup, Web-page design, or other important stuff even less complicated than you feared it might be.

This icon points out information that you shouldn't pass by — don't overlook these gentle reminders (the life you save could be your own).

Be cautious when you see this icon. It warns you of things you shouldn't do; the bomb emphasizes that the consequences of ignoring these bits of wisdom can be severe.

When you see this spiderweb symbol, it flags the presence of Web-based resources that you can go out and investigate further. You can also find all these references on the "Jump Pages" on the *XML For Dummies* CD!

When you see this symbol, it indicates a resource, a tool, or a pointer to resources that you can find on the *XML For Dummies* CD that comes with this book.

We use this icon to tell you how various businesses are currently using XML.

Where to Go from Here

This is where you choose a direction and hit the road! *XML For Dummies,* 3rd Edition is a lot like a recipe for goulash; you begin by tasting the final dish, proceed to assembling the ingredients necessary for your own "document stew," and then get to work on cooking up what you need for yourself (or your organization).

To keep up with the latest version of these references, please visit the related "XML For Dummies Update" site on the authors' Web site at www. lanw.com/books/xmlfd3e/. Here, you find the results of our best efforts to keep the information in the book current and a list of errata to straighten out any of the mistakes, boo-boos, or gotchas that we weren't able to root out before the book went to publication. We hope you find this a convincing demonstration that our hearts are in the right place (we already know we're not perfect).

Please share your feedback with us about the book. We can't claim that we'll follow every suggestion or react to every comment, but you can be pretty certain that suggestions that occur repeatedly or that add demonstrable value to the book will find a place in the next edition!

Good luck on your journey, and don't forget to keep your eyes on the road and your hands on the wheel as you cruise the information highway.

Enjoy!

Part I
Why XML Is "eXtreMely cooL"

In this part . . .

Here, you get a gentle but formal introduction to the eXtensible Markup Language, also known as XML. Starting in Chapter 1, you find out about XML's capabilities, its relationship to other markup languages including SGML, HTML, and more. You also ponder the basics of XML markup and the many applications and forms of output it enables. You conclude this chapter by building a minimal but complete XML document of your very own. In Chapter 2, you explore XML's relationship to XHTML and look at XML structure and syntax as it applies when converting HTML to its XML equivalent, XHTML. Finally, in Chapter 3, you have a chance to explore some excellent exemplars for XML, re-examine a simple document in light of what you now know, find out what formal descriptions for XML documents (known as DTDs and XML Schemas) do, and how they can be handy.

Chapter 1

Understanding What XML Is — and Why You Should Care

*H*ave you ever wanted a document format that you could use to exchange data across the Internet? Well, eXtensible Markup Language (XML) may be just the solution for your problems. Various software products in many different industries widely employ XML to present and organize their data.

XML is a programming language based on the Standard Generalized Markup Language (SGML). The flexibility of XML has made it a necessity for exchanging data in a multitude of forms. Accessing information with XML is so much easier than with HyperText Markup Language (HTML). For example, with XML, you can send the same information to both a person using a mobile phone and a person using a Web browser. In addition, you can customize the information to be displayed appropriately on the various devices. Welcome to a new age!

Getting started with XML isn't difficult. Just check out this chapter, and you'll find out what markup languages are, what XML is, what you can use XML to do, and what types of XML applications exist — waiting for you to take advantage of them.

Getting to Know Markup Language Lingo

Although having a working knowledge of HTML is a good idea when getting started with XML, you don't have to be a markup pro to read this book or to use XML. If you're new to the markup world or if you need to brush up on your vocabulary, the following list should help you out.

These terms are the most common ones that you need to become familiar with to understand markup languages in general (including XML):

- ✔ **Attribute:** In XML, a property associated with an XML element that's also a named characteristic of the element. An attribute also provides additional data about an element, independent of element content.

- ✔ **Document Type Definition (DTD):** An SGML-based statement of rules for an XML document that specifies which elements (markup tags) and attributes (values associated with specific elements) are allowed in your documents. A DTD also governs the order in which the elements and attributes may or must appear.

- ✔ **Element:** A section of a document defined by start and end tags or an empty tag, including any associated content.

- ✔ **Metalanguage:** A language used to communicate information about a language itself; many experts consider both SGML and XML to be meta-languages because they can be used to define markup languages.

- ✔ **Nesting:** An ordering of elements whereby a child element is opened and closed before its parent element is closed (child elements nest within parent elements).

- ✔ **Schema:** An XML-based statement of rules that represents an XML document's data model and defines its elements (or objects), their attributes (or properties), and the relationships between different elements.

- ✔ **Syntax:** The rules that govern the construction of intelligible markup fragments.

- ✔ **Tag; empty tag:** The markup used to enclose an element's content. An empty element employs a single tag; a regular element (which isn't empty) has an opening and a closing tag.

- ✔ **Valid:** A markup language document that adheres to the rules outlined in an associated DTD or schema document.

- ✔ **Well-formed:** A markup language document that adheres to the syntax rules for XML, which are explicitly designed to make that document easy for a computer to interpret.

A Wee Bit of Background: Markup Languages

A *markup language* is a language used to label, categorize, and organize data or document content. *Markup* is what describes document or data structure and organization. *Content,* such as text, images, and data, is what markup contains and is also generally what's of greatest interest to humans who read or interact with data or documents.

XML is a markup language and so is HTML. In fact, both of these markup languages derive from the same parent: SGML. And eXtensible HTML (XHTML) is a reformulation of HTML using XML. Figure 1-1 shows you a diagram of the happy markup family tree.

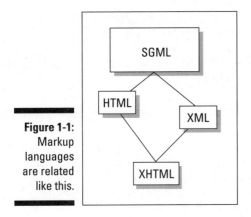

Figure 1-1:
Markup
languages
are related
like this.

Introducing SGML: The mother of all metalanguages

SGML is a powerful metalanguage; its primary job is to define other markup languages, including HTML, XHTML, and XML itself. In other words, SGML is the parent of HTML, XHTML, and XML, among many other markup languages. (Refer to Figure 1-1.)

SGML is a "kitchen sink" metalanguage: That is, it incorporates everything but the kitchen sink — all the facilities and capabilities that are intended to make it as complete as possible. These extra bells and whistles, however, make SGML software difficult to implement and slow and unwieldy to run.

The purpose of SGML was to create a powerful, general-purpose tool for defining markup languages that could work faster and better on more focused tasks. XML is a markup language that defines a carefully chosen subset of SGML meant to work efficiently to better support the World Wide Web (WWW) and other networked applications across the Internet.

Introducing HTML

HTML is a markup language that was originally developed to describe and deliver textual documents across the Internet. HTML tags define only basic text elements, such as paragraphs and divisions, and offer only limited presentation controls for text.

HTML is not a general-purpose tool to label and organize text (or data). It uses a predetermined set of markup elements that can be expanded only by agreement and alteration of HTML's underlying markup language description. This makes HTML a *closed* markup language in the sense that adding new markup elements is not part of its built-in capabilities.

The closed nature of HTML explains why it has gone through so many versions. Starting with the public introduction in 1993 of HTML 1.0, up to its "final definition" as HTML 4.01 in 1999, each of its new incarnations represents incorporation of new markup and capabilities to meet document designers' ever-expanding desire for more functionality.

Introducing XML

In a very real sense, XML is the child of dire necessity because the custodians of HTML realized that a closed markup language couldn't be maintained and still meet demands for document- and data-handling on the Web. With daily demands for change and schedules that led to an average interval of about 1.5 years between HTML versions, its keepers simply couldn't keep up.

XML was developed by a working group under the umbrella of the World Wide Web Consortium (W3C). To solve the problem at its root and to create an *open-ended* markup language that could easily accommodate future expansions and additions, the W3C created a working group to define such a markup language. Officially called the XML Working Group, this gang consisted of researchers and experts from many parts of the computer industry, including Internet and intranet technology gurus, publishing wizards, and markup language mavens. The primary goal of this merry band of technologists was to bring the kinds of capabilities found in SGML to the Web, without all the extra bells, whistles, fat, and calories. Rather than calling it *SGML Lite*, they called it *XML*.

By February 1998, version 1.0 of the XML specification was unleashed on the world, and the XML markup revolution began in earnest.

Introducing XHTML

XHTML closes the loop between XML and HTML. The W3C calls XHTML "a reformulation of HTML 4 in XML 1.0." In simpler terms, XHTML represents the latest incarnation of HTML, using XML markup and syntax to re-express HTML in XML terms. Because XML is open-ended, by recasting HTML in its terms to create XHTML, XHTML is open-ended, too. That's why the *X* in XHTML stands for *eXtensible*.

In its simplest application, XHTML uses markup that differs only slightly from its HTML predecessor and works as well as HTML in the vast majority of Web browsers. More ambitious applications of XHTML take advantage of the *X*, so to speak, adding markup definitions to the basic set originally defined for HTML 4.0 so that document developers can expand the set of markup elements that they employ within their XHTML documents.

Understanding Why XML Suits So Many Dang Applications

If you take a close look at today's Internet industry and at the many different research and development initiatives underway, you soon recognize that pinning down a single, definitive function for XML is nearly impossible. The W3C created XML as a way to disseminate complex, structured data and documents over the Web. In other words, the open-ended nature of XML is what makes it so useful for many different things and so difficult to put into a single, small box.

In fact, case studies of XML never fail to mention new and exciting possibilities where XML adds value to existing environments or solves previously intractable problems. That's probably why XML applications have been defined and are widely used for everything from chemical formulas to genealogies (family trees). Nonetheless, many key XML implementations fall into one of two categories:

- ✔ **Complex document creation,** such as a large, multisection description of a software application, with an auto-generated index, table of contents, and working code examples.

- ✔ **Data exchange,** where complex data structures, such as patient medical records, can be completely and comprehensively described and where such data can easily be reformulated to view in a report, print in a document, or imported into a database.

Experts in many applications and industries have already created specific markup languages that you can use as is. We describe a few popular examples in Chapter 22.

The universe of XML-based markup languages, also called *XML applications*, is constantly expanding. The odds are high that you can find a markup language suitable for your particular needs. If the language doesn't completely satisfy you, extend it — after all, XML is the *eXtensible* Markup Language.

Using XML for a Variety of Output Options

Authors of XML-based Web documents don't make any assumptions about how the documents will be used on the client side. HTML pages, on the other hand, are designed for one particular purpose: to display information inside a browser. Browsers process HTML documents easily, but software sometimes has a difficult time post processing the information that such documents contain. This limitation doesn't apply to XML documents.

The phrase *post processing* means taking information delivered within a document and using that information in some other process or program. For example, suppose that you receive a purchase order in the form of an XML document. An application that understands XML purchase orders can use that data to determine which items in what quantities have been ordered and can even send instructions to another piece of software to generate a pick-list so the order can be picked, packed, and shipped from the warehouse. Now that's what we call post processing! To achieve the same goal in an HTML-based environment, you'd have to write a special purpose program to read and interpret the HTML document. Comparatively, with XML you can use standard tools to parse and process document contents directly — with no extra markup needed!

XML is not a replacement for HTML. XML enables the Internet industry to invent a new set of powerful tools for many purposes.

In many cases, XML documents are used with style sheets to provide high-quality output on-screen. You can use the same data, however, to send information to a speech-synthesis program that reads the text to a person who is vision impaired. Alternatively, that same data might also create output on a Braille reader. The same document with a layout program and a style sheet also might be used for high-quality printouts. See Figure 1-2 for an illustration of this post processing.

The beauty of this concept is that you never need to change the XML data to create output for different devices. You need only to use different pieces of software that can provide the output for a particular format or output device.

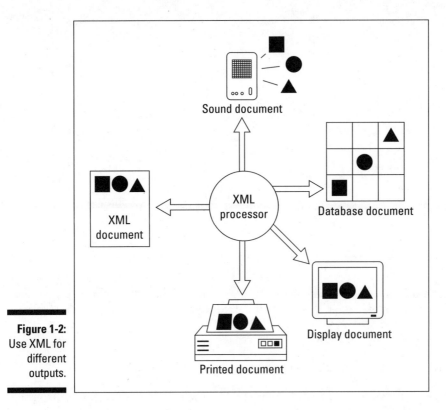

Figure 1-2:
Use XML for
different
outputs.

Using XML for data and HTML for display

You may often see a combination of XML and HTML in everyday online use. XML is all about preserving information. HTML is all about, or at least is accomplished at, displaying information within a browser. Why not combine the best of these two worlds? The basic idea is to have the original data based on XML, where all the rich markup and additional information about a document is available. Then you can use the same document for many different purposes and use the "intelligence" in the data to build powerful applications to display the data on-screen and translate it into HTML, a concept illustrated in Figure 1-3.

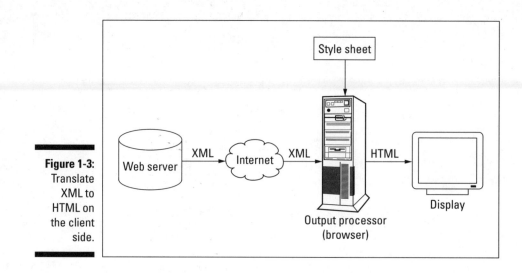

Figure 1-3:
Translate
XML to
HTML on
the client
side.

XML stores and organizes the data, and HTML renders it inside your browser by using a style sheet. The methods differ depending on when the XML data is translated into HTML for display inside a browser, as well as on the type and version of the browser.

The conversion experience can occur in the following ways:

✔ XML data is sent to the client (your browser), and your browser uses a style sheet — extra information that helps your browser make XML look interesting — to display HTML.

✔ The XML data resides on the server where it passes through an XSL Transformation and is converted to HTML before being sent to a browser.

Using XML for enhanced post-processing functions

HTML is a display-oriented language. That's its primary function, plain and simple. And that's why HTML isn't the best option for post-processing functions, such as constructing searchable local indexes. You can see the poor-quality results of HTML's lack of post-processing capability when you query a search engine to find Web pages on a particular subject. Very often, you get back either 0 hits or 100,000.

The XML Files and other XML phenomena

Those in the W3C's XML Working Group keep most of their materials, including text for speeches, presentations, and technical specifications, freely available on the W3C Web server. Visit this site to find out what you need when you need it most — that is, when you're slaving over some hot XML markup. The address is

```
www.w3.org/XML
```

Not only have these XML gods declared their collective wills, but they've also started a regular e-zine called — you guessed it! — *The XML Files.* Keep up with the latest and greatest information on XML and its development by visiting

```
www.gca.org/whats_xml/whats_xml
     _xmlfiles.htm
```

In addition, you may want to visit `www.xml.com` and click the <u>Annotated XML 1.0</u> link to take a peek at Tim Bray's annotated version of the specification.

Because XML data preserves both context and semantics, building applications that apply some smarts to electronic documents is a lot easier than it would be in HTML. Suppose that some XML documents contain an `Author` element. Because you can search any XML document to elicit the content of specific elements, this means you can search the Web for all XML documents in which *Ed Tittel* appears in the `Author` element. XML makes it possible to focus on any specific piece of information within a document because it can identify and access individual document elements.

Likewise, XML enables search engines to access information inside documents because those engines can use XML element contents and attributes to find specific entries or text. So instead of relying on the document titles and headings that robots usually gather from HTML documents to index their contents, they can access all the content (and markup) inside XML documents and get more accurate results. Imagine actually being able to use the results of a search on the first try!

Using XML for data exchange

Suppose that you want to exchange database information across the Web. In particular, suppose that you want to use a Web browser to send information from a user questionnaire back to a Web server. To accomplish this and many other tasks, you need a document format that's extensible, open, and nonproprietary. An *extensible* format is one that can be tailored or customized for specific applications. An *open* format is one that's well documented and widely available to would-be users. And finally, a *nonproprietary* document is one that's expressed in an accepted or standard form of notation that isn't the exclusive property of some individual, company, or organization. These characteristics are what make it possible to adapt to changing conditions, to leverage the work of others, and to avoid extra expense or legal liability.

You could use import/export filters to interchange file formats, but XML is the best solution for data exchange because XML can constantly be improved upon to provide a single platform for data interchange between multiple applications.

Building XML Documents

Regular old-fashioned editors such as Notepad will do the job if you're just getting your feet wet with XML, but text editors that are built specifically for XML are the way to go if you plan on using XML regularly. These editors often look like a blend of traditional word processors and HTML editors. In fact, most XML editors work so much like word processors that you could easily forget that you're working with XML.

XML editors can make your job easier and help keep those creative juices flowing! (Tracking tags and cleaning up structures can interrupt, and sometimes completely destroy, the creative train of thought.) XML editors have two distinct features that are essential for creating good XML documents:

- ✔ **Ease of markup:** XML editors, such as XML Spy and XML Pro, can add markup to text as simply as you can turn text **bold** in today's word processors. All XML editors provide the capability to select text with a cursor and choose which markup you want to apply from a menu of selections. (See Chapter 20 for more on XML Spy, XML Pro, and other XML authoring tools.)

- ✔ **Enforcing document rules:** For many applications, XML editors can determine which element types can appear in certain contexts. In this way, the editor helps you avoid making syntax or structure mistakes. For example, if you specify that the `ChapterTitle` element is valid only at the beginning of a chapter and never within an ordinary paragraph, the editor can make sure that your rule is enforced if you accidentally break it.

XML is a subset of SGML, so many authoring tools and editors previously used for SGML have been recast and are now ready to take on XML.

Breaking Out Your Text Editor

To create your own XML documents, you don't need anything more than a plain old ASCII-based text editor such as Notepad. If you plan to use XML more often than once in a while or for a lot of pages, however, think about getting an XML editor.

If you're using Windows, you can access Notepad by choosing Start➪ Programs➪Accessories➪Notepad. A new Notepad window opens. You can save the files just as you would in a word processor and do simple functions such as copy and paste. Aside from that, though, Notepad is a pretty bare-bones program.

Check out Chapter 2 for steps on creating an XML document by hand. But before you skip on, here are some handy text-editing tips:

- ✔ **Be specific with filenames.** When you save a document for the first time, most text editors have predefined settings for the document's extension. If you use generic XML, just use .xml as the extension. With a specific XML application like Channel Definition Format (CDF), for example, use .cdf.

- ✔ **Beware of binary.** You can create XML documents by using one of the more sophisticated document-authoring programs such as Microsoft Word or Corel WordPerfect. Keep in mind, however, that the native File➪Save format of such programs is a binary format. For example, the native and default file format for a Word file is the .doc format. That format is not suitable for XML (or HTML). Make sure to save your XML document as a text file (.txt) if you use one of these programs.

- ✔ **Hand coding means you have to do a lot of typing.** You must insert all markup yourself when using a text editor such as Notepad. If you have a paragraph such as

```
This section is about XML editing
```

you need to type the required markup tags by hand. If your XML markup for a paragraph was Para, your text would look like this:

```
<Para>This section is about XML editing.</Para>
```

Chapter 2

Comparing and Combining HTML and XML

In This Chapter
▶ Understanding the limitations of HTML
▶ Comparing HTML with XML
▶ Converting HTML to XML
▶ Getting the best of both worlds: XHTML

*T*his is the most important thing that you should know when comparing eXtensible Markup Language (XML) and HyperText Markup Language (HTML): Despite their similarity in appearance, they are two very different markup languages. You may not need to convert all your HTML documents into valid XML; rather, you may need to decide which markup language is best for your content and information handling needs. However, if you do want to convert your HTML document to XML, we show you how in the upcoming section "Converting HTML to XHTML."

What HTML Does Best and Where Its Limits Lie

Although you purchased this book to find out about XML, you wouldn't get your money's worth if we didn't take some time to talk about HTML. As a Web designer, you're forced to work in an imperfect world. For example, new markup language capabilities take center stage every few months, but new browser versions don't always follow suit. Therefore, a user's browser doesn't always support every bit of standard or nonstandard markup. The two main browsers, Microsoft Internet Explorer (IE) and Netscape Navigator, still don't fully support Cascading Style Sheets (CSS) level 2 . . . so don't expect their next versions to support XML completely, either. If your target audience is the world-at-large, you may have to use HTML or eXtensible HyperText Markup Language (XHTML) on the Web for some time to come rather than switching entirely over to XML markup.

HTML makes our Web world look pretty. In some instances, *pretty* is all that's needed for a Web page, such as a personal site that you create for your family. You want an easy, cheap way to let others know what you've been doing and to post a few pictures of your new baby, kitten, Chia pet, or electronic gadget.

Most Web sites use straight HTML to display data — say data that shows your family tree (see Figure 2-1). The site would have little need for flexibility and wouldn't need a database. (If you need a database for your family's site, we wouldn't want to run your next family reunion!)

If you want to sell the infamous widget from your Web site, however, you have to jump through additional hoops. You may want to create a database with product codes, styles, and colors, and you also may want your customers to be able to select any combination of this data. In this case, HTML isn't the best tool to represent widget data in text form: You want something that can do a better job of representing (and presenting) database fields and values as such.

The idea behind HTML is modest: HTML is meant to describe only basic page contents, providing rudimentary controls over how that content should appear in your browser. Since its public introduction, however, HTML has been forced to provide solutions for problems it was never meant to solve. HTML was enlisted to do the following:

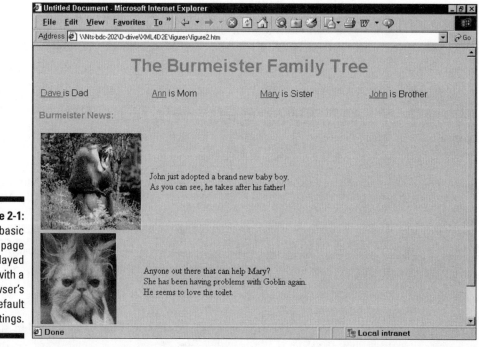

Figure 2-1:
A basic HTML page displayed with a browser's default settings.

✔ **Allow tight control** over document display

✔ **Provide the flexibility** to describe different, specific types of information and data

✔ **Convey information** from a variety of media and in various formats

✔ **Define complex linking relationships** between documents

✔ **Publish a single set of information** across a variety of media

Web designers (like us, for example) sometimes catch themselves thinking, "But my heading has to be in 45.5-point Arial type, centered in the second two-thirds of the page." Although this sentiment is a bit overstated, many Web designers do expect that much from their HTML; then they're left wondering why HTML can't live up to those expectations.

Today's Web designers want to achieve the same formatting control over Web documents that they have over printed documents. They want what they see on their screens with their browsers to be exactly what any visitor to their sites may also see. Two overarching problems prevent Web designers from achieving this control with HTML:

✔ **HTML lacks fine controls.** First and foremost, HTML by itself doesn't include mechanisms for fine control. You can't specify a document's display size or control the size of a browser window. A user's monitor size and display settings can dramatically affect how a browser displays HTML documents. Although HTML 4.0 does include a `font` element to help you manipulate font style, size, and color, users can override your settings with their own.

✔ **Browsers' displays vary.** Along with the different versions of the two most common browsers (IE and Navigator), other graphical browsers such as Mosaic and HotJava make it impossible to know exactly on which browser and platform users view your pages. And you can't realistically test every Web page on every available browser on every platform just to see what your users see.

Although adding style sheets and elements to your arsenal gives you more flexibility in comparison to earlier versions of HTML, doing so doesn't solve every Web design problem. That's where XML comes in.

Style sheets have become an integral part of the XML discussion. For an in-depth look at the use of style sheets and XML, please visit Part IV.

Comparing and Contrasting XML and HTML

Right off the bat, we want to tell you in no uncertain terms that XML won't — and can't — replace HTML. XML and HTML are not the same kind of markup language. But XML and HTML both derive from the same parent, SGML, so they must be similar, right? The answer is: "Yes, they're similar, but not identical."

HTML and XML both use tags and attributes. Indeed, XML and HTML look similar. But whereas HTML defines basic text elements and includes defaults (and more explicit controls) for how text may be displayed in a browser window, XML tells us only what each element means. XML says nothing about how elements should or must be displayed.

Using tags, elements, and attributes to describe data

Unlike HTML, XML is not limited to any fixed set of *tags* or *element types* (which is the proper name for the whatchamathingies that show up between the opening < and closing > characters in XML markup). By using XML, you can define your own sets of elements and even your own attributes that you may then use within your documents. On the other hand, XML has already been used to define lots of specific markup languages, called *XML applications,* that you can use within your documents as well.

Although it might seem that the terms *tag* and *element* are interchangeable, they're not. One example of a tag is the opening `<p>` tag; an example of an element is `<p>text</p>`. An *element* includes the opening and closing tags for a tag pair and everything in-between. A *tag* is just a tag, all by itself.

With this power, XML enables you to give meaningful names to your markup. In HTML, the paragraph element (p) is one of the most frequently used elements. In XML, you can replace the paragraph element with something more descriptive.

For example, suppose you have HTML text that looks like this:

```
<html>
<p>
This book is about the foundations of the Extensible Markup Language (XML)
 and how to use it for your own applications.
</p>
<p>
The authors are Ed Tittel and Frank Boumphrey.
</p>
</html>
```

Used as a plain-old HTML document, you know nothing about the meaning of the data. In other words, the first sentence could be a very long title, a description in a catalog, the first line of a book, the chorus of the new O-Town song, or something else entirely.

HTML is used to describe the display of data as seen through a Web browser. We could have just as easily written

```
<html>
<p>
Blah blah blah blah blah blah blah blah blah blah blah blah blah blah blah (XML)
 blobbity blobbity blobitty blah blah blah blah.
</p>
<p>
Blah blah blah Ed Tittel blah Frank Boumphrey.
</p>
</html>
```

and you would have gained just as much (or as little, depending on your point of view) insight as to the function of this data. But you *would* know that the data is displayed in two distinct paragraphs because the tags identify the appearance of the data.

Consider this alternate form of expression, in which cover copy (the information found on the cover of a book) is provided and broken into specific, named elements:

```
<Cover>
<Abstract>
 This book is about the foundations of the Extensible Markup Language (XML)
 and how to use it for your own applications.
</Abstract>
<AuthorInfo>
<Para>The authors are <Author>Ed Tittel</Author> and
 <Author>Frank Boumphrey</Author>. </Para>
</AuthorInfo>
</Cover>
```

The `Cover`, `Abstract`, and `AuthorInfo` elements identify the previous markup as XML-based. By using the elements in this markup language, you can now identify cover copy and specify further that cover copy includes an abstract plus a section for author information. In addition, this markup identifies each of the book's authors individually. Never fear, XML also provides numerous ways to translate this information so that it displays like you want it to: These ways include CSS and the eXtensible Stylesheet Language (XSL). See Part IV of this book for more about CSS and XSL.

XML enables you to define and use your own elements and attributes. This is what XML is all about and explains why XML is called the *eXtensible* Markup Language.

After you get your head wrapped around the differences between XML and HTML, you won't find that thinking of ways to increase the information associated with particular elements is at all difficult. For example, perhaps the `Author` element should include not only an author's name but also a brief biography.

In the earlier section, "What HTML Does Best and Where Its Limits Lie," we outline the limitations of HTML. Perhaps you're wondering why you would want to use it at all. HTML does have some advantages (see the following section); and in the short term, you have no real choice in the matter. Besides, HTML can create a reasonably consistent Web page presentation for users. As the expectations of businesses and end-users increase, however, so does the need for more flexible markup languages. XML rises to meet that challenge.

The benefits of using HTML

Why use HTML? Because it's quick, easy, and cheap. In addition, HTML is way easier than the alternative, too, which is to use an XML-based source document along with an XSL (or something similar) document to define display attributes for the document's contents.

Anyone can create an HTML document by using a text editor and a little knowledge. Even if you don't know HTML, you can use an HTML editor — a What-You-See-Is-What-You-Get-style (that is, WYSIWYG-style) editor such as FrontPage or Dreamweaver — to produce readable Web pages in minutes.

The most important reason not to write off HTML just yet lies in where it's headed: XHTML. HTML isn't out of the game. (See the section, "XHTML 1.0: Best of Both Worlds," later in this chapter for more information.)

The benefits of using XML

XML seems to be brimming with benefits. Here's a list of these benefits in a nutshell:

- **Unlimited elements:** You get to create your own elements and attributes instead of working with a restricted, predefined set of elements.

- **Structured data:** Applications can extract information that they need from XML documents.

- **Data exchange:** Using this enables you to exchange database contents or other structured information across the Internet or between dissimilar applications.

- **XML complements HTML:** XML data can be used in HTML pages.

- **XML documents are well formed:** XML documents must follow certain rules. This makes such documents easier to read and create.

- **Self-describing:** No prior knowledge of an XML application is needed. Of course, knowing HTML can really help you understand more about XML (but software thrives on self-describing documents and data).

✔ **Search engines:** XML delivers a noticeable increase in search relevancy because it provides ample contextual information and explicit labels for document elements.

✔ **Updates:** No need to update an entire site page by page; the Document Object Model (DOM) built into XML documents permits individual elements to be accessed (and updated).

✔ **User-selected view of data:** Different users can access different information or can present the same information in various ways.

As a user, the potential for intelligent XML-based pages that contain human-readable data is exciting. For example, HTML-based search tools use keywords and text strings. XML-based search tools can use them, too, but they can also use metadata and data structures. This means that your searches produce more relevant results more quickly.

A Web designer reaps several benefits from XML as well. For example, if you maintain a site that sells widgets and inflation kicks in, raising prices by $1.50 per widget is easy to implement across an entire site. No late nights spent changing each page — you're working with intelligent data now.

The benefits of XML are endless. Trust us, large corporations have good reasons for using XML-based markup languages to maintain their intranets. These benefits also explain why XML is all that Web designers (like us) want to talk about.

XHTML 1.0: Best of Both Worlds

Simply put, XHTML is a reformulation of HTML 4.0 as an application of XML 1.0. By definition, this offers you the benefits of XML in any XHTML documents. If you're familiar with HTML 4.0, XHTML concepts won't seem all that revolutionary as long as you don't let the new acronym scare you. If it helps, please think of XHTML as HTML 4.0 with a face-lift.

Why do we like XHTML? The benefits of XHTML aren't clear until you understand what's great about XML. For one thing, the strictness of XML provides an increase in predictability. Unlike HTML, with XML (and sometimes XHTML), either your markup works without a hitch or you get an error message. To a Web designer, this is wonderful news — no more late nights praying that a universal browser will be mandated!

Here's a list of some of the advantages of XHTML over HTML:

✔ XHTML documents can be viewed, edited, and validated using XML tools.

✔ Well-formed XHTML documents mean better-structured documents.

✔ XHTML documents can be delivered using different Internet media types, such as hand-held computers.

Making the Switch: Conversion

Because XML is still a relatively new technology, creating viewable documents in XML by using current tools *can* be problematic. Although Netscape is adding XML support to its browsers (in versions 6.1 and 6.2), how this support will be implemented remains foggy. IE 5 and higher-number versions, however, offer decent support for XML. Using an XML editor such as XML Spy, or a special XML-capable browser such as Internet Explorer, is the best way to view your work in native XML format.

Converting HTML to XHTML

Before you even write your first line of XML markup, you can benefit from it by converting HTML documents to XHTML because it's an XML-based markup language. Creating a well-formed XHTML document from an HTML document isn't as difficult as you might think, especially if the original HTML document uses correct syntax. When converting HTML to XHTML, the most important characteristics are

- ✔ All XHTML tags must be written using only lowercase.
- ✔ All tags must include distinct start and end components.
- ✔ All tags must be nested correctly.
- ✔ All attribute values must be quoted.

XHTML is intended to conform to XML syntax and structure. Thus, if you follow some simple guidelines, XHTML operates well within HTML 4.0-conforming user agents (for example, Web browsers). Table 2-1 summarizes the rules for correct XHTML and how markup looks in HTML and XHTML.

Table 2-1	Correct Formats for XHTML versus HTML	
Rule	*Looks Like This in XHTML*	*Looks Like This in HTML*
XHTML tags must be written using only lowercase.	`<b>This text is bold</b>`	`<B>This text is bold</B>`
Empty tags in XHTML must include a space before the trailing / and > in all empty elements.	`<img src="goblin.gif" alt="goblin" />` ` `	`<img src="goblin.gif" alt="goblin">` ` `
All nonempty elements in XHTML must have closing tags.	`<p>Closing tags mean no errors</p>`	`<p>Closing tags mean no errors`

Rule	Looks Like This in XHTML	Looks Like This in HTML
All elements in XHTML must be nested properly; elements can't overlap.	`<b>this text is in <em>bold</em></b>`	`<b>this text is in <em>bold</b></em>`
In XHTML, attribute values must always be in quotes.	`<col width="20" />`	`<col width=20>`

With HTML, Web designers could be sloppy. For example:

```
<body>
<p>I am late for lunch and have to run
<p>My boss is yelling at me, I must finish that report!
</body>
```

XHTML demands respect — and closing tags:

```
<body>
<p>I am late for lunch, but I cannot forget my closing tag.</p>
<p>My boss is yelling, but those creators of XML will yell if I don't close
my tags.</p>
</body>
```

The first three requirements are pretty straightforward, even though they aren't strictly necessary in HTML. XML doesn't allow you to use HTML short-cuts and is unforgiving of syntax errors because XML documents must be well formed. HTML documents must be altered to transform them into acceptable XHTML (an XML-based application). On the other hand, these requirements make XML and XHTML documents easy for computers to read and digest.

Our sample HTML page — which we also convert into XHTML — is a document that contains a bean burrito recipe. It appears in Figure 2-2, and uses the following HTML markup in Listing 2-1.

Listing 2-1: The HTML Document to Convert to XHTML

```
<html>
 <head>
  <title>Bean Burrito</title>
 </head>
 <body>
<p>This recipe was written by <i><b>The XML Gourmet</i></b>.<br>
This yummy recipe can be classified as tex-mex.
 <h1 id=ingredients>Bean Burrito Ingredients</h1>
  <ul>
   <li>1 can refried beans
   <li>1 cup longhorn colby cheese, shredded
   <li>1 small onion, finely chopped
   <li>3 flour tortillas
  </ul>
```

(continued)

Listing 2-1 *(continued)*

```
<h1 id=cooking instructions>Bean Burrito Cooking Instructions</h1>
 <ol>
   <li>Empty can of refried beans into medium saucepan.
   <li>Heat over medium-high heat until beans are smooth and bubbly.
   <li>Warm tortillas in microwave for 30 seconds.
 </ol>
<h1 id=serving instructions>Bean Burrito Serving Instructions</h1>
 <ol>
   <li>Spread 1/3 of warm beans on each tortilla.
   <li>Sprinkle with cheese and onions.
   <li>Roll tortillas and serve.
 </ol>
 </body>
</html>
```

All elements have explicit starts and ends

The first requirement when converting HTML to XML is that all nonempty elements (that is, those that contain actual text) must have a start tag and an end tag. Several HTML elements, such as p and li, act as text containers but didn't explicitly require end tags. Those tags work in nonpair containers because a special SGML shortcut allows the parser to assume an end tag must occur before another start tag for the same element. So, in effect

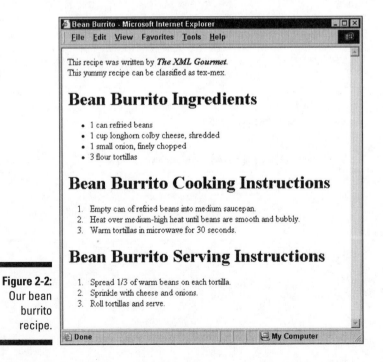

Figure 2-2:
Our bean
burrito
recipe.

```
<p>text text text
```

is the same as

```
<p>text text text</p>
```

Doing without an end tag doesn't fly in XHTML. You need to add closing paragraph tags where they belong. In our bean burrito recipe, that means adding a closing paragraph tag to this line of markup:

```
<p>This recipe was written by <i><b>The XML Gourmet</i></b>.<br>
This yummy recipe can be classified as tex-mex.
```

You also need to add ending list item tags (`</li>`) if you have list items, whether those lists are numbered or bulleted.

Tags are nested correctly

The rules of XML, XHTML, and HTML syntax say that tags must be nested in a certain order for HTML-to-XHTML conversion to work.

The rule is always to close first what you opened last, working your way from the inside to the outside tags. So, even though this HTML markup

```
<p>This recipe was written by <i><b>The XML Gourmet</i></b>.<br>
```

looks fine in a browser, the line is technically ill formed. To make it well formed, you must make this change:

```
<i><b>The XML Gourmet</b></i>.
```

All attribute values are quoted

HTML requires that only some attribute values, such as text strings and URLs, be quoted. Other values, such as image dimensions and font sizes, produce the desired results whether quoted or not. In XML, all attribute values must be quoted.

That means more changes. Even though the following markup works just fine on an HTML page, if you want burritos in XML, you need to put quotation marks around all the id attribute values; for example:

```
<h1 id="cooking instructions">Bean Burrito Cooking Instructions</h1>
```

Both single quotation marks (') and the double quotation marks (") are legal in XML and XHTML. However, you see double quotation marks used more, mostly because they're easier to see.

Empty elements are formatted correctly

The XML way to format empty elements may seem a bit strange, but remember that all other XML elements must use both a start tag and an end tag to be correct.

Empty elements are singleton tags (also called *empty tags*); they have no text sandwiched between a pair of tags.

The br element looks like this in our HTML example:

```
<br>
```

In, XHTML, it looks like this:

```
<br />
```

For backward compatibility, you must use a space in front of the closing slash that occurs near the end of XHTML empty elements (like this: <br />). This permits older, XML-ignorant Web browsers to recognize empty elements anyway. When native XML markup is used (or more to the point, interpreted properly), that extra space isn't necessary.

If you changed our original HTML markup for that yummy bean burrito recipe as we indicate in the preceding section, the result would be a proper XHTML document that looks like Listing 2-2. (We've bolded the additions and changes so they're easier for you to see.) We're not even going to show you the figure for this because it looks the same as Figure 2-2!

Listing 2-2:   Bean Burrito Recipe Converted to XHTML

```
<html>
<head>
 <title>Bean Burrito</title>
</head>
<body>
<p>This recipe was written by <i><b>The XML Gourmet</b></i>.<br />
This yummy recipe can be classified as tex-mex.</p>
 <h1 id="ingredients">Bean Burrito Ingredients</h1>
 <ul>
  <li>1 can refried beans</li>
  <li>1 cup longhorn colby cheese, shredded</li>
  <li>1 small onion, finely chopped</li>
  <li>3 flour tortillas</li>
 </ul>
 <h1 id="cooking instructions">Bean Burrito Cooking Instructions</h1>
```

```
  <ol>

    <li>Empty can of refried beans into medium saucepan.</li>
    <li>Heat over medium-high heat until beans are smooth and bubbly.</li>
    <li>Warm tortillas in microwave for 30 seconds.</li>
  </ol>
<h1 id="serving instructions">Bean Burrito Serving Instructions</h1>
  <ol>
    <li>Spread 1/3 of warm beans on each tortilla.</li>
    <li>Sprinkle with cheese and onions.</li>
    <li>Roll tortillas and serve.</li>
  </ol>
  </body>
</html>
```

Convert your HTML document to an XHTML document with ease by using HTML Tidy, an open-source program available at `www.w3.org/People/Raggett/ tidy/`. Better yet, use HTML-Kit (available at `www.chami.org`) to hide Tidy's ugly command-line settings and details!

Converting XHTML to XML

After you build a valid XHTML document, which is already technically in XML form, you may want to use more descriptive elements. For example, the list item (`li`) element doesn't really tell you what kinds of list items appear in a recipe. Of course, you know recipes must include lists of ingredients, cooking instructions, and serving instructions — but how can you make that clear to both humans and machines that read them?

Step 1: Create an XML declaration

The first step in crafting an XML document is to create an XML declaration. An XML declaration is optional (but highly recommended) and includes up to five parts. All together, these parts look like this:

```
<?xml version="1.0" standalone="no" encoding="UTF-8"?>
|--1-|-----2------|------3--------|------4---------|5|
```

Each part of this sample declaration works as follows:

1. `<?xml` begins the XML declaration.

2. `version="1.0"` describes the version of XML in use. Currently, XML 1.0 is the only version; therefore, `version` must equal `1.0`.

3. `standalone="no"` specifies whether external markup declarations exist. You may set this attribute equal to `yes` or `no`. The `yes` value means that you don't use external declarations; `no` means that you do reference external declarations.

4. `encoding="UTF-8"` specifies the character encoding the author uses. UTF 8 corresponds to what most of us know as 8-bit ASCII characters.

5. `?>` closes the XML declaration.

For now, we keep our XML markup simple because we're concentrating on converting from XHTML to XML. For a more detailed look at creating XML documents, see Chapter 4.

Step 2: Create a root element

The root element is the most important element in any XML document. In any well-formed HTML document, `html` is always the root element. In XML, however, the root element can be just about anything that you want it to be. In XML, you create a root element and all related XML elements; then, you can use them in more or less the same way that you use predefined HTML elements.

For our example, it makes sense for us to designate `Recipes` as the root element. Because our document contains one or more recipes, our root element name sets the stage for our sample document, which can contain a single recipe or many recipes.

What we have so far is:

```
<?xml version="1.0" standalone="no" encoding="UTF-8"?>
<Recipes>
</Recipes>
```

Step 3: Create XML Markup

Next, we pick parts of our recipe XHTML document and provide them with new element names. Look back at Listing 2-2. You already know to change the `html` element to the `Recipes` element, so what's next? Well, you know you want to have at least one or more recipes in your document, so you need a `Recipe` element to contain each recipe. Then, each recipe should have a title. But wait, our example already has a title, so we can just leave that title like it is. Thus, we arrive at the following state:

```
<?xml version="1.0" standalone="no" encoding="UTF-8"?>
<Recipes>
<Recipe>
<Title>Bean Burrito</Title>
</Recipe>
</Recipes>
```

If you examine the markup a little more closely, other element names should jump out at you. Look back at Listing 2-2 and try it yourself once. Then read the following steps to see what we came up with:

1. The following line of markup tells you specific information about the document: Who wrote it and what type of recipe it is:

```
<p>This recipe was written by <i><b>The XML Gourmet</b></i>.<br />
This yummy recipe can be classified as tex-mex.</p>
```

   Just from the way this text is written, it makes sense to create a `cook` attribute for the `Recipe` element and then create a `Category` element that tells you the name of the type of food. So, our document shapes up to look like this:

```
<Recipes>
<Recipe cook="The XML Gourmet">
<Category name="tex-mex"/>
<Title>Bean Burrito</Title>
</Recipe>
</Recipes>
```

In XML, you don't need to insert a space before the trailing slash in empty elements.

2. Next you find a heading 1 called *Bean Burrito Ingredients*. It makes perfect sense to change that to an Ingredients element.

3. Under the Ingredients element, you have an unordered list of ingredients. We call each list item simply an Item. This produces markup like this:

```
<Ingredients>
<Item>1 can refried beans</Item>
<Item>1 cup longhorn colby cheese, shredded</Item>
<Item>1 small onion, finely chopped</Item>
<Item>3 flour tortillas</Item>
</Ingredients>
```

4. The next heading 1 introduces a numbered list of cooking instructions for the recipe. We think it makes sense to use a CookingInstructions element followed by individual Cinst elements to separate individual cooking instructions to make our markup look like this:

```
<CookingInstructions>
<Cinst>Empty can of refried beans into medium saucepan.</Cinst>
<Cinst>Heat over medium-high heat until beans are smooth and
    bubbly.</Cinst>
<Cinst>Warm tortillas in microwave for 30 seconds.</Cinst>
</CookingInstructions>
```

5. The last bit of text contains a heading 1 that introduces a numbered list for serving instructions. We follow what we did in the preceding step and create a ServingInstructions element with Sinst elements to separate the individual serving instructions. So now we have

```
<ServingInstructions>
<Sinst>Spread 1/3 of warm beans on each tortilla.</Sinst>
<Sinst>Sprinkle with cheese and onions.</Sinst>
<Sinst>Roll tortillas and serve.</Sinst>
</ServingInstructions>
```

There you have it. Listing 2-3 shows the complete XML markup and documents that you'll never want to see again after you finish this book! We sincerely hope it doesn't spoil your taste for Tex-Mex, either (we still like it; so should you).

Listing 2-3: Our Recipe Document

```
<Recipes>
<Recipe cook="The XML Gourmet">
  <Title>Bean Burrito</Title>
```

(continued)

Listing 2-3 *(continued)*

```
    <Category name="tex-mex"/>
    <Ingredients>
     <Item>1 can refried beans</Item>
     <Item>1 cup longhorn colby cheese, shredded</Item>
     <Item>1 small onion, finely chopped</Item>
     <Item>3 flour tortillas</Item>
    </Ingredients>
    <CookingInstructions>
     <Cinst>Empty can of refried beans into medium saucepan.</Cinst>
     <Cinst>Heat over medium-high heat until beans are smooth and bubbly.</Cinst>
     <Cinst>Warm tortillas in microwave for 30 seconds.</Cinst>
    </CookingInstructions>
    <ServingInstructions>
     <Sinst>Spread 1/3 of warm beans on each tortilla.</Sinst>
     <Sinst>Sprinkle with cheese and onions.</Sinst>
     <Sinst>Roll tortillas and serve.</Sinst>
    </ServingInstructions>
 </Recipe>
 </Recipes>
```

Step 4: Checking your document

An XML document with an error is a dead document. Even omitting a single
closing bracket renders a document unreadable. Instead of staring at your
document for hours, trying to find a minute error (such as that missing
bracket), use a *parser,* a program that checks your XML document for errors.
Find out more about validation in Chapter 4.

Chapter 3

Getting XML Basics Down Pat

· ·

· ·

*O*ne of the best things about eXtensible Markup Language (XML) documents is that they're text based. Text isn't proprietary (like a Windows or Mac application file might be), so you can share XML documents with all your friends and family — okay, how about your coworkers and business partners — without considering which computer operating system that they use.

With flexibility like this, we're sure that you're chomping at the bit to get started with XML. In this chapter, we start off by proving to you that XML really is as powerful as we claim by providing you with a bit of inspiration. We showcase two real-world XML solutions and introduce you to the sample XML that we use throughout the book in our examples and discussions. Finally, we dive into the particulars of XML with a discussion of two very important components of XML: Document Type Definitions (DTDs) and schemas. You also get a glimpse of how style sheets can make your complex data useful to a variety of computer systems and people.

XML by Excellent Example

Large numbers of individuals, organizations, and businesses plan and implement XML solutions every day. You know this or you wouldn't be reading this book. To show that XML applies across a variety of industries and is useful in ways too numerous to count, this section includes a short review of how XML is being used in two very different ways.

Using OFX to describe financial data

The applications Money (from Microsoft) and Quicken (from Intuit) are the two most popular personal financial software packages that individuals use to balance their checkbooks and track their expenses. A majority of banks, large and small, offer Web-based access to account information. Some even provide that information in Money and Quicken formats. To serve the widest possible audience, the bank has to make checking account information available in as many as four formats: the bank's, Web-based for online access, Money, and Quicken.

Wouldn't it be easier if financial data existed in one standard format that the banks, the Web, and your personal financial software could all understand? The Open Financial Exchange (OFX) accomplishes this goal by using XML to describe bank data and then transfer that data electronically via the Internet. Although Microsoft and Intuit compete in the software world, they've come to realize that standardizing on one datatype is a good thing. They can still compete for your hard-earned dollars based on their respective program's different functionalities, as well as how easy these programs are to use. The data format should be irrelevant.

Because Microsoft, Intuit, and the banking organizations can agree on a single format to describe banking data, information exchange is as easy as pie. They chose XML because it's a standard in — and is becoming the de facto format for — data exchange. To discover more about OFX, check out www.ofx.net.

Tracking ancestry with GedML

Thanks in large part to the efforts of the Mormon Church, genealogical data is abundant and widely available. One of the hardest parts of tracking your ancestors is reconciling all the information that you uncover. You may find a birth record here and a hospital record there, and of course you hear all sorts of stories. After you gather this information, you must put it together and see what it adds up to.

The *Genealogical Markup Language* (GedML) is a set of XML elements used to describe genealogical data. GedML is based on GEDCOM, an existing common format for describing this kind of information that uses XML to describe the data involved.

One of the best ways to find out about implementing a solution is to see what others are already doing with it. In Chapters 21 and 22, among others, we take a detailed look at a variety of XML implementations already at work in the world.

A Truly Simple XML Document

You're probably thinking, "Enough hype already. Show me the money." (Or the XML, in this case.) Your wish is our command. One simple XML document coming up, as shown in Listing 3-1.

Listing 3-1:   A Simple XML Document

```
<?xml version="1.0" standalone="yes"?>
<Recipes>
 <Recipe cook="The XML Gourmet">
 <Title>Bean Burrito</Title>
 <Category name="tex-mex"/>
 <Ingredients>
  <Item>1 can refried beans</Item>
  <Item>1 cup longhorn colby cheese, shredded</Item>
  <Item>1 small onion, finely chopped</Item>
  <Item>3 flour tortillas</Item>
 </Ingredients>
 <CookingInstructions>
  <Cinst>Empty can of refried beans into medium saucepan.</Cinst>
  <Cinst>Heat over medium-high heat until beans are smooth and bubbly.</Cinst>
  <Cinst>Warm tortillas in microwave for 30 seconds.</Cinst>
 </CookingInstructions>
 <ServingInstructions>
  <Sinst>Spread 1/3 of warm beans on each tortilla.</Sinst>
  <Sinst>Sprinkle with cheese and onions.</Sinst>
  <Sinst>Roll tortillas and serve.</Sinst>
 </ServingInstructions>
 </Recipe>
</Recipes>
```

Listing 3-1 is a sample XML document that uses our own markup language, the Recipe Markup Language (RML). Huh? We just made up a markup language? That we did.

You see, it's easy to think of XML as a language (and it's okay with us if you do), but to be truly accurate you should think of it as a *meta-markup language* — a markup language for defining other markup languages. XML provides a set of rules for creating markup that describes a particular kind of content — for example, financial data, genealogical data, or recipes. In turn, you can use the content described with that markup as part of an XML-based application that specifically addresses a need. In the case of our RML, the need is to manage recipes.

Whether you understand this markup versus meta-markup explanation isn't important. What's important is that you keep in mind that XML was created to *do* something — specifically, to describe data in a constant and predictable way so that it's usable across a variety of systems and applications. We cannot emphasize this fact enough. If you want to use XML to create a language to describe your family tree, you could call it the Family Markup Language (FML). If you want to use it to create a language to help solve world hunger, we encourage you give it your best shot (but keep in mind that XML does have *a few* limitations). You can call it the No More World Hunger Markup Language (NMWHML). (When you receive the Nobel prize, don't forget to thank us in your acceptance speech.)

The role of markup

The function of the simple markup in our RML is to describe a recipe — any recipe. The markup that we define in the previous section describes the different components of a recipe, including its title, author, ingredients, and steps for preparing and serving the finished dish.

All the different kinds of content in the recipe are described with markup, and you (or the computer system of your choice) can easily identify its different pieces and parts based on that markup. For example, without knowing much about the syntax of markup, you can tell what kind of information each bit of markup is designed to describe. For example, Ingredients identifies the recipe ingredients, and CookingInstructions identifies cooking instructions. Content description is what XML is all about. Add some descriptive elements and poof! — you have an XML document. It's almost as easy as making a bean burrito.

Not all markup is as reader-friendly as ours is. Because our markup exists primarily to support the discussions of this book, we've been particularly careful to make it human-readable. When you create your markup language — or learn to work with someone else's — keep in mind that the markup should fit the content like a glove. In the end, you want the computer or the programming that processes the XML to be able to best understand it.

We're sure that you can think of different ways to describe this same recipe by using more or different markup elements. You might include a Preparation element that would precede the CookingInstructions element, in which you could instruct readers to shred the cheese and chop the onion finely. Or maybe you'd rather see the author of the recipe identified as author instead of cook. As you discover in the Chapter 4, a large part of working with XML is analyzing what content you have to work with and finding the right markup to describe it.

Beyond the markup

With a little time, we could build an application that uses RML to feed recipes into a deeply complex system with a database of ingredients, a way to increase and decrease the number of servings, tools for customizing meals and shopping lists, and more. You'll discover as we go along that the markup and XML documents are only one part of the solution — albeit a key part. Content described with markup works in conjunction with other tools, such as programming languages and databases, to create the final XML application.

So if you have a burning desire to flesh out our RML and devise a complete recipe-management solution of your own, go for it. And as you work your way through other chapters in the book and discover the fine points of creating XML — including DTDs, schemas, documents, style sheets, and more — change our RML as you see fit. You'll end up with a tool for describing your favorite recipes as you exercise your XML know-how.

Getting Comfy with DTDs and Schemas

In XML, you can use any combination of elements and attributes to describe the pieces and parts of your content. If you'd like, you can make up your markup as you go along and never use the same markup twice. Remember, however, that one of the main reasons that you use XML to describe content is to make that content easy to share with other systems and applications. You also want other people to be able to create content that works well with any applications that you have.

In the real world, this means you want to give others (human or digital) a map to the markup you've used. Or if you want your content to play well with a different system, you can use markup already defined by someone else's map. For example, OFX and GedML have maps that enable a lot of different people to use their markup to define financial data or genealogical data, respectively.

The reason that XML works so well as a tool for data description and exchange is that everyone (and every system) using a particular flavor of markup agrees to use that markup. The map provides the lowdown on the particulars of the markup so that everyone is on the same page.

In XML, the two methods for defining the map for a particular set of markup elements are DTDs and schemas. Both define what kind of markup elements you can use — what kinds of tags such elements require, what attributes go with them, and so forth — to describe data in an XML document. Each flavor of markup that you may want to use to describe your content — usually called an XML *vocabulary* or *application* — has its own DTD or schema.

A *DTD* or *schema* specifies how a document's elements can work together to create a specific structure. For example, in our recipe markup, the Item element relies on the Ingredients element to completely identify different ingredients for the recipe. Without the Ingredients element, you don't know very much about the content of the Item element — it could be a grocery list item, for all you know. The Ingredients and Item elements together identify each recipe ingredient as an individual ingredient item. Together, all the elements in the RML describe a complete recipe.

When you don't need a DTD or schema

Technically, you need a DTD or schema to create XML documents and use them in an XML solution. Of course, you *can* just make up tags as you go along and not worry about creating a map to your markup. But, there's really only one circumstance for which we can recommend this practice: When you're first creating a new flavor of XML.

Rarely do DTD and schema developers get their markup exactly right on the first try. Remember that markup needs to describe content well, and you can use any combination of elements and attributes for the description. DTDs and schemas usually go through several iterations before they're done, and most developers start by taking a sampling of data and writing markup sans DTD or schema. After they have a good set of working markup, they usually create the final DTD or schema from it. Find out more about this particular approach in Chapter 4.

The rare instance may pop up when you'll describe some content with markup and then never need to use the markup again. Our experience tells us that this isn't very common. Because the whole point of XML is for systems (or people) to agree on a common set of rules for describing data and then use those rules, you almost always need a map to those rules. If you plan to share your data, want to be able to take data from others, or want someone who comes after you to know how your XML documents work, you want a DTD or schema to go with them.

Another good example of how elements work together in markup is a document that describes the books in a library. If you want to catalog all your books using XML, you could create a document with a collection of Book elements each with a corresponding Title element. In this example, you don't know what the Title element is the title of without the Book element. The DTD or schema provides the map to how all the elements work together.

Even though DTDs and schemas do the same thing — define the rules for a particular set of markup — each does it in a different way. Chapters 6–9 include a complete overview of how each works and help you figure out which one you want to use when.

Predefined DTDs and schemas

Lots and lots of DTDs and schemas are already available for your use. For example, you can use an eXtensible HyperText Markup Language (XHTML) DTD that governs how you can use combinations of elements and attributes to define Web pages. Among other things, the DTD specifies that every XHTML document should be contained within the html element and that all tables should be contained within the table element. OFX and GedML are examples of other predefined DTDs and schemas that are already completely developed and ready for use. (See the earlier section, "XML by Excellent Example," for real-world examples of OFX and GedML.)

When you create a document according to a DTD or schema, you use a predefined structure that specifies how the components of markup (elements, attributes, and such) should be used to describe a particular kind of content. Predefined DTDs and schemas usually come from a couple of different sources:

 ✔ **Industry groups or organizations** that want to establish a common format for standard data — OFX is a perfect example of this source. Another good example is the Chemical Markup Language (CML), created by chemists to describe chemical equations.

 ✔ **Application builders** who created their systems to run with content described by a particular set of markup. The ColdFusion Markup Language (CFML) is a good example of this source. Allaire/Macromedia defined a particular set of markup for describing applications written to run in the ColdFusion system. ASP.NET from Microsoft also uses a similar predefined flavor of XML for creating Active Server Pages (ASP).

Of course, these aren't the only sources for predefined DTDs and schemas, but they are two of the most prominent. Browse some of the currently available DTDs and schemas at Schema.net (`www.schema.net`).

We bring this topic of predefined DTDs and schemas up because we think it's important that you look around for predefined schemas and DTDs before you try to create your own. If you find one that meets your needs, you can save yourself a lot of time because you're building on markup that at least one other person or group is using. If you're trying to work with an established system such as ASP, for example, you won't have a choice; you need to use that particular DTD to make your instructions work with that system.

Your own DTD or schema

Sometimes, however, even with all the predefined DTDs and schemas available, you can't find one that does your data justice. You just have to build your own. If you don't like our specialized RML, for example, you can write your own DTD or schema and make it as complex or as simple as you like. (See the earlier section, "A Truly Simple XML Document," to look at how we define RML.) You can then use your own set of elements to define the same bean burrito recipe that we describe with RML. Because the sets of elements would be different, however, the recipe would have two different structures.

When you're trying to decide whether you need to build a new DTD or schema for your content or use an existing one, remember that the most important issue is the way that the markup fits your content. The goal of XML is to make your content as accessible to a system as possible. That goal is thwarted when you force your content into an existing markup scheme because the markup doesn't accurately reflect the content.

Because the topic of using the right DTD or schema (your own or someone else's) is so important, we discuss it in more detail later in the book. In Chapter 4, we show you how to analyze your content so that you have a good idea of what information that the markup needs to describe. If you don't know your content, you won't be able to find the right markup to go with it.

Then, because DTDs and schemas are such crucial parts of XML development and are also an in-depth topic that you must understand to some extent if you want to build customized XML solutions, we devote a rather large section of this book to their ins and outs. See Chapters 5–11 for the complete skinny on DTDs and schemas: How to read them, how to build them, and how to use them with your XML documents and solutions. Finally, in Chapter 13, we show you how to analyze your whole XML solution to find out whether predefined markup or a customized set of markup will best fit into your grand scheme of things.

All about Context

One of the most powerful features of XML is that it enables you to describe data in a consistent way even though the data's context may change. "But when would the data's context change?"

Think about our bean burrito recipe again for a second. If you store a recipe as part of your personal collection, it has one context. If you submit that same recipe to an online recipe repository, its context changes.

That said, how does XML deal with changing contexts? And more importantly, why should you care?

Having that liberating feeling that only context-free data gives you

Unlike a Microsoft Word document, which really only works inside of Microsoft Word itself, XML documents aren't tied to any particular context. Because they're built of simple text, XML documents can be stored anywhere and processed on any platform or application. They don't depend on a particular application for display; in fact, their contents may never be seen, even though they can make an application hum. (See Chapter 22 for some examples of XML at work behind the scenes of a solution.)

Because an XML document isn't tied to one system or application, another bonus of its open nature is that you can use a variety of tools with an XML document and the data that it describes. Here are just some of the possibilities for our bean burrito recipe when described with XML:

✔ We might submit it to an online recipe repository to share with the world.

✔ It might be read by a meal-planning software program on a Windows XP system and be accessible for menu planning and shopping list creation.

✔ It could appear on a miniature countertop recipe computer that has a 6 x 4-inch screen and displays recipes in a simple way with no graphics or other splashy effects.

✔ We might submit it to a publisher for inclusion in a printed recipe book.

Same data, same markup, different context.

The previous scenario assumes that all the systems that we sent our recipes to accepted XML — and more specifically, our RML. In the real world, this isn't necessarily true. In fact, although many systems accept XML as their default data format, sometimes the data needs to use a different set of markup from one system to another. Never fear, XML has a solution for that, too. More on this interesting twist in Chapter 13.

Because a recipe is usually meant to be displayed, all our scenarios for the bean burrito recipe have some display component (on the Web, in a book, and so on). This doesn't mean, however, that all XML data has to be displayed. For example, if you pay your bills online, you may never see the XML that your bill-pay service exchanges with your credit card company. What you *do* see is its effects: The balance in your checking account goes down, as does your credit card bill.

Creating context with style

Okay, are you with us? We have one bean burrito recipe and many potential contexts. To dig a little deeper into the issue of context, we now narrow the possibility down to two: a countertop recipe computer and an online recipe repository. Both are XML-aware, and both can display the recipe. However, the context for display is different in each case.

The recipe computer has a small 6 x 4-inch screen and displays recipes in a simple way with no graphics or other splashy effects. The Web-based recipe repository is designed for users with computer monitors that can display resolutions of 800 x 600 pixels or larger. This means that the site displays recipes using an advanced layout, colors, and more goodies that the countertop recipe computer just can't handle.

See Figure 3-1 to see how the burrito recipe might look as displayed on a countertop computer. Figure 3-2 shows how it might look if you view it online at the repository's Web site.

If you've been following along at home (nod your heads), your question now should be, "How can one document be displayed differently, without the markup changing?" Remember that XML only *describes* data. It doesn't include information about how that data should be treated in any way, including its display. This is a good thing because single XML documents are incredibly flexible and support many possible forms of display. Style sheets help make that display possible.

In the traditional sense of the word, a *style sheet* is a file that holds the layout settings for a certain category of a document. Style sheets, like templates, contain settings for headers and footers, tabs, margins, fonts, columns, and more. One kind of style sheets for XML — eXtensible Stylesheet Language Formatting Objects (XSL-FO) — control how the XML documents are displayed by specifying how certain elements in a document should look. The style sheet for the countertop recipe computer specifies that the entire recipe should be displayed in a monospace font. The style sheet for the recipe repository Web site adds a title banner and a navigation bar and displays the recipe in a standard serif font — same document, two different displays.

Style sheets take on a whole new meaning in XML. They not only make it possible to display a single XML document in several different ways, but they also help you convert content from one flavor of XML to another if it means that the content will work better with your system. Because style sheets are the driving mechanisms behind the delivery of content in an XML solution, they're a major topic in and of themselves. We dedicate all of Part IV to this important topic. Turn to it for all you need to know about stylin' your XML.

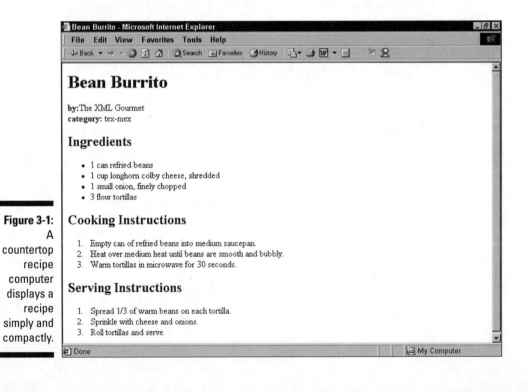

Figure 3-1:
A countertop recipe computer displays a recipe simply and compactly.

Figure 3-2:
An online
recipe
repository
adds flash
and
substance
to the
recipe's
display.

Context often has nothing to do with display; we use it here to help you visualize the power of context-free XML. And remember that a lack of context also means that a standalone XML document can't do much. It's ultimately up to the processing application — be it recipe repository or online banking system — that makes use of the data described with XML.

XML Doesn't Work Alone

On its own, XML can't do much, and an XML-based solution can have a variety of elements from databases to display and more. Although we haven't torn a complete XML solution apart just yet (don't worry, we get to that in Chapter 13), we hope you know by now that XML is just one component of a total solution. In XML-based applications, XML and the content that it describes are often driving forces behind the application and its functionality.

As you begin to discover more about the inner workings of XML, think about what kind of solution that you need or want to build and the role or roles that you think XML could play. As you delve more into XML and how it works, you can begin to refine your thoughts about the solution so that you have a good idea of how it can help you solve a problem or meet a need.

Part II
XML Basics

In this part . . .

*I*t's a good idea to get a thorough grounding in the pieces and parts that make up any XML document. Starting in Chapter 4, you consider the requirements for markup that a deceptively simple bean burrito recipe can pose and work your way through the exercise of understanding what kinds of elements, attributes, and potential document structure lie buried in this tasty little concoction!

In Chapter 5, you begin to plumb the mysteries of the markup descriptions known as a Document Type Definition (DTD) and XML Schema, which govern most XML documents. Chapter 5 takes you through the concepts and related terminology that control what DTDs and XML Schemas do and how they behave. Chapters 6 and 7 describe what's involved in understanding and creating your own DTDs (and hence, your own customized XML markup). Chapters 8 and 9 cover the same topics for XML Schema — namely understanding and creating XML document descriptions using an "all-XML" approach instead.

Chapter 4

Planning an XML Document That Does Something Great

*E*xtensible Markup Language was created to help people *do* things, so making an XML document really isn't all that much fun if the document doesn't have a function . . . or even worse, won't function at all. This chapter gives you a brief overview of the different components that you should include in every XML document so that it's well formed. To add to the fun, we show you how to be sure your documents are also valid. (If you haven't figured it out already, as soon as you start creating your own XML documents, you'll understand the importance of these classifications.)

You can create syntactically perfect XML, but if it doesn't fit your content, you're right back where you started. Because proper syntax is only half of the XML battle, the remainder of this chapter is devoted to helping you get a handle on the content that you're creating so that you can use XML to describe it well. Content analysis isn't nearly as scary as it sounds, and a little analysis early on (tell us what you see in these ink blots) can save you from going loco later.

Gettin' Down with Some Basic XML Rules

Obviously, a document that describes the elements in a complex chemical formula is a bit more intricate than one that describes the different pieces and parts of an address book, a recipe, or a novel.

No matter. XML documents are exactly as simple or as complex as they need to be to do the job that you have in mind for them. They don't need any extra fluff added along the way just for good measure. And whether an XML document is extremely complex or very simple, it must — we repeat, *must* — follow a basic set of rules.

XML documents that play by all the official rules are *well formed*. Figure 4-1 shows our XML document with some pointers to the different parts of the document that make it well formed.

A document that isn't well formed doesn't go far in the XML world because XML documents that aren't well formed aren't technically XML documents. You'll be sorry if you don't take the time to make sure that every document that you create plays by these very basic rules. (They aren't that hard to follow, actually.)

Root element

Attribute

Attribute value   XML declaration

Empty tag

Closing tag

```
Untitled - Notepad
File  Edit  Format  Help
<?xml version="1.0" standalone="yes"?>
<Recipes>
 <Recipe cook="The XML Gourmet">
  <Title>Bean Burrito</Title>
  <Category name="tex-mex"/>
  <Ingredients>
   <Item>1 can refried beans</Item>
   <Item>1 cup longhorn colby cheese, shredded</Item>
   <Item>1 small onion, finely chopped</Item>
   <Item>3 flour tortillas</Item>
  </Ingredients>
  <CookingInstructions>
   <Cinst>Empty can of refried beans into medium saucepan.</Cinst>
   <Cinst>Heat over medium-high heat until beans are smooth and bubbly.</Cinst>
   <Cinst>Warm tortillas in microwave for 30 seconds.</Cinst>
  </CookingInstructions>
  <ServingInstructions>
   <Sinst>Spread 1/3 of warm beans on each tortilla.</Sinst>
   <Sinst>Sprinkle with cheese and onions.</Sinst>
   <Sinst>Roll tortillas and serve.</Sinst>
  </ServingInstructions>
 </Recipe>
</Recipes>
```

Figure 4-1: Dissecting the different parts of an XML document.

Root element

Opening tag

✔ **You need an XML declaration.** The first thing to include in every XML document is a simple declaration that specifies the document is XML compliant. (See Chapter 6 for more on the XML declaration.) In our burrito recipe, the declaration always is the first line and always looks like this:

```
<?xml version="1.0" standalone="yes"?>
```

The attribute `standalone` with a value of `yes` means that the document isn't dependent on any other document to be complete. You can still reference style sheets, Document Type Documents (DTDs), schemas, and other such documents, but what you're saying with this attribute is the application that processes the document won't have to go looking for any other documents for a complete set of content. Most XML documents are standalone. Look for more information on this topic in Chapter 6.

✔ **You need a root element to contain all the other elements.** All elements and content within an XML document must live within a single top-level element, appropriately called the *document element* or *root element*. In our sample, `Recipes` is the document element. This means that every document that uses our Recipe Markup Language (RML) should begin with `<Recipes>` and end with `</Recipes>`.

Sound familiar? If you're well versed in HTML, you can think of this rule like the one that says that every HTML document has to begin with `<html>` and end with `</html>`.

✔ **Every element must have a start tag and an end tag.** If you open an element, make sure that you close it. If the burrito recipe were missing `</CookingInstructions>` somewhere in the document after the opening `<CookingInstructions>`, the document wouldn't be well formed. If you've worked with HTML, this ought to be a bit of a change for you. There are no exceptions. Well. . . .

✔ **Empty elements have to end with a slash (/).** Okay, we lied. There's one exception to the open/close rule that we mention in the previous bullet, but even this exception means paying very close attention to the details. Elements that consist of only a start tag, such as the `Category` element in our example, are called *empty elements* because they don't hold content between opening and closing tags. To avoid confusion and to prevent XML tools from searching endlessly for closing tags that don't exist in the first place, identify all empty elements with a slash (/) before the closing greater than sign (>), like this:

```
<Category name="tex-mex"/>
```

In the upcoming section, "Using trial and error for the best fit," we give you some guidance on how to choose what kind of markup structures to use as you define your content. In Chapter 6, you find out all about the ins and outs of elements in general.

✔ **Elements should be nested like measuring cups.** Nesting elements means including one within the other, as we do with our `<Ingredients>`. . . `</Ingredients>` and `<Item>`. . .`</Item>` elements:

```
<Ingredients><Item>1 can refried beans</Item></Ingredients>
```

To avoid breaking this cardinal rule, always close *first* the tag that you opened *last*. In other words, DON'T go out of order:

```
<Ingredients><Item>1 can refried beans</Ingredients></Item>
```

The closing `Item` tag shouldn't come after the closing `Ingredients` tag. This is incorrect. Bad reader.

A good tool for remembering to nest elements correctly is to think of nested suitcases. Before you can close and zip the outer suitcase you have to close and zip the inner suitcase. Think of tags as suitcase tops: You can't close the one on the outside until you close the one on the inside.

✔ **All attribute values should be quoted.** You *must* enclose every attribute value in quotation marks (either single or double quotes — double quotes are used most often) as we do in our burrito recipe when we identify the recipe's cook `<Recipe cook="The XML Gourmet">`. If you forget even one set of quotation marks, you can count on the markup to break somewhere along the line.

✔ **Tags and entities have to be built the right way.** Every XML tag must begin with a less than sign (`<`), and every XML entity must begin with an ampersand (`&`). XML tools don't know what to do with tags and entities that don't play by this rule, and usually treat them as plain ol' content. Not a total disaster (if you fix the error) but certainly not a boon for the document if you leave it alone.

An *entity* is a virtual storage unit that can contain text, binary files such as graphics or sound clips, or non-ASCII characters such as the copyright symbol. You reference an entity in an XML document by using a string of characters that begins with an ampersand (`&`) and ends with a semicolon (`;`).

XML supports non-ASCII characters. In Chapter 10 we discuss the XML use of characters and entities in depth.

XML is very flexible; its syntax is rigid. This is a good thing because it guarantees that all XML documents adhere to the same basic rules (and computers like data that follows the rules).

Some Rules Aren't Meant to Be Broken

If you that think some of these rules are a bit nit-picky, you're right. Remember, the intended audience for your XML isn't a human being who can intuit what you "meant to mark," but a computer that can only work with what you give it.

If you're worried that building well-formed documents by hand will be tedious and not worth the effort, don't abandon us (and XML) here. Take a look at the sidebar "Staying well formed with good tools" elsewhere in this chapter to find out how a good XML tool picks the nits for you.

To put the rules in action (just for fun — this pop quiz isn't being graded), see whether you can find the problems with the version of the bean burrito recipe in Listing 4-1. (***Hint:*** There are seven mistakes — one for each rule — that would have to be corrected to make this document well formed.)

Listing 4-1:   A Broken XML Document

```
<Recipes />
<Recipe cook=The XML Gourmet">
  <Title>Beef Nachos
  <Category name="tex-mex">
  Ingredients>
    <Item>1 can refried beans</Item>
    <Item>1 cup longhorn colby cheese, shredded</Item>
    <Item>1 small onion, finely chopped</Item>
    <Item>3 flour tortillas</Item>
  </Ingredients>
  <CookingInstructions>
    <Cinst>Empty can of refried beans into medium saucepan.</Cinst>
    <Cinst>Heat over medium-high heat until beans are smooth and bubbly.</Cinst>
    <Cinst>Warm tortillas in microwave for 30 seconds.</CookingInstructions>
  </Cinst>
  <ServingInstructions>
    <Sinst>Spread 1/3 of warm beans on each tortilla.</Sinst>
    <Sinst>Sprinkle with cheese and onions.</Sinst>
    <Sinst>Roll tortillas and serve.</Sinst>
  </ServingInstructions>
</Recipe>
```

If you're playing along at home, here's a list of the errors that we made:

- **The XML declaration is missing.** Remember that the first line of every document needs to be an XML declaration similar to this:

  ```
  <?xml version="1.0" standalone="yes"?>
  ```

- **The document element isn't complete.** The `Recipes` document element is missing its closing tag. Because the document element must contain every other element in the document, it can't be an empty tag, as in the broken document; you have to use a tag pair.

  ```
  <Recipes />
  ```

  The well-formed markup is

  ```
  <Recipes>
  . . .
  </Recipes>
  ```

- **There's an attribute value that's not enclosed in quotes.** The value of the `cook` attribute in the `Recipe` element is missing its open quotation mark. The well-formed version is

```
<Recipe cook="The XML Gourmet">
```

✔ **An element is missing a closing tag.** We forgot to close the `Title` element:

```
<Title>Beef Nachos
```

The well-formed XML is

```
<Title>Beef Nachos</Title>
```

✔ **An empty element is missing its closing slash.** To be well formed,

```
<Category name="tex-mex">
```

should be

```
<Category name="tex-mex"/>
```

✔ **An opening tag isn't properly built.** All tags must begin with a less-than sign (<), and our opening `Ingredients` tag is missing its less-than sign:

```
Ingredients>
```

The proper syntax is:

```
<Ingredients>
```

✔ **Elements aren't properly nested.** The final `Cinst` element isn't nested properly within the `CookingInstructions` element:

```
<CookingInstructions>
<Cinst>Empty can of refried beans into medium saucepan.</Cinst>
<Cinst>Heat over medium-high heat until beans are smooth and
        bubbly.</Cinst>
<Cinst>Warm tortillas in microwave for 30 seconds.</CookingInstructions>
</Cinst>
```

The well-formed XML looks like this:

```
<CookingInstructions>
<Cinst>Empty can of refried beans into medium saucepan.</Cinst>
<Cinst>Heat over medium-high heat until beans are smooth and
        bubbly.</Cinst>
<Cinst>Warm tortillas in microwave for 30 seconds.</Cinst>
</CookingInstructions>
```

We've found that people with HTML experience have a harder time learning to adhere to the rules of well-formedness simply because Web browsers seem to encourage breaking the rules instead of following them. Although this shift in thinking happens gradually (some may say *painfully*), with a little practice you'll be over the HTML hump. (We made it without too much discomfort.)

Staying well formed with good tools

You're probably wondering how you can possibly remember all the rules that we describe in this chapter when you develop XML documents. Even veteran document designers forget a quotation mark or two here and there — not to mention occasionally forgetting a closing tag or a slash at the end of an empty tag. If you try to send a malformed XML document to the application that is going to work with it, the application will spit it right back out at you, or spit out error messages that are just as bad. Before you get your document to your application, it pays to ensure that it's well formed and valid (if necessary).

The best way to make sure your documents are well formed is to build your XML document with a text editor built specifically for XML documents. XML editors can check documents as you build them so that easy-to-make mistakes don't fester long enough to grow into ugly, malformed documents. Believe us, you'll be a happier and less-stressed camper if you go out and

find yourself a good editor — we promise! XML editors are available for a variety of platforms and range in price from free to fairly expensive. Every editor has extra gimmicks and functions, but no XML editor is worth its salt if it can't check documents to make sure that they're well formed.

In Chapter 20, we focus entirely on XML-related tools, including a section on XML editors. Read more about the editors available for your platforms of choice and then download a few and try them out. The best online resource that we've found for XML software is www. xmlsoftware.com.

For fun, and to see how a good XML editor can help you avoid common mistakes, try recreating Listing 4-1 in an XML editor. Depending on the editor, it will ring warning bells with each new mistake that you intentionally create, or will run a check on your final document and list all the errors.

Seeking Validation with DTD and XML Schema

A step up from well-formedness is validity. In addition to being well formed, a *valid* XML document adheres to a DTD or an XML Schema. Although all XML documents must be well formed — or else they aren't XML — not all XML documents have to be valid. As we mention in Chapter 3, DTDs and schemas give your XML documents an extra layer of organizational structure. This extra organization makes your life easier when you want to make a document actually do something (which is all the time) because it helps developers share expectations about document structures. In Chapter 3, we stress (okay, harp on) the idea that DTDs and schemas give you a map to follow when you're creating XML documents.

To be or not to be (valid): That is an ASP.NET question

The issue of whether your XML documents need to be valid or not depends entirely on what you want your XML document to do. If you plan to use your XML document with other systems and across applications (a likely scenario, we think), you need to be aware that the data is defined in a particular way: that is, consistent with other XML documents of its type. The only way to accomplish standardization is to create valid documents.

A good example of this is the Microsoft ASP.NET system for creating dynamic Web sites that can be tied to a database. Because you pass all the programming instructions that guide the development of a Web site to the system in the form of Active Server Pages (ASP) code, the ASP.NET system needs to know what to expect from you and how your code is structured. To pass code to ASP, you must create valid XML so that the system can give you the results you're looking for.

To create a valid document, you have to follow the map to the letter. DTDs and schemas spell out:

- ✔ Which elements and attributes are required in valid documents
- ✔ How all the components of markup work together in valid documents
- ✔ Which elements and attributes are optional in valid documents

We give you more details about XML Schemas and DTDs in Chapters 6 through 11.

If you're in doubt about the necessity of validity in XML, just remember that XML documents are cool because they're malleable enough to enable users to access vital data across platforms. DTDs and schemas make this important function possible by allowing programmers to set up common rules for specific types of functions.

Here are a couple of ways that you can use DTDs and schemas:

- ✔ **You've come up with a brand-new solution or function that you want to make accessible to others:** Say that you create a recipe repository that enables users worldwide to search for recipes. If we decide to submit our burrito recipe to the repository, we have to follow your rules because you're the one who decided which standard information to include and which format the data should appear in. If you come up with a cool tool that you want others to be able to use, you write the book, so to speak, and the rules.

✔ **You want your XML document to be used according to someone else's rules:** Say that you want to submit your famous enchilada recipe to an online repository. It just so happens that the repository accepts XML documents but it's already set up rules that require every recipe to contain the same, standard information — ingredients, instructions, and so on. Some additional information, such as the author or cook, may be optional. The repository's DTD or schema lays out all these rules for marking up recipes so that they contain standard information in a standard format. To ensure that your recipe is widely accessible, you've got to follow the rules that are already in place, which means applying an existing DTD or schema in your own document. If your document is described with one set of markup, like our RML for example, you may have to redescribe it with the XML the repository expects so that the system will accept it.

When you submit the recipe, the first thing that the repository does is check to see whether your document is valid. If the document is valid, the repository happily accepts the recipe, and the world can glory in your enchilada masterpiece. If you've left something out, your document is invalid (even if it's well formed), and the repository doesn't allow you to submit your recipe. Instead, it gives you an error message letting you know your document is invalid and wasn't accepted by the system. If the repository application was well written, it might even be nice enough to tell you which parts of the DTD or schema that you violated. One way or the other, it won't accept your recipe until it's valid.

Content Analysis and You

In earlier chapters of this book (and earlier in this chapter), we stress over and over again the importance of making sure that your markup fits your content like puzzle pieces, or peas and carrots, or a hand in a glove (choose the simile that you prefer).

The process of becoming best friends with your content is often called *content analysis* or *information analysis*. Whatever name it goes by, analysis requires breaking down content into bite-size chunks to see exactly what pieces are going to become key components when you describe the data with markup.

 When we use the term *components,* we're referring to types of data that run throughout a document. Ingredients and cooking instructions are two key components of a recipe, for example. Until you have a good handle on the components of your content, you can't create markup that fits it or even use an existing markup language to describe it.

Why start from scratch when you can use other people's work?

Not to sound like a broken record, but here we go anyway. Because XML describes how data is supposed to be used, it s the ideal markup language for making good on a very simple but very important idea: to customize a solution to fit the problem instead of trying to solve a problem by modifying it to fit a predefined solution. XML is optimized for maximum tweakage, so go ahead — take someone else's predefined markup, study its DTD or schema, and use it to describe your own, specially-modified, markup. After all, that's the main reason to analyze data that you're working with — to customize

markup (or create brand-new markup) to perform a particular function.

Visit www.schema.net to read about existing DTDs and schemas; choose a DTD or schema that sounds interesting to you. When you look at how the DTD or schema developers broke down the content, ask the following questions:

✔ Do you agree with their choices?

✔ What would have done differently?

Exercises like these go a long way towards learning to analyze your own content.

We usually start our analysis by trying to understand what the key components of the content already do, and then we determine how we want to extend the components' existing functions.

Getting started by gathering some content

To get started analyzing data, you need to gather up several samples of the data content to work with so that you can create as complete a composite of the key data components as possible.

The more complete that your collection of samples is, the better chance that you have of creating markup that fits all your content. Here are some ideas:

✔ **Get data from multiple sources:** If you want to describe recipe content, find several different kinds of recipes, from main dishes to deserts, and preferably from different sources.

If you're working with data for a business, gather invoices, receipts, and other data that comes from multiple vendors or customers. One vendor may exclude vital info that another vendor includes.

✔ **Get a lot of data:** If you need to describe data that will eventually go into an existing database, see whether you can get sample data that's already in the database so that you can be sure that your markup and the database's requirements match.

You may have to make modifications to the database to make sure that the information is gathered and used to its fullest extent.

✔ **Get a lot of data from multiple sources:** If you need to describe complex reports, lay your hands on several different reports, written by different people if possible.

You're getting the drift, aren't you?

To create a complete picture, try to find five or six samples, at least, to work with.

If you're familiar with the content that you're working with, you've already got a leg up on the process. If you're unfamiliar with the content, however, take some time to talk to those people who create or frequently process the data. Find out

✔ What users do with individual pieces of information

✔ What data users think is impossible to live without (and why)

✔ What data is unnecessary or optional (and why)

Gather enough information to sufficiently understand what the key components of the content are, why the content was created, and what the people who created it need to make it useful to them.

Because your content is ultimately destined for a processing system of some kind, you should talk with the people building that system to see what kind of data requirements it has (assuming there's no predefined DTD or schema already in place). You want your markup to work with their system, so a little bit of communication up front about their needs and expectations goes a long way towards avoiding a complete rework of your DTD or schema.

Slicing and dicing recipe content

When we created our RML, we went through the same data-analysis process that we're sharing with you. After we gathered our sample recipes and familiarized ourselves with them (we like to cook, so we had plenty of sample recipes to work with), we took a good hard look at what we learned about the content of recipes. Here's what we came up with:

✔ **Recipes may be categorized.** Some include:

- Type of cuisine

- Type of recipe (for example, vegetarian)

- Ingredients needed

- Time needed to prepare and complete the recipes

✔ **Recipes usually have a title and a list of ingredients.**

Recipes may also include an author or source, step-by-step preparation instructions, cooking instructions, and serving instructions.

✔ **Some recipes may also include pictures.**

Sometimes only a photograph of the finished dish is included. Other recipes may also include photographs or drawings to depict particularly tricky operations (such as boning a fowl, trussing a roast, and so forth).

In the end, we discovered that recipes can be very complex and have a variety of component types. Some components are consistent across all recipes (such as ingredients), but others are only found in some (such as pictures). We created RML to help you understand XML — not as an elaborate markup language that covered all the bases. (We left images out of the fray, for example.) That decision was as much of the content-analysis process as discovering that pictures are a possible content element. Knowing the purpose of your markup can help you keep your goals in check.

Jumping right in and making markup

You might be surprised by this tidbit, but one of the best ways to start analyzing content is to jump in and write some markup that describes how it should be used — after you have a good understanding of what it takes to create and use the content, of course. What you start with may only slightly resemble your finished markup language, but you do have to start somewhere.

During this process of writing markup, you're really doing a detailed analysis of the content and you have two products in the end: a solid content analysis and a working draft of the markup that you need to describe it.

To create RML, we picked a recipe and started creating elements. In our initial round of markup, we used Recipe as the document element because we thought that each recipe would have its own document. After giving it some thought, we realized that we might want to put several recipes in one document (such as a document containing nothing but vegetarian Mexican cuisine). Thus we made Recipes the document element and set the Recipe element to delineate each individual recipe in a document.

Using trial and error for the best fit

We're not going to lie: A lot of this stuff is plain old-fashioned trial and error. As you work with your markup, experiment with using combinations of elements and attributes until you get the best results. For example, initially, we used two nested elements to specify the category for a recipe:

```
<Category>
  <Name>tex-mex</Name>
<Category>
```

This option would work very well if we thought that a recipe could have more than one category to work with. The markup would use as many Name elements within the Category element as there were categories, with at least one required. In the end, we decided to go with name as an attribute of the Category element instead because we thought that we'd want to predefine the category names and require that valid documents choose one of the names from the list in our DTD or schema. This choice narrows the category to one but allows us to enforce category names. The final XML turned out like this:

```
<Category name="tex-mex"/>
```

As you become more comfortable with content analysis, you will instinctively know that some data components work best as attributes and other data components work better as elements. As you discover the details of element and attribute syntax and how they work together (see Chapters 6 through 9), you'll have a firm basis for making decisions about what should be an element and what should be an attribute.

While you create your initial markup, you may find that you have new questions about the content that you need to answer before going on. That's okay. We might even say that's a good thing, but that's because we're perfectionists. Just try to keep in mind that analysis is part science and part intuition.

Testing your content analysis

The best way to test your final (or final draft) markup is to apply it to as many content samples as you can lay your hands on. With each test, you may find something that you need to tweak or change outright. However, after much testing, you'll end up with a final product that serves you well.

In a perfect world, you would have talked with the system's developer early in the process to find out what content the system needs to work with, using that knowledge while conducting data analysis. (We'll pretend that's exactly what you did.) Show your markup to the system developers and be sure that it has the information that they were expecting. Expect more tweaks and changes. Feed sample documents into the system and see what happens. Tweak and change some more.

Building a Better (Or Different) Bean Burrito

You may develop a preference for element naming conventions — `CookingInstructions` versus `cooking_instructions`, for example. (Either option works, but maybe you just don't like capital letters.) For those of us who analyze content for fun (and occasionally profit), the most important thing is the final feel of the markup and how well it works with the content.

To give you an idea of how two different sets of markup can be used for the same content, take a look at the version of the bean burrito recipe marked up with Alternative Recipe Markup Language (ARML), shown in Listing 4-2. This version incorporates some of our discussions from the previous section about attributes versus elements, using a different element naming convention. Note the different feel that it has. ARML also incorporates images and preparation times to show you how to add new components.

Listing 4-2:   The Bean Burrito Recipe in ARML

```
<?xml version="1.0" standalone="yes"?>
 <recipes>
  <recipe cook="The XML Gourmet">
   <title>Bean Burrito</title>
   <category>
     <name>tex-mex</name>
   </category>
   <time>
     <prep_time>10 minutes</prep_time>
     <cook_time>15 minutes</cook_time>
   </time>
   <difficulty scale="easy"/>
   <ingredients>
    <item>1 can refried beans</item>
    <item>1 cup longhorn colby cheese</item>
    <item>1 small onion</item>
    <item>3 flour tortillas</item>
   </ingredients>
   <preparation>
     <step>finely shred colby cheese</step>
     <step>chop onion</step>
   </preparation>
   <cooking_instructions>
    <cinst>Empty can of refried beans into medium saucepan.</cinst>
     <cinst>Heat over medium-high heat until beans are smooth and bubbly.</cinst>
     <cinst>Warm tortillas in microwave for 30 seconds.</cinst>
   </cooking_instructions>
   <serving_instructions>
    <sinst>Spread 1/3 of warm beans on each tortilla.</sinst>
    <sinst>Sprinkle with cheese and onions.</sinst>
    <sinst>Roll tortillas and serve.</sinst>
   </serving_instructions>
```

```
<images>
  <image_small href="/images/bean_burrito_thumbnail.gif/>
  <image_large href="/images/bean_burrito_large.gif/>
</images>
</recipe>
</recipes>
```

The content analysis that led us to this set of markup was a little different. We included more key elements because the goal of this markup was to be as complete as possible . . . not to teach XML. See how a subtle shift in thinking can change the final analysis of the content components and even how they are displayed? Yet another testament to the flexibility of XML.

Content analysis with XML in mind is much easier when you have a handle on the ins and outs of XML Schemas and DTDs and how to put them together. Once again, keep what you read here in mind as you check out how to build custom DTDs and schemas in Chapters 7 and 9.

Chapter 5

Defining XML Documents

· ·

· ·

*I*f you want to play the eXtensible Markup Language (XML) game, you have to know the rules. But the *X* in XML means *eXtensible*; the element names that you use and define are unlimited. That is, you get to make up as many (or as few) rules as you want or need to make the markup do what you want it to. For example, you can create a document definition for a recipe to define precisely what kind of data can go into any future XML documents that adhere to that definition.

The rules that you create with XML can dictate which elements make up an XML document, which kinds of content these elements can contain, and how such elements may be ordered. Document descriptions even support rules about which elements are optional, which ones are required, and how many times that certain elements can (or must) appear.

Creating XML document descriptions enables you to state the rules that a whole class of documents must follow. In this chapter, you explore why making such rules can be important or helpful, and you find out how to create or discover such rules. You also get an introduction to the primary techniques used to create XML document descriptions so that you can understand their differences and similarities.

The Magic of Metadata

Literally, the term *metadata* means data that describes other data. Computer scientists in general — and XML document wizards in particular — recognize document descriptions as a form of metadata. Document descriptions are considered metadata because they incorporate lots of crucial information, including:

✔ Named elements within the type of document described.

✔ What kinds of content named elements can contain.

✔ How named elements may be further qualified, distinguished, or labeled.

✔ The order in which elements can or must appear.

✔ Ranges of values from which element attribute values or actual element content must be chosen.

✔ Rules governing the occurrence of specific elements. (They may be optional or required, and if required, may be constrained to occur some specific number of times.)

✔ The relationships between and among elements in a document.

The metadata definitions *don't* contain the actual data that you care about; they just contain rules for describing the data.

An XML document description is nothing more than a formal statement of the rules that govern how content can or must appear in any XML document that claims to follow those rules. Because such document descriptions can be digested by software and then used to check the structure and content of individual documents against those rules, it becomes easy to determine whether a document adheres to or breaks those rules.

The ability to check individual documents against a governing collection of rules is what gives XML so much power. This also enables you to use a general-purpose approach (XML itself) to create all kinds of document types or XML applications. In turn, this kind of open-ended extensibility puts few limits on the imagination and ingenuity of individuals who design document descriptions.

To create an XML document description, you just need to understand the requirements of a particular description language (such as Standard Generalized Markup Language [SGML] or XML Schema). Therefore, to define XML documents, you need to become facile with a description language with which to state the rules for some particular type or class of XML documents. This means that a further set of rules exists for how XML document rules are stated — and this is why we use the term *metadata* to explain the role that document descriptions play for the XML documents that they govern.

Why Describe XML Documents?

At this point, you may be asking yourself why you need to bother creating a customized formal XML document description. The answer to this question is both interesting and telling: Creating a custom document description may be a good idea for numerous reasons, but not always necessary for other reasons. In Table 5-1, we describe both the pros and cons of creating your own customized XML document description.

Table 5-1	XML Document Description Pros and Cons
Pros	**Cons**
When you need to accommodate or incorporate specific types of content or document structures not readily available elsewhere, creating a custom document description helps meet those needs.	When an existing document description can accommodate your data or documents, you don't need to create a customized document description. Why bother if the work's already done for you?
When you want to check documents automatically against a set of formal rules (be it for quality control or other purposes), using a document description and a validator makes it easy to automate and apply such checks.	Well-formed XML documents that refer to no DTD or XML Schema needn't conform to a document description; they need only to conform to XML syntax rules. For single-use or trivial applications, invoking a formal document description may be overkill.
When you have a great deal of specific data to collect, store, and maintain, a detailed formal document description for such data helps organize and control that process.	When data or document collections are small or very simple in structure and/or content, creating a document description may be overkill. On the other hand, when numerous instances abound, see item to left!

As you explore the kinds of data and documents that XML can capture and represent, remember that the term *XML document* embraces a whole lot more than text. XML can handle many kinds of data, and its ability to accommodate or point to binary information means that it can supply data to other computer applications outside XML's control. Thus, an XML document can reference anything that a computer can represent, including video, graphics, multimedia, and other specialized kinds of data!

In general, it's not worth creating your own formal XML document descriptions unless one or more of the following conditions is true:

- You've got sizable collections of documents or data to manage.
- Your data collection (whether large or small) is pretty complex; therefore, you could benefit from the analysis and documentation that a document description represents.
- You want to promote a new industry standard.

Even then, creating custom document descriptions is worthwhile only when what you've got doesn't fit nicely into some existing, predefined XML markup language. This is what is also known as an *XML application*. XML applications invariably include one or more document descriptions at the core of their formal specifications, so lean on them if they meet your needs.

The extensible part of XML (*X* marks that spot) also means that you can extend existing XML document descriptions as well as XML documents. Before creating document descriptions from scratch, survey the landscape of existing XML applications. Don't be afraid to reuse pieces and parts of existing document description. You, too, can stand on the shoulders of the XML giants who've gone before you!

Creating XML Document Descriptions

XML documents can be described formally in many ways, but two languages for creating such descriptions are most widely used today.

- ✓ **Document Type Definitions (DTDs):** Documents created using the SGML
- ✓ **Schemas:** Documents created in XML that adhere to a document description markup language

As we discuss in Chapter 2, HyperText Markup Language (HTML) uses a set of SGML DTDs to describe specific versions (3.2, 4.0, and 4.01). The same is true for eXtensible HyperText Markup Language (XHTML) versions 1.0 and 1.1. DTDs describe many, if not most, existing standard XML applications.

XML Schema (one of many schema languages) is a purist's dream. It uses XML structure and syntax to create XML document descriptions. This also enables XML-literate professionals to rely on what they know about XML when building XML document descriptions. Because SGML is a complex markup language with syntax and structure different from XML, doing away with DTDs means one less learning curve to climb — or so goes the thinking of XML Schema aficionados, anyway.

XML Document Descriptions Compared and Contrasted

In the inner circles of the XML cognoscente, the argument continues as to which markup language is better for describing XML documents. Both DTDs and XML Schema have adherents and detractors. Not only is it difficult to separate the wheat from the chaff in the debate between these two camps, it's sometimes hard to know whom to believe.

Adding to this controversy, you can find lots of public discussion that XML Schema is overly complex for the kind of representational power that it confers. In simpler words, "Too much work, too few results, and too little flexibility." Multiple XML-based alternatives to XML Schema are available, such as REgular LAnguage for XML Next Generation (RELAX NG), Schematron, and the Microsoft XML-Data Reduced (XDR) schema language (see Chapter 8 for more information). In fact, some of these alternatives get higher marks for ease of learning and use than XML Schema does!

What's a body to do when it comes to building XML document descriptions? You can never go wrong by using your head and following some common sense rules. Most experts agree that the kinds of data that XML captures can be characterized along a spectrum from document- or text-intensive to what's called data-intensive.

On the document or text end of that continuum, the content to be captured and represented fits typical notions of text or hypertext materials — that is, a collection of words, graphics, and other information meant to be read or viewed as a structured object. Examples on this end of the spectrum include books, articles, magazines, narratives, training materials, and so forth.

On the data end of the spectrum, you find collections of data like those that reside in a database. These collections consist of a more or less arbitrary number of record structures, in which each record contains some kind of unique identifier or key (to help locate individual records), and each includes a common collection of named, organized values. Think of an address book, a card catalog in a library, or a set of medical records in your doctor's office.

Then, too, the capability of XML to capture and represent data that itself describes other collections of data — for example, start and stop dates for time-sensitive files, status information, modification data, and so forth — makes it easy to describe and use all kinds of helpful information that applies to document or data collections equally.

For example, we use a special form of XML markup to describe online classes in a Web-based course delivery environment that we've built. This markup describes class start and end dates, module counts, plus per-module quiz, exam, and interactive exercise links. This markup gives us a neat way to describe and manage all the pieces and parts of individual online classes. This also enables us to create and manage multiple online classes in the context of an ongoing Web service, where we may have as many as several dozen or only a handful of classes running at once. In general, this kind of information may also be considered to be data-intensive as well because it has no narrative structure. Because the flexibility of XML is so great, you can create one set of XML markup to manage and control other collections of XML markup. We call this *leverage*, and we like it!

Choosing between DTD and XML Schema

One simple rule for solving the DTD versus XML Schema dilemma is to examine the data to be described in order to pick one approach over the other. In general, DTDs work better for document- or text-intensive collections; XML Schema works better for data-intensive collections.

Another simple rule for choosing between DTDs and XML Schema is "Go with what you know." If you're already familiar with DTDs and understand how they work, the learning curve is behind you. Ditto for XML Schema. If you work with a description language that you already know, you can concentrate on describing XML documents, rather than learning a description language.

Finally, if you're equally oblivious to the details of DTDs and XML Schema, you might be swayed by that favorite argument of XML Schema proponents: If you want to build XML documents, you're going to have to master XML structure and syntax anyway. Therefore, why not also use a document description language based on XML?

Of course, there are pros and cons for both languages. We cover each of these major approaches elsewhere in this book: Chapters 6, 7, and 10 focus on DTDs; and Chapters 8, 9, and 11 focus on XML Schema. You can pick whichever language you like best or try your luck at both of them.

Chapter 6

Understanding and Using DTDs

*W*hen an XML document invokes a Document Type Definition (DTD) — using a document type (DOCTYPE) declaration — the DTD defines the rules of the game for that document. In general, you use DTDs to add structure and logic and to make it easier to understand what all the elements in an XML document mean. Although DTDs aren't absolutely necessary when creating XML documents, understanding what they are and how they work is important.

Using a DTD properly means that your document will be valid. In Chapter 2, we outline what it takes for an XML document to be well formed. In this chapter, we discuss what it takes to create an XML document that's valid when interpreted according to the rules defined in a specific DTD.

When using DTDs, please understand that they define a set of rules for the documents that they govern. Keep in mind that if you break the rules in any DTDs that your XML documents invoke, those documents will fail to validate properly — and may therefore be unusable because some document processors quit processing when they find a syntax or structure error.

What's a DTD?

A *Document Type Definition* (DTD) is a set of rules that defines the elements and their attributes in any XML document that invokes the DTD. Some people say that a DTD defines the grammar for an XML document because it tells applications — and people — what each element means and how to use it. We're all accustomed to rules that govern the way that we speak and write a language. Well, when you use a DTD, you automatically become subject to a bunch of rules that tell you how to write — markup, that is.

DTDs consist of declarations for elements and their attributes. DTDs are really nothing new; in techno years, they're pretty darn old. DTDs were created as part of the Standard Generalized Markup Language (SGML) — XML's parent.

DTDs aren't required because unlike SGML, XML follows strict rules of construction. This enables XML processors to read a well-formed document and infer the rules that govern the document. The processors do this by building a tree of all elements and their children and then drawing conclusions from the patterns in which elements occur. It's kind of like drawing your family tree by knowing who's related to whom and how.

Table 6-1 lists some of the important components that you find out about in this chapter.

Table 6-1		DTD Lingo
Term	*Example*	*What It Does*
XML declaration	`<?xml version="1.0" encoding="UTF-8" standalone="yes"?>`	Tells the processor which version of XML to use
Document type (DOCTYPE) declaration	`<!DOCTYPE Root-Element SYSTEM "Root-Element.dtd">`	Tells the processor where a DTD is located
Element type declaration	`<!ELEMENT Name (#PCDATA)>`	Defines an element type
Attribute-list declaration	`<!ATTLIST Element-Name Name Datatype Default>`	Defines a name, datatype, and default value (if any) for each attribute associated with an element
Entity declaration	`<!ENTITY Entity-Name "text">`	Defines a set of information that can be referred to by its entity name
Notation declaration	`<!NOTATION NameSystem "externalID">`	Associates a notation name with information that can help find an external program to interpret that notation (used to accommodate data and executables within XML documents that XML processors themselves can't handle directly)

Reading a Simple DTD

Even if you don't plan to create your own DTDs from scratch, knowing how to read them is helpful. In theory — and we hope in practice — XML (and DTDs) should be easy to read and understand. You should be able to look at a DTD, list all elements and their attributes, and understand how and when to use those elements and attributes.

Create a document tree to help you better understand the hierarchy among document elements. A document tree begins with one root element. All other elements are children of (in other words, nest within) that root element. See Chapter 16 for more information on document trees.

In the following sections, we dissect a DTD. You need to understand all the pieces and parts of a DTD before you try to create one yourself. (If you already recognize all the pieces of a DTD, read Chapter 7 to find out how to build a DTD.)

Inspecting an XML prolog

The *XML prolog* is the first thing that a processor — or human — sees in an XML document. You place it at the top of your XML document, and it describes the document's content and structure. An XML prolog may include the following items:

- XML declaration
- DOCTYPE declaration
- Comments
- Processing instructions
- White space

Notice that we use the phrase *may include*. An XML prolog doesn't have to include any of that information. If you want to use a DTD, however, you must include a few items in your prolog in addition to an XML declaration. See Listing 6-1 for an example of an XML prolog.

Listing 6-1:   An XML Prolog

```
<?xml version="1.0" encoding="UTF-8" standalone="yes"?>
<!DOCTYPE Recipes SYSTEM "Recipes.dtd">
<!-- End of Prolog -->
<!-- Beginning of Document Body -->
<Recipes>
. . .
</Recipes>
<!-- End of Document Body -->
```

Take a second to look at what we include in the prolog:

- ✔ The first line is the XML declaration.
- ✔ The second line invokes a specific `DOCTYPE` declaration named `Recipes`.
- ✔ The next two lines are comments that denote the end of the prolog and the beginning of the document proper.

Examining an XML declaration

Generally speaking, a *declaration* is markup that tells an XML processor what to do. Declarations don't add structure or define document elements. Instead, they provide instructions for a processor, such as what type of document to process, what standards to use, and even where a DTD can be found. Specifically, the *XML declaration* tells the processor which version of XML to use. The XML declaration is found in the XML document prolog.

An XML declaration is easy to write. A simple XML declaration reads like this:

```
<?xml version="1.0"?>
```

This XML declaration tells the processor to use version 1.0 of the XML specification. Right now, version 1.0 is the only XML version on the market, but version 1.1 is under development as of the writing of this book, and version 2.0 is on a more distant development schedule. Until XML versions 1.1 and 2.0 are available, a simple XML declaration looks exactly like our example.

However — and there's always a *however* — you can write a more complex XML declaration, such as

```
<?xml version="1.0" encoding="UTF-8" standalone="yes"?>
```

The second part of the statement, `encoding="UTF-8"`, is called an *encoding declaration*. This statement describes the character coding used. The next set of markup, `standalone="yes"`, implies that the document doesn't rely on markup declarations defined in an external document, such as an external DTD. If `standalone` is set to equal `"no"`, it leaves the issue unresolved — translation, it may or may not reference one or more external DTDs.

Because the `standalone` declaration means that the DTD markup appears only in the body of an XML document itself, it's only seldom encountered in production environments. Because the amount of work involved in building a DTD is pretty substantial — be it inline code, as the `standalone` declaration indicates, or an external DTD, as the `SYSTEM` declaration indicates — `standalone` occurs typically when creating or experimenting with new DTD markup. Otherwise, it's far more common to use the `SYSTEM` declaration, perhaps with a bit of inline DTD markup to customize an external DTD.

Discovering a DOCTYPE declaration

The *document type (DOCTYPE) declaration* is markup that tells the processor where it can find a specific DTD. In other words, a DOCTYPE declaration links an XML document to a corresponding DTD. Please also note that the DOCTYPE declaration is an SGML construct, and therefore follows SGML syntax and not XML syntax. This explains why only some values appear in quotes in this statement.

While you read this chapter, don't confuse document type (DOCTYPE) declarations with Document Type Definitions (DTDs). The DOCTYPE declaration is the locator for the DTD.

Here's the basic markup of a DOCTYPE declaration:

```
<!DOCTYPE Recipes SYSTEM "Recipes.dtd">
```

<!DOCTYPE marks the start of the DOCTYPE declaration. Recipes is the name of the DTD used. The DTD name must correspond with the name of the root element for that document. SYSTEM "Recipes.dtd" tells the processor to fetch an external document — in this case, a file named Recipes.dtd.

We know that it may seem as if we're duplicating information by using Recipes twice, but keep in mind that the first instance of Recipes names the document's root element. The second instance — Recipes.dtd — identifies a DTD filename.

In the preceding example, Recipes.dtd is a relative Uniform Resource Identifier (URI). URIs are basically filenames — or locations. Recipes.dtd points to an external DTD that resides in the same folder as the XML document but not in the same document. We delve into how to reference external DTDs in the "Calling for outside support: Referencing external DTDs" section later in this chapter. *Hint:* You might notice the resemblance between the terms *URL* and *URI*. Well, a URL is a type of URI.

Listing 6-2 is a DTD included entirely in the prolog of an XML document:

Listing 6-2:   The Recipes DTD, Internal Version

```
<!DOCTYPE Recipes [
<!ELEMENT Recipes (Recipe+)>
<!ELEMENT Recipe (Title, Category, Ingredients, CookingInstructions,
 ServingInstructions)>
<!ELEMENT Title (#PCDATA)>
<!ELEMENT Category EMPTY>
<!ELEMENT Ingredients (Item)+>
<!ELEMENT Item (#PCDATA)>
<!ELEMENT CookingInstructions (Cinst)+>
<!ELEMENT Cinst (#PCDATA)>
<!ELEMENT ServingInstructions (Sinst)+>
<!ELEMENT Sinst (#PCDATA)>
]>
```

This listing is an example of an internal document type definition. In our first example (refer to Listing 6-1), we invoke an external DTD; here, we include the same DTD information within the `DOCTYPE` declaration itself.

We don't expect you to recognize most of the markup that makes up a DTD because we haven't defined it yet. We talk about each declaration later in this section. But for now, take a look at Listing 6-2 and see whether you can understand its structure. What you should notice is that the third line, `<!ELEMENT Recipe (Title, Category, Ingredients, CookingInstructions, ServingInstructions)>`, contains the names for the following element declarations in the same order in which they appear. So, without even being told, you know how these elements relate to each other (see Figure 6-1).

Understanding comments

Comments — use them and read them! An author (yes, we mean you) can use comments to include text that explains a document better without that text being displayed or even processed. The syntax is the same as for HTML comments (`!– comment text –`), because HTML is built on SGML.

Comments are like an owner's manual; they can help you find your way through a document when something breaks down or even when you need to make changes. Use them liberally but know why and how to use them!

As long as you follow the correct format, comments remain visible only when you're viewing the markup itself. If you don't follow the correct format, parts of your comments may show up when users view your document or your document may not display correctly. The correct format is

```
<!-- Include your comment here -->
```

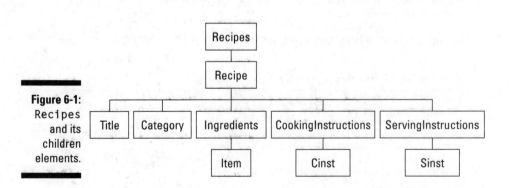

Figure 6-1:
Recipes
and its
children
elements.

You have two rules to live by when using comments:

- ✔ Never nest a comment inside another element.

- ✔ Never include - (hyphen) or -- (double hyphen) in the text for a comment. Those characters might confuse processors into thinking that you're closing the comment and thus treat remaining comment content as a syntax error!

Processing instructions

Using comments enables you to leave instructions (or comments) to someone who reads the markup without interfering with the document's structure. *Processing instructions* are like comments, but they provide a way to send instructions to computer programs or applications — not humans.

Another common processing instruction that you're likely to find in XML documents includes style sheets in a document. For example,

```
<?xml:stylesheet type="text/xsl"?>
```

All processing instructions follow the same format shown in Figure 6-2.

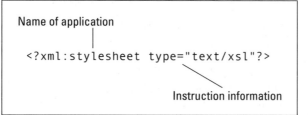

Figure 6-2:
Dissecting a processing instruction.

Name of application

```
<?xml:stylesheet type="text/xsl"?>
```

Instruction information

All processing instructions must begin with <? and end with ?>.

What about that white space?

White space consists of invisible characters such as spaces, tabs, carriage returns, or line feeds. The XML specification allows you to add white space outside markup; it's ignored when the document is processed.

Think of it this way: If we wrote a book without paragraph breaks, readers would give up reading after a few pages. A line of white space between each paragraph (a break) is easier on the eyes. The same logic applies to XML documents. When you write markup, consider adding a line of white space between sections. That way, when someone reads your XML document, he or she can read it (if not understand it) without a hitch.

Some elements treat white space in a special way. Including white space *outside* XML elements is safe, but do your homework before you add extra white space *inside* them. If you find yourself intrigued by the use of white space, read up on the xml:space attribute, which lets applications know when white space matters and when it doesn't. For more information on the xml:space attribute, check out the W3C site at www.w3.org/TR/REC-xml#sec-white-space.

Using Element Declarations

Because the heart of an XML document is made up of its elements, you must define them in your DTD. To do so, you use *element type declarations*. Element type declarations are important because they not only name your elements but also define any *children* that an element might have. Calling nested elements children makes sense when you sketch out the element hierarchy (refer to Figure 6-1) that looks so much like a family tree.

We start with the root element for a document based on our example DTD:

```
<Recipes>
. . .
</Recipes>
```

All other elements occur inside the root (if not more deeply nested), and all other elements relate back to the root somehow. Therefore, the root element is topmost in a document's hierarchy of elements. Part of what makes XML so great is that the element hierarchy is logical and easy to read or understand.

Elements can be defined to contain four types of content, listed in Table 6-2.

Table 6-2	Types of Content Found in Elements	
Content Type	*Example*	*What It Means*
ANY	<!ELEMENT *Name* ANY>	Allows any type of element content, either data or element markup information
EMPTY	<!ELEMENT *Name* EMPTY>	Specifies that an element must not contain any content

Content Type	Example	What It Means
Mixed content	`<!ELEMENT Name (#PCDATA | ChildName)>`	Allows an element to contain character data or a combination of subelements and character data
Element content	`<!ELEMENT Name (Child1, Child2)>`	Specifies that an element can contain only subelements, or children

Perhaps you're wondering what the commas (,) and the pipe bars (|) in the table's examples mean. We discuss them in the upcoming section, "Adding mixed content to the mix."

Using the ANY element type and the EMPTY element type

Sometimes you may want an element type to remain empty with no content to call its own. Suppose that you use an image that's located in an external file. In that case, you reference the image file but you don't have to include anything between opening and closing tags in an image element. Therefore, you use an empty element instead of an element with an opening tag and a closing tag. (Check out Chapter 2 to see the proper XML markup for empty elements.) To work with empty elements, you first must declare them like this:

```
<!ELEMENT Name EMPTY>
```

You may want to use another type of content specification: ANY. If you declare an element to contain ANY content, you allow that element type to hold any element or character data. Using the ANY content specification creates no structure to speak of, however, so it's rarely used except when testing a DTD.

Adding mixed content to the mix

Mixed content allows elements to contain character data, or character data and child elements. In other words, it allows elements to contain a mixture of information types. Even if an element contains only character data, it's still said to contain mixed content.

Keep in mind that mixed content is one of four valid types of element content. (The other three are element content, ANY, and EMPTY.)

The basic structure for an element declaration is as follows:

```
<!ELEMENT Name (#PCDATA | Child1 | Child2)*>
```

In the following example, we take some liberties with our basic example DTD and fiddle with the declaration for the Ingredients element. The string that begins an element definition in SGML, <!ELEMENT, begins the declaration; Ingredients is the element name.

```
<!ELEMENT Ingredients (#PCDATA | Item )*>
```

Including #PCDATA means that the element contains *parsed character data*, which is text that the document processor actually looks at and interprets to display both content and markup. Whenever you want your element to contain parsed character data, use the #PCDATA keyword. If you simply want an element to contain character data with no markup, use (#CDATA) by itself for the content definition part.

In the preceding example, you also find the element name Item. This means that the element named Item may nest within the parent element Ingredients. The * in the preceding markup is required in element type declarations that contain both text and elements. See the following section and Chapter 7 for more information on symbols in declarations.

But what does | signify? In this example, | means that the Ingredients element may contain parsed character data *or* an Item element. With mixed content, you can't control the order of the elements or even how many times they appear. The purpose of mixed content is to enable the author to specify an element that may contain both text and other elements.

You don't have to create or define symbols, such as |, in your DTD. They're already defined as part of SGML. Wait, we have one more helpful hint. White space is not significant within parentheses in SGML. For example, (#PCDATA) is the same as (#PCDATA).

You can work with mixed content in one of the following two ways:

- ✔ Use only parsed character data
- ✔ Allow an element to contain both text and other elements (and in that case, don't forget the asterisk!)

Using element content to keep children in line

An *element content model* is a little more involved than mixed content. Element content describes the child elements that an element can contain.

This type of specification says that an element may contain only child elements, for example:

```
<!ELEMENT Element (Child*)>
```

In the following example, as with all element declarations, !ELEMENT begins the declaration. Then the element receives its name, Recipes. Next comes the content specification, which states that Recipes may have a child, Recipe. The + is an occurrence indicator that states the Recipe element must occur at least once but that it can be used as many times as needed. For clarity, the + is also called the *one or more times* occurrence indicator.

```
<!ELEMENT Recipes (Recipe+)>
```

The element content model uses occurrence indicators to control the order and number of times that elements can occur. In fact, the element content model almost always uses one. Take a look at Table 6-3.

Table 6-3	Occurrence Indicators	
Symbol	*Example*	*What It Means*
, (comma)	`<!ELEMENT Recipe (Title, Category, Ingredients, Cooking Instructions, ServingInstructions)>`	All child elements listed must be used in the order shown.
| (pipe bar)	`<!ELEMENT Recipes (#PCDATA | Recipe)>`	Either parsed character data or the Recipe element may occur inside Recipes.
(No symbol)	`<!ELEMENT Recipes (Recipe)>`	Indicates that a single occurrence of Recipe must occur inside Recipes.
+ (plus sign)	`<!ELEMENT Recipes (Recipe+)>`	The Recipe child element must be used one or more times inside Recipes.
* (asterisk)	`<!ELEMENT Recipes (Recipe*)>`	The Recipe element may be used zero or more times within Recipes.
? (question mark)	`<!ELEMENT Recipes (Recipe?)>`	The Recipe element may be used once or not at all within Recipes.

Apply what you just read to our example. You may use the , (comma) occurrence indicator to imply sequence when listing elements. The example DTD uses the following content model for the Recipe element:

```
<!ELEMENT Recipe (Title, Category, Ingredients, CookingInstructions,
    ServingInstructions)>
```

The preceding declaration means that Title must precede Category, which must precede the Ingredients element, and so on when nesting within a parent Recipe element. To find out more about creating element type declarations, read Chapter 7, where we use them to build a DTD.

Getting a Handle on Attribute-List Declarations

In the "Using Element Declarations" section earlier in this chapter, you explore how to declare an element. In this section, you need to define an element's better half — its attributes. In techie terms, you need to include *attribute-list declarations* in your DTD whenever you want elements to use associated attributes. The attribute-list declaration lists all attributes that may be used within a given element and also defines each attribute's type and default value.

The attribute-list declaration begins with the !ATTLIST string, followed by white space. Remember, SGML is case sensitive, so don't forget to use capital letters.

So far, we have !ATTLIST with a space. Next comes the element name, the associated attribute's name, its type, and a default value. We dissect an example for you in Figure 6-3.

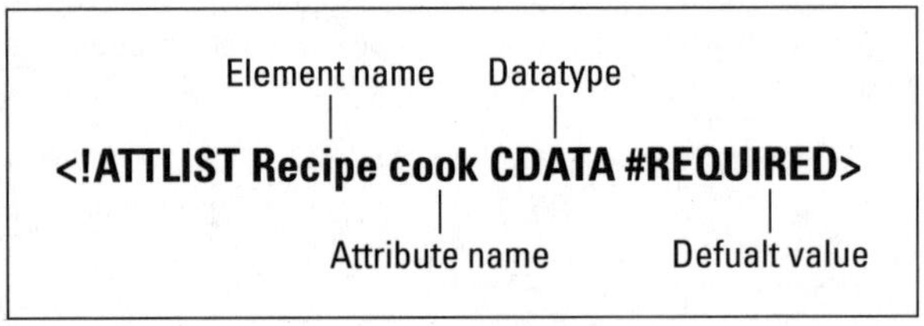

Figure 6-3:
The dissection of an attribute declaration.

```
          Element name    Datatype
              |              |
<!ATTLIST Recipe cook CDATA #REQUIRED>
                   |              |
              Attribute name   Defualt value
```

The following list defines the terms that appear in Figure 6-3:

- **Element name** is the name of the element to which the attribute belongs (Recipe, in this case).
- **Attribute name** is the name given to the attribute (cook, in this case).

- ✔ **Datatype** is one of the following ten kinds of datatype attributes:

  - CDATA, **or character data,** enables the author to include any string of characters that doesn't include the ampersand (&), less than and greater than signs (< or >), or quotation marks ("). These four characters may be represented using special escape sequences (&, <, >, or ", respectively).

  - Enumerated is a list of possible values for the attribute, separated with vertical bars (|). The XML author has a choice!

  - ID creates a unique ID for an attribute that identifies an element. This type is most often used by programs that process a document.

  - IDREF allows the value of an attribute to be an element somewhere else in the document.

  - IDREFS is just like IDREF but the value may be made up of multiple IDREFs.

  - ENTITY allows you to use external binary data or unparsed entities.

  - ENTITIES allows you to link multiple entities.

  - NMTOKEN restricts the value of the attribute to any valid XML name.

  - NMTOKENS allows the value of the attribute to be composed of multiple XML names.

  - NOTATION allows you to use a value already specified with a notation declaration in the DTD.

- ✔ **Default value** consists of one of the following four options:

  - #REQUIRED means you must always include the attribute when the element is used:

  ```
  <!ATTLIST element-name attribute-name CDATA #REQUIRED>
  ```

  - #IMPLIED means the attribute is optional. The attribute may be used in an element type, but no default value is provided for it if the attribute isn't used:

  ```
  <!ATTLIST element-name attribute-name CDATA #IMPLIED>
  ```

  - #FIXED means the attribute is optional. If used, the attribute must always take on the default value assigned in the DTD:

  ```
  <!ATTLIST element-name attribute-name #FIXED "value">
  ```

  - value simply defines a specific value as the default value — end of story. Whereas the first three options use keywords to require a specific use of attributes, this last option provides the value to be used if none is set. If the element doesn't contain the attribute, the processor assumes that the element has an attribute with the default value:

```
<!ATTLIST element-name attribute-name (option1 | option2 | option3)
   "default-value">
```

Discovering Entity Declarations

Entity declarations are a little trickier than other declarations, but they sure save you time! An *entity declaration* defines an alias for another block of text. This means you can attach a name to a specific block of text and then insert the whole block using just one name.

Think about how quickly you could include your company's address in different documents if they all used the same DTD. Or what if the company moved? If your company address were defined as an entity, you wouldn't have to change the address in each document — that address is centralized.

An entity declaration in a DTD looks like this:

```
<!ENTITY Name "text">
```

Name is the name of the entity and is used to call up the *text* in your document. Nice, huh? This allows you to take those long footers — that you normally have to type again and again and again — and reference them with one word. No more extraneous typing — almost.

The two types of entities are internal and external:

- **Internal (or general) entities** occur within the document and don't reference outside content — for example, `<!ENTITY Copyright "Copyright 2002, Hungry Minds, Inc.">`.

- **External entities** refer to content that may be found outside the document using a system or public identifier. Both parameter and general entities may be used as external entities, for example, `<!ENTITY entity-name SYSTEM "file.gif">`.

A parameter entity is both defined and used within a DTD. For more on parameter entities, see Chapter 10.

Understanding Notation Declarations

Notation declarations allow XML documents to refer to external information. They announce to the XML processor that information from an outside source is needed and can be processed. Nine times out of ten, this external information is non-XML information. Take a look at the syntax:

```
<!NOTATION Name SYSTEM "file.exe">
```

As with other declarations, you have a declaration name followed by the name given. In our example, we use the `SYSTEM` keyword, but you may also use `PUBLIC` identifiers. The file found in the quotation marks, *file.exe*, is an external ID.

`SYSTEM` is an SGML and XML keyword that indicates an entity appears in a URL or URI. `PUBLIC` indicates that a standard name for an entity is used.

Deciding Whether to Include a DTD

In the "What's a DTD?" section at the beginning of this chapter, we mention that XML doesn't require you to use a DTD. The first step in including DTDs in a document is to decide whether you want to jump off that bridge.

Why would you want to use a DTD? Well, here are several reasons:

- ✔ **To create and manage** large sets of documents for your company. DTDs allow you to create and maintain rules that all documents must follow.

- ✔ **To define clearly** what markup may be used in certain documents and how markup should be sequenced. DTDs make document rules explicit.

- ✔ **To provide a common frame of reference** for documents that many users can share. Big name XML applications such as XPath, XLink, XPointer, and others covered in Parts V and VI all have associated DTDs.

Therefore, when it comes to working with DTDs, standardization and control is what they're all about!

Why might you want to scrap this chapter and create an XML document without a formal description? You may not need to use a DTD if

- ✔ You're working only with one or a few small documents. Remember why you create DTDs: to make your life easier. If a DTD is bigger than the document that it describes, you may be wasting your time.

- ✔ You're using a nonvalidating processor to handle your XML documents. If the processor checks only for well-formedness, you don't need an external DTD.

In general, let the XML documents or data that you work with drive you toward or away from creating formal document descriptions. Our experience has been that any application that involves more than a one-time or throwaway document or data collection is worthy of its own formal description (or at least, customization or outright use of an existing standard DTD). Because the XML's rules let you to skip the document description if you like, you may certainly decide otherwise.

Ways to Include DTDs or Definitions

In this section, we outline the differences between an internal and an external DTD. Formally called *internal* and *external subsets*, respectively, these two approaches follow the same markup structure but have some key differences, such as where they live.

Often, the best approach is to combine both internal and external DTD subsets. But before we go there, here are some differences.

The inside view: Internal DTD subsets

The most important drawback to using internal DTDs is that they may be used only by the document that contains them. When you create an internal DTD, you're essentially keeping all the information in one single document. However, internal DTDs have a few benefits, as follows:

- ✔ A single file processes faster than multiple files.

- ✔ Validity and well-formedness are kept in the same place. Any processor can process your document without looking elsewhere.

- ✔ You can use internal DTDs on a local system without connecting to the Internet — you can take that file on the plane and run it on a laptop!

Calling for outside support: Referencing external DTDs

Although internal DTDs are quicker, easier, and more mobile, we don't necessarily recommend them over external DTDs. Compared with internal DTDs, external DTDs have many advantages:

- ✔ They're recyclable. You can use one DTD file for multiple documents. (For internal DTD's, there's one in every file.)

- ✔ Your external DTD can simply be a public one already created by someone else. (Internal DTDs are totally private and isolated.)

- ✔ Editing an external DTD can be a breeze when you need to change one item found in multiple documents. (You can only edit internal DTDs one at a time.)

- ✔ Because you can manage and maintain external DTDs in single, discrete documents (rather than multiple instances of the same in-line SGML markup in multiple XML documents), there's less work involved in keeping external DTDs up to date than internal ones.

Two is sometimes better than one

Sometimes you need a large, complex external DTD; other times you not only need a monster DTD, but you also want to define more information internally. We find that more often than not, authors combine internal and external DTDs to get the most from their XML document structure.

You already know how to read internal and external DTDs. Combining DTDs isn't much different. Live by these two major rules when mixing these two types of DTDs:

- ✔ An XML processor always reads the internal subset first. Therefore, the internal DTD takes precedence.
- ✔ Entities declared in the internal subset can be referenced in the external subset.

For a complete example of building DTDs, see Chapter 7.

Chapter 7

Creating Custom DTDs

· ·

· ·

*I*f you're trying to build your own custom XML documents, creating a Document Type Definition (DTD) is one of the most important tasks you need to perfect. DTDs define the different pieces of data you want to present and explain the relationships between them. However, DTDs are based on an older, very complex markup language called the Standard Generalized Markup Language, or SGML. A newer alternative to DTDs called XML Schema has the advantage of being just another XML application, so you may want to investigate Chapters 8 and 9 to check out this "all-XML" alternative to DTDs.

Without further ado, this chapter gives you the skinny on building your own DTD, step by step. (By the way, if you need an introduction to DTDs and want to review the key terms and syntax that you need to know, skip back to Chapter 6.)

Step 1: Understanding Your Data

Here's what you need to do to make sure you have a firm grasp of data before you even think about creating DTDs (see Chapter 4 for some details about conducting data analysis):

> ✔ **Figure out where the data comes from and get it organized.** If you take a sample of some of your favorite book titles and want to use XML to organize that material as a detailed resource for others, your task may not be so huge, but if you want to start building multiple databases, you need to plan and organize accordingly.

✔ **Make form follow function and start whittling.** Create a structure that makes the markup easy enough for almost anyone to manage and understand. That may require taking a gander at DTDs that have already been created to get a sense of how other people are doing this work. Then you can begin to chop it up into small, manageable pieces.

Step 2: Defining Some Element Types

After you've done proper data analysis, you should be able to come up with some specific items of data (we refer to them as components) that you know you'll need to map. For example, to keep track of recipes, you should be able to identify specific items of data that must be present in any recipe, such as the title, category, and ingredients, right away. You can identify these items as *element types,* for example:

```
<Title>
<Category>
<Ingredients>
```

Step 3: Understanding Hierarchy and Adding Order to Your Elements

Element types are nothing but empty shells until you begin organizing them and determining their attributes.

On their own, elements don't *mean* anything; they simply exist to make your life easier by creating labeled containers for your data. The data — the content between the start and end tags — is where the real meaning lies. That said, good element organization leads to good data description. And DTDs (which don't hold any data at all, only rules about how data should be used) are there to make things go even more smoothly.

Understanding the family tree

The elements in an XML document are like one big happy family that comes together to describe your content. Imagine a family tree with a single trunk that splits into branches that, in turn, further split into branches with leaves at the end. An XML document has the same structure: The root element is the trunk that forms the foundation for the tree, and the branches and their branches are the elements and content in your document.

The terminology we use to explain how the different elements in your document relate to one another even uses this family tree metaphor. We discuss the root element in the "Choosing a root element" section, coming up next. The other family members that play a part in your XML documents are:

- ✔ **Parent elements:** An element becomes a parent element when it contains other elements. An element is just an element until you nest another element inside of it, at which time it becomes a parent element.

- ✔ **Child element:** A child element is — yep, you guessed it — an element that sits inside of a parent element.

- ✔ **Sibling element:** When a parent has more than one child element those elements are siblings of one another.

But what about grandparents, aunts, uncles, and cousins? XML doesn't take the family tree metaphor to such an extreme. These terms exist only to help describe the immediate relationship among elements. For example, take a look at this snippet from our bean burrito recipe:

```
<?xml version="1.0"?>
<Recipes>
 <Recipe>
 . . .
  <CookingInstructions>
   <Cinst>Empty can of refried beans into medium saucepan.</Cinst>
   <Cinst>Heat over medium-high heat until beans are smooth and bubbly.</Cinst>
   <Cinst>Warm tortillas in microwave for 30 seconds.</Cinst>
  </CookingInstructions>
  <ServingInstructions>
   <Sinst>Spread 1/3 of warm beans on each tortilla.</Sinst>
   <Sinst>Sprinkle with cheese and onions.</Sinst>
   <Sinst>Roll tortillas and serve.</Sinst>
  </ServingInstructions>
 </Recipe>
</Recipes>
```

In our recipe, Recipes is the root element and Recipe is its child. Recipe, in turn, is a parent to both CookingInstructions and ServingInstructions (who are siblings). Cinst is a child of CookingInstructions and Sinst is a child of ServingInstructions.

CookingInstructions isn't, however, called an aunt or uncle to Sinst, nor are Cinst and Sinst called cousins. Finally, even though Recipe would appear to be the grandparent of Cinst and Sinst, and Recipes their great-grandparent, the description of the relationships in the document doesn't go to that level. When you use the family tree terms, you stick with parents, children, and siblings.

Choosing a root element

Now is a good time to take a few moments (or paragraphs) to focus on how to choose your document (or root) element. You know it's important — or at least we've done our best to let you know it's important — and that every document should have one. The question is, how do you go about choosing one?

There's no simple answer to this question, but we can tell you that you want your root element to be able to contain the information you need in your document without needing to be duplicated or a child of another element. The scope of your individual documents is important here as well.

Think about a DTD that describes books. Two possible root elements for this DTD might be Books and Book. The difference between the two (besides the "s") is that the Books document element, by virtue of its plurality, can hold more than one book description, whereas the Book document element seems to be specific to a single book. If you know you want your document to describe more than one book, Books is the better choice. If, however, you know you want to limit each document to describing a single book, Book is a better choice.

When you think about your root element, keep in mind that every other element has to fit neatly inside it. Therefore, a couple of candidates for your root element should appear. With a little trial and error, you can find the one that is right for you.

Creating a hierarchical map of elements

Once you're clear on the family dynamics of an XML document, here's some key terminology to help you get a handle on how hierarchy and data elements work:

- **Sequence:** When using a DTD, you can define the order, from the top of the document to the bottom, in which element types may appear.

- **Hierarchy:** DTD element declarations can add another dimension to the document by specifying parent-child relationships between or among elements. The sequence sets the initial order of elements, and hierarchy specifies within each individual element what other elements can appear and in what order.

- **Occurrence:** Element declarations may use occurrence indicators (such as ?, *, and +) to specify the number of times an element type may be used or must occur. (See the "Step 4: Developing and Defining Your Elements and Their Content" section later in this chapter for some examples.)

Before you define your element types, you must identify relationships and any resulting hierarchy among elements. The best way to understand what we mean is to work through an example. Here goes:

```
<Recipes>
<Recipe>
 <Title> . . . </Title>
 <Category/>
```

```
<Ingredients>
    <Item> . . . </Item>
</Ingredients>
<CookingInstructions>
    <Cinst> . . . </Cinst>
</CookingInstructions>
<ServingInstructions>
    <Sinst> . . . </Sinst>
</ServingInstructions>
</Recipe>
<Recipes>
```

Because we want to demonstrate only the relationships between element types, we didn't include any content in this example.

Table 7-1 maps out the sequence and hierarchy of data components in the sample RML that we use here.

Table 7-1		Data Used in Valid RML		
Data	*Element Type*	*Child Of*	*Parent Of*	*Sibling Of*
Recipes	Recipes	Nothing (Root element)	Recipe	Nothing (Root element)
Recipe	Recipe	Recipes	Title,Category, Ingredients, Cooking Instructions, Serving Instructions	Nothing
Title	Title	Recipe	Nothing	Category, Ingredients, Cooking Instructions, Serving Instructions
Category	Category	Recipe	Nothing Ingredients,	Title, Cooking Instructions, Serving Instructions
Ingredients	Ingredients	Recipe	Item	Title,Category, Cooking Instructions, Serving Instructions

(continued)

Table 7-1 *(continued)*

Data	Element Type	Child Of	Parent Of	Sibling Of
Item	Item	Ingredients	Nothing	Nothing
Cooking instructions	Cooking-Instructions	Recipe	Cinst	Title,Category, Ingredients, Serving Instructions
Cooking instructions item	Cinst	Cooking-Instructions	Nothing	Nothing
Serving instructions	Serving-Instructions	Recipe	Sinst	Title, Category, Ingredients, Cooking Instructions
Serving instructions item	Sinst	Serving-Instructions	Nothing	Nothing

Using attributes to shed light on relationships

Now that you understand a little about elements, you need to turn your attention to the attributes that modify or manage the content that elements may contain. Not only can attributes help clarify what content elements may contain, but they can also help define what an element does and how it relates to other elements. As with elements, attributes have a few rules of their own, as you see a bit later.

Later in this chapter, we define the two ways that attributes provide information: by defining a data type and by defining a default value.

The way attributes are handled in a DTD is particularly important because the DTD must cover all conceivable usage scenarios. To help you decide when to use an attribute with an element in a DTD, ask yourself:

✔ Are you defining a particular aspect of an element, such as size, height, or color?

✔ Do you need a way to provide more information about individual instances of an element?

✔ Do you want to be sure that every time an element is used certain information is included with it?

✔ Are you pointing to an object such as a graphic or a cross-reference?

If the answer to the first question is yes, you might want to consider handling that kind of information in a style sheet instead. (We cover style sheets in Part IV.)

But if you want a mechanism for making an individual instance of an element more specific, you want to be sure an element always includes certain information, or you're associating an element with external data, you should definitely consider adding an attribute, or several, to an element. For some good working examples of how to use attribute and elements together, see Chapter 6 for our discussion of the attributes in our RML DTD — specifically, the `cook` attribute for the `Recipe` element, and the `name` attribute for the `Category` element.

Step 4: Developing and Defining Your Elements and Their Content

When you're on top of the elements you're using in your document, the next step is to create the element declarations in your DTD. You declare elements like this:

```
<!ELEMENT name (content specification)>
```

In our example recipe in RML, you would define elements this way:

```
<!DOCTYPE Recipes [
<!ELEMENT Recipes (Recipe)+>
<!ELEMENT Recipe (Title, Category, Ingredients, CookingInstructions,
 ServingInstructions)>
<!ELEMENT Title (#PCDATA)>
<!ELEMENT Category EMPTY>
<!ELEMENT Ingredients (Item)+>
<!ELEMENT Item (#PCDATA)>
<!ELEMENT CookingInstructions (Cinst)+>
<!ELEMENT Cinst (#PCDATA)>
<!ELEMENT ServingInstructions (Sinst)+>
<!ELEMENT Sinst (#PCDATA)>
]>
```

Our RML DTD uses content specifications that include mixed content models and element content models. A *mixed content model* specifies that an element's content can be a combination of regular text and other elements. An *element content model* only allows for other elements. For all the gory detail on content models, see Chapter 6.

The content model for the `Recipe` element sets up the basic structure for each recipe:

```
<!ELEMENT Recipe (Title, Category, Ingredients, CookingInstructions,
  ServingInstructions)>
```

`Recipe` has an element content model that specifies that `Title`, `Category`, `Ingredients`, `CookingInstructions`, and `ServingInstructions` must appear exactly once and in the order shown. This content model guarantees that every recipe has the same basic structure, and that key components like the ingredients aren't left out.

The content models for `CookingInstructions`, `ServingInstructions`, and `Ingredients` also include only elements:

```
<!ELEMENT CookingInstructions (Cinst)+>
<!ELEMENT ServingInstructions (Sinst)+>
<!ELEMENT Ingredients (Item)+>
```

`CookingInstructions` and `ServingInstructions` must each have at least one instance of `Cinst` or `Sinst`, respectively, and `Ingredients` must have at least one instance of `Item`. This guarantees that each recipe has at least one cooking instruction, one serving instruction, and one ingredient.

The remaining elements in the DTD all utilize mixed content models because these elements are designed to hold the actual recipe text (`PCDATA`):

```
<!ELEMENT Title (#PCDATA)>
<!ELEMENT Category EMPTY>
<!ELEMENT Item (#PCDATA)>
<!ELEMENT Cinst (#PCDATA)>
<!ELEMENT Sinst (#PCDATA)>
```

Step 5: Declaring Attributes

Declaring attributes is similar to working with elements, because you have to include a bunch of information within those pesky little greater than and less than signs — and don't forget the exclamation mark (!). To jog your memory, take a look at the syntax for creating attribute declarations:

```
<!ATTLIST elementname attributename (datatype) defaultvalue>
```

When you create your own attributes, the first decision you must make is what type of data to use in an attribute, as well as the default values to use. We list your options in Chapter 6.

The following defines some attributes for our example:

```
<!ATTLIST Recipe cook CDATA #IMPLIED>
<!ATTLIST Category name ENUMERATED (chinese, japanese, home cooking, tex-mex,
  continental, haute cuisine, other)>
```

In this example, the element type Recipe can include more information about the person who created the recipe, and is cited with the cook attribute. The declaration for the cook attribute states that the XML document doesn't always have to include a cook attribute. The second declaration follows similar logic. Category is required to have a name attribute, and the legal values for that attribute are explicitly listed (or enumerated) as indicated. (Can you tell what kind of food we like?)

When we put these declarations together, it was important for us to be sure each recipe was categorized using a particular set of values. If we let XML authors come up with their own values for the name attribute, the variety of values would be endless. For chinese alone we could expect asian, oriental, stir-fry, and more. We chose to use a required datatype to be sure that we had one of several specific categories set for each recipe. Along the same lines, we didn't really care whether the information on the recipe author was included, which is why cook is an optional attribute.

When you create your own customized DTDs, you can use attributes much as we did to control when an element has particular information associated with it, and even what that information is. You can also use attributes as a way to help authors provide additional information without making it required.

Step 6: Creating Shortcuts with Entities

The XML specification supports two types of general entities: internal and external. *Internal entities* hold their values in the entity declaration, whereas *external entities* point to an external file.

Beyond general entities, XML also supports parameter entities and character entities. Parameter entities make building complex DTDs easier and character entities allow you to include non-ASCII characters like the copyright symbol and accented characters in your XML document. Look for more information on these two types of entities — as well as more detail on general entities — in Chapter 10.

Internalizing entities

Suppose you create your own recipes and your name is Madeline Margaret Murphy-Morrison. Imagine typing that same string of letters every time you entered a new recipe. Wouldn't it be nice if you could take a shortcut and use the string &mmmm; instead?

You can if you define an internal entity with the identifier &mmmm; to contain your name. When the document is processed, the entity reference is replaced with the entity's value (your name), and you can be assured that you get the same text in every location — spelled the same way!

To declare a general entity, you must use the following syntax:

```
<!ENTITY entityname "replacement text">
```

or

```
<!ENTITY mmmm "Madeline Margaret Murphy-Morrison">
```

To reference an internal entity anywhere in the text of your document, you use an ampersand (&), followed by the entity's name, followed by a semicolon (;).

Try turning common strings of text, like your company name or a standard copyright disclaimer, into entities.

Five commonly used internal entities are already defined as part of XML for your use and are listed in the following table. You don't have to define these entities in your DTD before you use them; you can simply use them.

Entity	Refers To	Symbol
<	Less than sign	<
>	Greater than sign	>
&	Ampersand	&
'	Single quotation mark or apostrophe	'
"	Double quotation mark	"

Externalizing entities

External entities help you integrate other documents and files into your XML document. In general, you use them

- As a mechanism to divide your document into logical pieces. Rather than creating a single, large, and unwieldy document, such as a book stored in a single document that holds all of the chapters, you can store each chapter in a separate file and use external entities to include those files in a book document whose only job is to bring the chapters together.

- To reference images, multimedia clips, and other non-XML files. Before you can include any non-XML file in your document, like a picture of a bean burrito for example, you first have to reference it as an external entity.

To declare an external entity, you use the following syntax:

```
<!ENTITY entityname SYSTEM "system-identifier">
```

The *system-identifier* is defined as a URI (or a URL). The most common URI is a filename. You may also use the following syntax to refer to a public identifier not stored on your system (for example, your local computer or the system running your XML application):

```
<!ENTITY entityname PUBLIC "system-identifier">
```

The benefit of using external entities is that they're reusable. If you want to use the same arrow image over and over again in a document, you only have to create the entity for it once, and you can reference it time and again. Or if we had a standard legal disclaimer — for example "Warning, we can't promise you'll like our recipes" — that you want to include at the end of every recipe, you can save the disclaimer as a separate file, create an external entity that points to it, and then reference that entity at the end of every recipe.

If you create an external entity that references a non-XML file, like an image, Word document, or media clip, you can only reference that entity in an attribute value. You can find out more about this in Chapter 10.

Step 7: Calling Your DTD

When working with a simple DTD, you can use it in two ways: internally (within the existing XML document) or as an external file. If you opt to include your DTD in your XML document, you work with what's called an *internal subset*. When you reference an external DTD, you work with an *external subset*. All this really means is that *internal* DTDs are contained within your XML document and *external* DTDs live in a separate document. The guts of the DTD stay the same, but it resides in different places in each case.

We delve into the differences between internal and external DTDs in Chapter 6. The following sections discuss how to invoke them in markup.

Internal DTDs

DTDs that appear inside of the document are located in the prolog of the XML document, within the document type (DOCTYPE) declaration. Remember that your first line of markup in an XML document is an XML processing instruction (the declaration). If you have an internal DTD, the second line should be a DOCTYPE declaration.

Tricks of the trade

Here are some additional tips and tricks to remember when you're creating and working with DTDs and XML documents:

✔ **<!— Comments document your work —>:** Always use comments to add notes and navigational information.

✔ **<!ENTITY first:** Declare your entities before element and attribute declarations. This enables you to define entities you can use in the declarations that follow.

✔ **<!ENTITY practice:** Practice using entities; they can save you tons of time in the long run!

✔ **Tools do DTDs, too:** Visit Chapter 20 to find XML editors that can generate a DTD from an XML document on demand.

✔ **Remember your CAPS:** XML is case sensitive, so don't forget to capitalize all reserved DTD terms, such as <!ENTITY.

When declaring your DTD internally, all the declarations that make up the DTD site are within the DOCTYPE declaration, like so:

```
<?xml version="1.0" standalone="yes"?>
<!DOCTYPE Recipes [
<!ELEMENT Recipes (Recipe)+>
<!ELEMENT Recipe (Title, Category, Ingredients, CookingInstructions,
 ServingInstructions)>
<!ELEMENT Title (#PCDATA)>
<!ELEMENT Category EMPTY>
<!ELEMENT Ingredients (Item)+>
<!ELEMENT Item (#PCDATA)>
<!ELEMENT CookingInstructions (Cinst)+>
<!ELEMENT Cinst (#PCDATA)>
<!ELEMENT ServingInstructions (Sinst)+>
<!ELEMENT Sinst (#PCDATA)>
]>
<!-- Begin Document Body -->
<Recipes>
 . . .
</Recipes>
```

External DTDs

Creating an external DTD file has many advantages. The main advantage is that an external DTD file is reusable. You can reference the same external DTD in a single document or in 10,000 documents. All of them use the same DTD, and if you need to make an update or a change, you only have to change one document instead of every one of the 10,000. The bottom line is, if you want to use your DTD in more than one document, make it external.

Here's how to reference an external DTD within your XML document:

```
<?xml version="1.0" standalone="no"?>
<!DOCTYPE Recipes SYSTEM "Recipes.dtd">
<Recipes>
   . . .
</Recipes>
```

For the previous sample XML document to be valid, it must adhere to
`Recipes.dtd`. Note that the root element must be listed in the document
type declaration.

Creating a Simple External DTD

Now that you can write all the parts and pieces, it's time to put them
together. We discuss the heart of a DTD and identify each piece as we go
along. At the end of this adventure, you find a simple, yet thorough, DTD.

Insert comments to identify the beginning of the DTD:

```
<!-- Begin Recipes.dtd last updated January 1, 2002 -->
```

Declare entities first so they can be referenced within element and attribute
declarations, as well as in the XML document. Remember, the &mmmm; entity
is an internal one.

```
<!ENTITY mmmm "Madeline Margaret Murphy-Morrison">
```

State your element declarations. You can then use these elements in your
XML documents.

```
<!ELEMENT Recipes (Recipe)+>
<!ELEMENT Recipe (Title, Category, Ingredients, CookingInstructions,
 ServingInstructions)>
<!ELEMENT Title (#PCDATA)>
<!ELEMENT Category EMPTY>
<!ELEMENT Ingredients (Item)+>
<!ELEMENT Item (#PCDATA)>
<!ELEMENT CookingInstructions (Cinst)+>
<!ELEMENT Cinst (#PCDATA)>
<!ELEMENT ServingInstructions (Sinst)+>
<!ELEMENT Sinst (#PCDATA)>
```

Now it's time to declare all your attributes. As shown, an attribute declaration
usually follows the corresponding element declaration:

```
<!ATTLIST Recipe cook CDATA #IMPLIED>
<!ATTLIST Category name ENUMERATED (chinese, japanese, home cooking, tex-mex,
 continental, haute cuisine, other)>
```

Throw in a closing comment for good measure.

```
<!-- End of Recipes.dtd -->
```

Don't forget to save your document with a .dtd file extension. As with naming elements, you may name your DTD anything you want. Remember that XML is case sensitive and don't forget to reference your DTD in your XML document. That's all she wrote.

Here's a look at an XML document with the DTD defined internally in the prolog:

```
<!-- Begin Recipes.dtd last updated January 1, 2002 -->
<?xml version="1.0" standalone="yes"?>
<!DOCTYPE Recipes [
<!--
   Description : Recipes
   Author : The XML Gourmets
   Update : January 1, 2002
-->
<!ENTITY mmmm "Madeline Margaret Murphy-Morrison">
<!ELEMENT Recipes (Recipe)+>
<!ELEMENT Recipe (Title, Category, Ingredients, CookingInstructions,
 ServingInstructions)>
<!ELEMENT Title (#PCDATA)>
<!ELEMENT Category EMPTY>
<!ELEMENT Ingredients (Item)+>
<!ELEMENT Item (#PCDATA)>
<!ELEMENT CookingInstructions (Cinst)+>
<!ELEMENT Cinst (#PCDATA)>
<!ELEMENT ServingInstructions (Sinst)+>
<!ELEMENT Sinst (#PCDATA)>
<!ATTLIST Recipe cook CDATA #IMPLIED>
<!ATTLIST Category name ENUMERATED (chinese, japanese, home cooking, tex-mex,
 continental, haute cuisine, other)>
]>
<!-- Begin document body -->
<Recipes>
 <Recipe cook="The XML Gourmet">
  <Title>Bean Burrito</Title>
  <Category name="tex-mex"/>
  <Ingredients>
   <Item>1 can refried beans</Item>
   <Item>1 cup longhorn colby cheese, shredded</Item>
   <Item>1 small onion, finely chopped</Item>
   <Item>3 flour tortillas</Item>
  </Ingredients>
  <CookingInstructions>
   <Cinst>Empty can of refried beans into medium saucepan.</Cinst>
   <Cinst>Heat over medium-high heat until beans are smooth and bubbly.</Cinst>
   <Cinst>Warm tortillas in microwave for 30 seconds.</Cinst>
  </CookingInstructions>
  <ServingInstructions>
   <Sinst>Spread 1/3 of warm beans on each tortilla.</Sinst>
   <Sinst>Sprinkle with cheese and onions.</Sinst>
   <Sinst>Roll tortillas and serve.</Sinst>
  </ServingInstructions>
 </Recipe>
</Recipes>
<!-- End document body -->
```

Chapter 8

Understanding and Using XML Schema

· ·

· ·

*A*lthough you can use any old markup to describe your XML documents, chances are they will be more valuable in a final solution if they include a structure that the solution can work with. An XML schema (created according to the XML Schema specification) defines rules for the structure and content of an XML document. Schemas specify the overall structure of an XML document and identify all of the components of the XML document. Like documents that adhere to DTDs (covered in Chapter 6), documents that adhere to an XML schema are called valid documents.

A valid document is not the same as a well-formed document. All XML documents must follow certain standards — they must contain a root element, all additional elements must be nested, and documents must follow proper syntax, among other things (we cover well-formed documents in Chapters 2 and 4). On the other hand, not all XML documents have to adhere to a schema, or DTD, for that matter. As long as you have a well-formed document, you don't have to worry about validity unless the application that is ultimately going to process your document requires that the document be valid.

If you're building an XML document according to a schema, you probably want it to be valid. A well-built schema can help you construct a well-structured document when you follow its rules.

What's an XML Schema?

You build an XML Schema document (we'll just call it a schema for ease of both typing and reading) according to the rules of the XML Schema specification defined by the Worldwide Web Consortium (W3C). A schema lays down the rules a valid XML document should follow to ensure that the information contained in the XML document is in the right form. In other words, the schema acts like a template within the document that specifies the form that the XML document must take. When a program processes an XML document written against a schema, it validates the document against the schema.

As you see a bit later in the chapter, the XML Schema specification is nothing more than a guide to creating an XML document that defines the structure other XML documents should follow. In other words, schemas are just XML documents. You use XML markup to create them, and the XML Schema specification specifies what markup you use and how.

If you've read up on DTDs yet, you know that a DTD can be partially or totally included in the XML document it governs. This means the DTD and XML document can be contained in one file. Look back to Chapter 7 for all of the details on the factors that govern where you put your DTD. We bring this facet of DTDs up here because it's important for you to know that schemas don't work this way. Schemas are stored in a totally separate file from the XML documents they govern. In other words, all schemas are external. You can't combine a schema and its XML document into a single file.

A schema consists of declarations for elements and attributes, and specifies how those elements and attributes work together to define content and to establish a document structure. In addition, a schema allows you to restrict the content of these elements and attributes by using and defining very specific datatypes (more on datatypes in the next section).

XML Schema is one of many schema specifications, but it's the one recommended by the W3C. You can use one of the other many other schema options, including REgular LAnguage for XML Next Generation (RELAX NG), Schematron, and Microsoft's XML-Data Reduced (XDR) schema language, but chances are support for it will be limited to a few systems. In this book, when we talk about schemas, we're always referring to those written according to the XML Schema specification, unless we say otherwise. For more information on the varieties of available schema mechanisms, see the XML Cover Pages at www.oasis-open.org/cover/schemas.html.

An XML Schema document includes many parts, listed in Table 8-1, along with some examples from our favorite Recipe Markup Language (RML).

Table 8-1		XML Schema Lingo	
Term	*Syntax*	*Example*	*What It Does*
XML declaration	`<xml version="version">`	`<xml version="1.0" encoding="UTF-8">`	Tells the processor which version of XML to use
Schema element	`<xsd:schema xmlns:xsd="namespace">`	`<xsd:schema xmlns:xsd="http://www.w3.org/2001/XMLSchema">`	Identifies the document as XML Schema
Element declaration	`<xsd:element name="name">`	`<xsd:element name="Recipes">`	Defines the element named Recipes
Attribute declaration	`<xsd:attribute name="name" type="datatype">`	`<xsd:attribute name="cook" type="xsd:string">`	Defines the attribute named cook

Even if you don't plan on writing your own schemas from scratch, it's useful to know how to read and understand them. You should be able to look at a schema, list all the elements, attributes, and datatypes, and understand how and when to use those elements and attributes and how to format the data in your XML document.

Unlike a DTD, schemas are simply XML documents that use XML's standard markup syntax to define the structure for other documents. When you write a schema, you're simply writing XML. This means you don't have to learn a new language; you only have to learn how to use a particular set of XML elements and attributes. Following a brief detour down the road to datatype land, you look at each part of a schema so that you understand each piece of it before you read someone else's schema or create your own schema. (If you're already familiar with the components of an XML Schema document, go to Chapter 9 to find out how to build a custom XML Schema.)

So Many Datatypes, So Little Time

Unlike Document Type Definitions (DTDs), which are great for directing the development of documents that consist mainly of groups of text, schemas are great for directing documents that include lots of data, such as phone numbers, addresses, part numbers, or prices. Schemas work much better when you want to be sure a document not only follows a particular structure, but also uses particular kinds of data — numbers versus strings for example — because it allows you to get very specific about the format of that data in the XML document.

Think about an invoice for a minute and the particular kinds of data it includes. It might include strings of text that describe services rendered or products sold, payment addresses, and terms of payment. It also includes a number of other things: the amount in dollars for a particular product or service, the quantity of something sold, the number of hours spent delivering a particular service. A schema allows you not only to break the invoice down into a basic structure defined by elements and attributes, but also to define what kind of data each element and attribute can hold. This means, for example, that you can specify the elements that describe amounts that can only hold numbers with two decimals.

In other words, schemas not only give you control over your document structure, but also give you control over your document data. The secret to the control of the kind of data an XML document includes is datatypes. A *datatype* specifies what kind of data you expect; the XML Schema specification supports 44 different datatypes. (We bet you didn't know there were that many types of data.)

We don't list all of the datatypes here, but a sampling of them includes:

- ✔ string: A collection of characters that are treated as a simple string of text.
- ✔ decimal: A number that includes a decimal point and some number of decimal places after the point. When you use the decimal datatype in your schema, you can specify how many decimal places the number in the element or attribute can include.
- ✔ dateTime: The date and time. You can specify what pattern the date and time should use.
- ✔ anyURI: A URI or URL.
- ✔ integer: A number without a decimal point. When you use this datatype, you can specify the total number of digits the decimal can include.

Each of the 44 datatypes has a list of *constraints* that you can use to further define the data described with an element or attribute. For example, the string datatype has both minLength and maxLength constraints that you can use to specify the minimum and maximum lengths for the string. If you want to be sure the value of a first_name element is a string with at least one character but no more than 20, you can specify that as part of the string datatype for the element.

Databases allow for similar datatype controls to carefully guide the data stored in the different database fields. If you're creating XML documents whose data will eventually be moved into a database, you can use a schema to create rules for the data in the document that are compatible with rules in the database.

Part 2 of the XML Schema Recommendation is entirely devoted to the particulars of datatypes. You can read about each of the 44 datatypes and their constraints at `www.w3.org/TR/xmlschema-2/`.

XML Prolog

The XML prolog is the housekeeping section of the document and contains useful information about the document that is helpful to both people and computers that may read the document.

Because a schema is simply an XML document, and the XML declaration is the first thing in an XML document, each schema starts with an XML declaration. Even though your schema is just an XML document with a particular purpose — to define a schema — you need to say, "Hello, this document uses XML Schema." You do that in the prolog. So at the very least, the prolog to your schema needs to include

- **An XML declaration:** An XML declaration identifies the document as an XML document and specifies its version:

  ```
  <?xml version="1.0" encoding="UTF-8"?>
  ```

  For more information about XML declarations, see Chapter 6.

- **A schema element declaration:** The `schema` element is similar to the root element in a DTD; it contains all the other elements in the XML Schema document and specifies the *namespace* for the schema. The namespace is a URL that points to the details of XML vocabulary, in this case, the XML Schema vocabulary that the document will adhere to.

  ```
  <xsd:schema xmlns: xsd="http://www.w3.org/2001/XMLSchema">
  ```

This is what a complete prolog for an XML schema looks like:

```
<?xml version="1.0" encoding="UTF-8"?>
<xsd:schema xmlns:xsd="http://www.w3.org/2001/XMLSchema">
```

Document Structures

Following the XML prolog is the meat of the schema that defines the schemas basic structures — elements and attributes. It also specifies how these structures work together: which elements are contained in other elements, and which attributes belong to which elements.

Element declarations

XML Schema documents always include elements. All elements included in a schema must be defined in an element declaration. This element declaration includes the element name and may also include the element datatype. There are two categories of element declarations:

- ✔ **Simple type definitions:** Declare elements that cannot contain any other elements and cannot include any attributes.

- ✔ **Complex type definitions:** Declare elements that can contain other elements and can also take attributes. The attribute declarations that go with these kinds of elements are part of the complex type definition.

Examples make this much clearer, so read on for a couple. In the following example, a *simple type* definition is used to specify an element named Title that can contain only text:

```
<xsd:element name="Title" type="xsd:string"/>
```

The type attribute specifies the datatype for the element, in this case, a string (just text).

In the following example, a *complex type* definition is used to specify an element named Category that includes a required attribute named name:

```
<xsd:element name="Category">
 <xsd:complexType>
  <xsd:attribute name="name" type="xsd:string" use="required"/>
 </xsd:complexType>
</xsd:element>
```

A content model defines what type of content — text, other elements, or some combination of the two — can be contained in an element. There are four basic content models for XML Schema elements. These four content models are:

- ✔ **Text:** The element can contain only text.

  ```
  <xsd:element name="Item" type="xsd:string"/>
  ```

- ✔ **Empty:** The element cannot contain child elements or text, that is, the content of the element must be empty.

  ```
  <xsd:element name="RecipeNumber" ID="555"/>
  ```

When you create an element that can only contain text or is empty, you can use a simple type definition to declare it. If your element's content model includes other elements (either element content or mixed content), you need to use a complex type definition.

✔ **Element:** The element can contain child elements.

```
<xsd:element name="Ingredients">
 <xsd:complexType>
  <xsd:sequence>
   <xsd:element ref="Item" maxOccurs="unbounded"/>
  </xsd:sequence>
 </xsd:complexType>
</xsd:element>
<xsd:element name="Item" type="xsd:string"/>
```

The Ingredients element is a complex type element that can contain an unlimited (maxOccurs="unbounded") number of Item elements. It could be used in an XML document as follows:

```
<Ingredients>
 <Item>2 cups cooked pinto beans</Item>
 <Item>2 cups pepper jack cheese, shredded</Item>
 <Item>6 cooked whole green chiles</Item>
</Ingredients>
```

Notice the xsd:sequence element that encloses the list of child elements (or element in this case) in the previous example. This element is a *compositor element,* and its job is to list the possible child elements and to specify the structure for those child elements. The three compositors included in XML Schema are:

- sequence indicates that the elements must occur in the specified order in the XML document. Use this compositor if you want to be sure every instance of an element includes all of its child elements in a particular order.

- choice indicates that any one of the elements may occur in the XML document. Think of this compositor as the multiple choice compositor. Use it if you want the element to contain only one of several possible children.

- all indicates that any or all of the elements may occur in the XML document. This is the free-for-all compositor. Use it if you don't care if the element contains one, none, some, or all possible children.

The following example shows a different complex type definition that also includes the sequence compositor:

```
<xsd:element name="Recipe">
 <xsd:complexType>
  <xsd:sequence>
   <xsd:element ref="Title"/>
   <xsd:element ref="Category"/>
   <xsd:element ref="Ingredients"/>
   <xsd:element ref="CookingInstructions"/>
   <xsd:element ref="ServingInstructions"/>
  </xsd:sequence>
 </xsd:complexType>
</xsd:element>
```

The elements that are referred to in the sequence must appear in this order in the XML document because they're contained with the `sequence` compositor. If we change `xsd:sequence` to `xsd:choice`, the `Recipe` element could contain only one of the elements listed. If we change it to `xsd:all`, the `Recipe` element could contain any number of the elements, or none, in any order.

✔ **Mixed:** The element can contain child elements and text and uses compositor elements to define the structure for child elements.

```
<xsd:element name="ServingInstructions">
 <xsd:complexType mixed="true">
  <xsd:sequence>
   <xsd:element ref="Sinst" maxOccurs="unbounded"/>
  </xsd:sequence>
 </xsd:complexType>
</xsd:element>
<xsd:element name="Sinst" type="xsd:string"/>
```

Mixed content as defined in the preceding example could be used in an XML document as follows:

```
<Serving Instructions>Friday's lunch menu includes stuffed green chiles.
 Please use the following instructions:
 <Sinst>Open the cooked green chile pods and remove all seeds.</Sinst>
 <Sinst>Stuff the green chiles with equal amounts of pinto beans and
  shredded jack cheese.</Sinst>
 Please check back for additional instructions tomorrow.
</ServingInstructions>
```

Attribute declarations

Attribute declarations include a name and a type. They are always simple type definitions because attribute declarations can't contain elements or other attributes. However, attribute declarations are contained within a complex type definition and they must be declared at the very end of the complex type, after all the other components of the complex type have been specified. In this example, the attribute `name` is specified as part of the complex type definition of the element `Category`:

```
<xsd:element name="Category">
 <xsd:complexType>
  <xsd:attribute name="name" type="xsd:string"/>
 </xsd:complexType>
</xsd:element>
```

Attributes are always optional unless you include a `use` attribute with the value `required` as in the following example:

```
<xsd:attribute name="cook" type="xsd:string" use="required"/>
```

Attribute groups

If the same set of attributes will be used with more than one element in an schema, you can create an attribute group that can be accessed by as many elements as you choose. This following markup snippet combines several different kinds of cheeses into a single attribute group. This group could be used over and over again with any element that would refer to cheese (a shopping list item, a recipe ingredient item, and nutritional information item, and so on).

```
<xsd:attributeGroup name="cheeses">
 <xsd:attribute name="cheddar" type="xsd:string"/>
 <xsd:attribute name="jack" type="xsd:string"/>
 <xsd:attribute name="swiss" type="xsd:string"/>
</xsd:attributeGroup>
```

An attribute group must be declared globally, that is, at the top level of your schema (right below the schema element declaration).

What about that white space?

White space includes invisible characters such as tabs, carriage returns, spaces, or line feeds. White space is ignored by XML processors as long as it is included outside the XML markup itself. For example, an extra carriage return between two element declarations is ignored.

However, white space within the XML document content is not always ignored by XML Schema. Element or attribute content that includes white space is normalized according to the value declared for the whiteSpace facet in the element or attribute definition. The possible values for the whiteSpace facet are as follows:

- ✔ preserve indicates that no white space normalization is done.
- ✔ replace indicates that tabs, carriage returns, and line feeds are replaced with spaces.
- ✔ collapse indicates that after tabs, carriage returns, and line feeds are replaced with spaces, sequences of spaces are collapsed to a single space.

Datatype Declarations

A datatype declaration is markup that defines the data format for the content of element or attribute and is included in the element or attribute declaration, for example:

```
<xsd:element name="Item" type="xsd:string"/>
```

The datatype declaration in this example is included in the element declaration for the element named Item. The type attribute specifies that the type is equal to xsd:string, which is the string datatype from the XML Schema namespace.

XML Schema includes 44 built-in datatypes and allows you to derive your own datatypes by specifying additional constraints on these 44 basic types. XML Schema not only includes more datatypes than any other schema language, but it's also the only schema language that lets you define your own, reusable datatypes. This makes it the language of choice for validating XML documents that include a lot of data.

Simple datatypes

A datatype can be used in a simple type definition, for example:

```
<xsd:element name="ounces" type="xsd:integer"/>
```

This specifies that the content of the ounces element in our XML document must be formatted according to the XML Schema definition for the datatype named integer.

Complex datatypes

A datatype can also be defined in a complex type definition, for example:

```
<xsd:complexType name="amount">
 <xsd:choice>
  <xsd:element ref="cups"/>
  <xsd:element ref="ounces"/>
  <xsd:element ref="tsp"/>
  <xsd:element ref="tbsp"/>
 </xsd:choice>
</xsd:complexType>
<xsd:element name="cups" type="xsd:float"/>
<xsd:element name="ounces" type="xsd:float"/>
<xsd:element name="tsp" type="xsd:float"/>
<xsd:element name="tbsp" type="xsd:float"/>
```

This creates a new type named amount that includes any one of the four elements listed. The content of each of these four elements is a float datatype. Other elements in this XML Schema may use this amount type, as shown in the following example:

```
<xsd:element name="Item1" type="amount"/>
```

Although a complex type definition can be used to create a new type, which can be used in an XML Schema document anywhere that a datatype can be specified, the new type is actually a *content model*, which you read about earlier in the element declaration section, not a datatype.

Defining constraints and value checks

New datatypes can be derived from any of the 44 built-in datatypes through the use of simple type definitions and a restriction constraint. A *restriction constraint* is a limit on a built-in datatype, which narrows the definition to be whatever you specify. In the following example, a simple type definition with an enumeration is used to specify a set of valid content values. For example, any element that is beanType can have a content value of pinto, kidney, white, or red:

```
<xsd:simpleType name="beanType">
 <xsd:restriction base="xsd:string">
  <xsd:enumeration value="pinto"/>
  <xsd:enumeration value="kidney"/>
  <xsd:enumeration value="white"/>
  <xsd:enumeration value="red"/>
 </xsd:restriction>
</xsd:simpleType>
```

This creates a new datatype named beanType, which restricts the string datatype to a set of specific values. Other elements in this schema can use this datatype, as in the following example:

```
<xsd:element name="Item2" type="beanType"/>
```

For additional information on the 44 built-in datatypes and on the use of the restriction element to create new datatypes, see Part 2 of the XML Schema Recommendation at www.w3.org/TR/xmlschema-2/.

Dealing with Entities, Notations, and More

Although *notations* (statements that tell a processor how to handle non-XML data, such as an image) and *entities* (structures that hold references to frequently used text or the location of external documents you want to include in your XML document) can be used in XML Schema, they can only be used in certain, very specific ways.

For starters, entities and notations in XML Schema can only be used as attribute values, and can only be used if there's a preceding notation declaration in the schema, as shown in this example:

```
<xsd:notation name="jpg" public="image/jpg" system="JPGViewer.exe"/>
```

In this example, the notation declaration includes the name of the notation, and values for the public and system attributes, which define the location of external non-XML data and an external application to handle the data.

For more information on notations and entities, and how to use them in a DTD, see Chapter 6.

If your XML document includes references to external non-XML data or external entities, you may want to use a DTD for validation rather than an XML Schema.

Annotations

Annotations are used in XML Schema documents to provide additional information to humans reading the document and/or to other applications. We start with an annotation element and then include either a documentation element (for information to be read by humans — similar to comments in XML and HTML) or an appInfo element (for information to be read by computer applications — similar to XML processing instructions). In this example, a documentation element is contained in the annotation element:

```
<xsd:element name="Recipes">
 <xsd:annotation>
  <xsd:documentation xml:lang="en">
   This is a collection of Recipes by the XML Gourmet.
  </xsd:documentation>
 </xsd:annotation>
</xsd:element>
```

The documentation includes a comment for the reader between the documentation tags.

In the following example, we add an appInfo element to our markup to include information from another XML schema language (in this case, Schematron) in our XML Schema document:

```
<xsd:element name="Ingredients">
 <xsd:annotation>
  <xsd:documentation xml:lang="en">
   This element specifies the ingredients in our recipe.
  </xsd:documentation>
  <xsd:appinfo>
   <assert test="beans &gt; rice">beans should be greater than rice</assert>
  </xsd:appinfo>
 </xsd:annotation>
</xsd:element>
```

Schematron is another schema language used to extend the capabilities of XML Schema documents. Schematron allows XML Schema documents to include conditional statements such as the one included in the preceding example.

Deciding When to Use a Schema

You do not have to use either a DTD or a schema to create and use XML documents. Validating your XML documents is entirely optional. However, when validity is important, you need to decide when to choose schemas versus DTDs.

Use XML Schema when you want

- To make sure that the information in your XML document is in a correct and consistent format and that all the necessary information has been included. An invoicing system is a good example. Invoices contain a lot of required information, and you want to be sure the different bits of information are in the right format and use the right data type (string, integer, date/time, and so on).

- To create a large set of XML documents that all have the same document structure. Payroll checks are a good example of this. Each check has the same format, and you need to closely control the structures and their data format.

- To share your document structure rules with others when you've built an application that requires valid documents with particular data formats. If you want people to send you data, you have to help them create and structure that data. In addition to being a validation tool, a schema is a great communication tool.

Schemas really make sense when your XML document contains large amounts of data. In this case, you can ensure that the data in the XML document is as accurate as possible by validating it against a schema. If your document validates, you can be sure that all required data is present and in the correct format. The XML Schema specification allows you to create schemas that are as specific as they need to be about what that format should be. If your document content is blocks of text rather than other types of data, it may be easier to use a DTD for validation instead of a schema.

Referencing XML Schema Documents

If you've built an XML document based on a schema, you can reference that schema document from your XML document. You can reference public schema documents as well as your own schema document.

The inside view: Referencing a schema in an XML document

Although you can't include an entire schema inside your XML document, as you can with an internal DTD, you can reference a schema namespace within the root element of your XML document.

For example, if we create a schema named Recipes.xsd based on our example recipe described with the Recipe Markup Language (RML), we can reference that schema in the following way:

```
<?xml version="1.0" standalone="yes"?>
<Recipe cook="The XML Gourmet"
    xmlns:xsi="http://www.w3.org/2001/XMLSchema-instance"
    xsi:noNamespaceSchemaLocation="http://www.lanw.com/Recipes.xsd">
```

In this example, we use the W3C Schema-instance namespace (http://www.w3.org/2001/XMLSchema-instance) and the xsi:noNamespaceSchemaLocation attribute to tie our XML document to the W3C XML Schema and to our XML Schema document (Recipes.xsd). This link is not required, but it does help XML Schema validators locate a schema.

Calling for outside support: Referencing external schemas in your schema

You can include references to multiple schemas written according to the XML Schema specification from within your schema document itself. Referencing multiple schemas enables you to include elements and attributes from other schemas in your own schema document.

REMEMBER

Namespaces are your friends

Because anyone can build their own elements using XML, it's possible — and most likely probable — that two DTDs, schemas, or documents will use the same elements. For example, our RML markup language uses Title in much the same way as HTML uses title.

A parser can deal with just about any set of XML elements. And a well-formed XML document can use elements from any DTD or schema. However, a special processor designed to work with documents written with one or two specific DTDs might not know what to do with a document that combines elements from several different DTDs, some of which may conflict, just like the RML Title element conflicts with the HTML title element.

Namespaces let the parser know which DTD or schema you're using so that you can use the markup from several different DTDs or schemas in one document. In the end, namespaces permit efficient sharing of vocabularies across documents and help eliminate confusion when two or more vocabularies use the same elements.

We cover namespaces in more detail in Chapters 11 and 17.

To refer to other schemas from within your schema document, you use a *namespace* reference and create a prefix for this namespace. Some prefixes are standard. For example, W3C XML Schema components usually have the prefix xs: or xsd: (including the colons) in front of the component name. You don't have to use the prefixes from the W3C's recommendations. You can use whatever prefix you choose, as long as the prefix you use in the namespace reference and the prefix you use in the schema document to identify components of that namespace are the same. (But why would you reinvent the wheel?)

You can also include new schema components that you create. For example, our schema, Recipes.xsd, could include references to as many namespaces as we choose to include:

```
<?xml version="1.0" encoding="UTF-8"?>
<xsd:schema xmlns:xsd="http://www.w3.org/2001/XMLSchema"
          xmlns:ck="http://www.example.com/cook.xsd"
          xmlns:bn="http://www.example.com/bean.xsd"
          xmlns:nm="http://www.newmexicocooks.com/Recipes.xsd">
```

In this example, we include references to three namespaces in addition to the W3C XML Schema namespace. We assign these prefixes to the additional namespace: ck, bn, and nm. If we use components from these namespaces in our schema document, we must use the appropriate prefix in front of the component. For example, to access a chile element from the Recipes.xsd namespace, we would create an element declaration that included the prefix we assigned to that namespace:

```
<nm:element name="chile">
```

Double-checking Your Schemas and Documents

After you've created your XML document and defined all the elements and attributes in a schema, you're ready to parse!

Be sure that your XML document is well formed before you try to validate it. If your XML document isn't well formed, it won't validate.

Here's a list of the tools that are available to help you:

- ✔ **Validating parsers:** Compare your XML document to the referenced schema. Validating your XML document involves using the constraints defined in your schema to check the structure and hierarchy of the elements and attributes in your XML document, as well as to check the structure of the content contained in the elements and attributes.

- ✔ **Schema validity testers:** Compare your schema to the W3C's XML Schema recommendation to be sure it is valid. It doesn't do you any good to validate an XML document against an invalid schema.

- ✔ **Conversion tools:** Convert DTDs to schemas and convert from one schema language to another.

In Chapter 9, we outline the steps to create custom schemas documents and to create a custom XML Schema document (`Recipes.xsd`) to validate our XML example bean burrito recipe.

For more information

For more information on the details of using and writing XML Schema documents, see the W3C XML Schema Recommendation documents on the W3C Web site. The W3C XML Schema Recommendation has three parts:

- ✔ XML Schema Part 0: Primer at `www.w3.org/TR/xmlschema-0/`

- ✔ XML Schema Part 1: Structures at `www.w3.org/TR/2001/REC-xmlschema-1-20010502/`

- ✔ XML Schema Part 2: Datatypes at `www.w3.org/TR/xmlschema-2/`

Chapter 9

Building Custom XML Schemas

*I*f you want to build custom XML documents, you'll probably want to create a map for the documents that defines how you want to use markup to describe your content. You also want to be sure all of your custom XML plays by the same set of markup rules, so you'll want to double-check them against your custom map — a process that you probably know is called *validating*.

The two most popular and useful methods for defining the structure (map) for an XML document are Document Type Definitions (DTDs) and schemas written according to the XML Schema specification. DTDs are most useful for defining the structure of XML documents with text content, although they can be used with any XML document. For more information on using and creating DTDs, check out Chapters 6 and 7. For data-intensive XML documents, schemas (which we also discuss in Chapter 11) have much more to offer in the way of structure definition.

An XML document is valid if it conforms to the rules you define in your schema. Validation against a schema is very useful if your XML documents contain a lot of data content that needs to be formatted in a particular way. For example, say the data content includes e-mail addresses and you want to be sure that the addresses contain alphanumeric characters before and after the @ symbol. A schema lets you specify a datatype to do just that!

Building a simple XML Schema requires these steps:

1. Understanding your data

2. Creating element declarations

3. Defining content models

4. Creating attribute declarations

5. Adding datatype declarations

This chapter takes you through the entire process of creating a custom schema that perfectly suits your XML document's every need.

We use the term schema throughout this chapter to refer to an XML document that is written according to the XML Schema specification and that is designed to describe the structure for other XML documents. The XML Schema specification isn't the only option for writing schemas, but it's the one published by the W3C to work with XML, so it's probably your best choice. Look over Chapter 8 for more information on other schema options.

XML Schema basics are covered in detail in Chapter 8. To jog your memory, here's a quick review of the essential pieces of a schema:

- **Element declarations:** Element declarations are a part of every schema. Element declarations are the basic structure of the schema document and show how each component of the document is related to every other component. Elements can be simple (containing only text content) or complex (containing other elements, attributes, and/or text content).

- **Attribute declarations:** Attribute declarations are contained within the complex type definition for the element that contains the attribute. Attributes are always optional unless you specify in the attribute declaration that an attribute is required. A group of attributes that will be used in more than one element in an XML document can be defined as an attribute group and accessed by any elements you choose.

- **Content models:** Content models define what type of content can be contained in an element. There are four basic content models for XML Schema elements: element (can contain other elements), text (can contain only text), mixed (can contain other elements as well as text), and empty (contain no content).

- **Datatype declarations:** Datatype declarations tell the processor the valid format for an XML element or attribute. You can use any of the 44 built-in XML Schema datatypes or build your own custom datatypes. The datatype declaration is included within an XML Schema element or attribute declaration.

Also remember that schemas are just XML documents that use a specific set of markup defined by the XML Schema specification to define the schema for other documents. You use elements and attributes in a schema to define elements and attributes for use in other documents. Cool, huh?

Step 1: Understanding Your Data

Before building a custom schema, you must understand the basic nature and function of your data. Is your data a collection of book titles, author names, and publishers? Or is your data a group of part numbers, phone numbers, and e-mail addresses? Take some time to look at the kind of data you'll be using in your XML documents so that you can use the right structures and datatypes to describe your content.

Before you design your schema, you also need to be clear about what you want to do with the data. Do you want to export data to a database from your XML documents, or do you want it available for access from wireless devices? Be sure your document structure matches up with the format you need for importing and exporting your data accurately and efficiently.

Step 2: Being the Root of All Structure: Elements

Elements define the basic structure for any XML document, including those created according to a schema. After you've got a good handle on your data and are ready to build a schema that fits it, you should first decide which elements will be included in your XML document.

Take another look at our sample XML document, a bean burrito recipe described with XML and saved in the file `Recipes.xml`:

```
<Recipes>
 <Recipe cook="The XML Gourmet">
  <Title>Bean Burrito</Title>
  <Category name="tex-mex"/>
  <Ingredients>
   <Item>1 can refried beans</Item>
   <Item>1 cup longhorn colby cheese, shredded</Item>
   <Item>1 small onion, finely chopped</Item>
   <Item>3 flour tortillas</Item>
  </Ingredients>
  <CookingInstructions>
   <Cinst>Empty can of refried beans into medium saucepan.</Cinst>
```

```
  <Cinst>Heat over medium-high heat until beans are smooth and bubbly.</Cinst>
  <Cinst>Warm tortillas in microwave for 30 seconds.</Cinst>
 </CookingInstructions>
 <ServingInstructions>
  <Sinst>Spread 1/3 of warm beans on each tortilla.</Sinst>
  <Sinst>Sprinkle with cheese and onions.</Sinst>
  <Sinst>Roll tortillas and serve.</Sinst>
 </ServingInstructions>
</Recipe>
</Recipes>
```

As a first step in declaring the elements for your schema, map out the basic structure of the document: What elements you think you'll need and how they fit together. The best way to go about this is to gather up several sample documents, and take a stab at defining markup that will fit their content. After you have that basic structure down in a marked-up sample document or two, you have your map.

A map makes deciding what kind of attributes, content models, and datatype you need to define a lot easier. Listing 9-1 shows the sample XML document with just the elements listed — without the content or attribute values.

Listing 9-1:   Recipes.xml without the Content or Attribute Values

```
<Recipes>
 <Recipe cook="">
  <Title></Title>
  <Category name="">
  <Ingredients>
   <Item></Item>
   <Item></Item>
   <Item></Item>
   <Item></Item>
  </Ingredients>
  <CookingInstructions>
   <Cinst></Cinst>
   <Cinst></Cinst>
   <Cinst></Cinst>
  </CookingInstructions>
  <ServingInstructions>
   <Sinst></Sinst>
   <Sinst></Sinst>
   <Sinst></Sinst>
  </ServingInstructions>
 </Recipe>
</Recipes>
```

As you can see in Listing 9-1, identifying the underlying structure of an XML document makes building your complete schema a lot easier because you can see the relationships between elements before you create attributes or values.

Elements that contain other elements and/or attributes are, by definition, *complex* types. We show you how to define complex type elements in the next section, "Step 3: Building Content Models." *Simple* element types contain only text content, and can't contain attributes or other elements. In Listing 9-1, the simple type elements are Title, Item, Cinst, and Sinst; the rest are complex.

Step 3: Building Content Models

A *content model* defines the type of content that can be contained in an element. The four content models for XML Schema elements are element (contains child elements), text (contains only text content), mixed (contains child elements and text), and empty (contains no content). For more details and examples of each of these content models, see Chapter 8.

For the schema you're building based on the Recipes.xml document, you only need to use two of these content models: element and text. Most of the elements in our XML document contain other elements, so you will need to create complex type definitions for these parent elements (Recipes, Recipe, Category, Ingredients, CookingInstructions, and Serving Instructions).

Complex type definitions can include *compositor* elements, which are containers for references to other element declarations. The three compositors included in the XML Schema language are as follows:

- ✔ sequence indicates the elements must occur in the specified order in the XML document
- ✔ choice indicates any one of the elements may occur in the XML document
- ✔ all indicates any or all of the elements may occur in the XML document

For more information on compositors, see Chapter 8. For the schema that works with the bean burrito recipe, you will use sequence compositors in most of the complex type definitions.

First, create a complex type definition for the Recipes element. In the DTD you created in Chapter 7, the Recipes element was the root element. In XML Schema, however, the schema element is always the root element and contains all the other elements of the document. The Recipes element in this case contains all the other elements in the schema document except for the schema element. The following markup shows the complex type definition for the Recipes element:

```
<element name="Recipes">
 <complexType>
  <sequence maxOccurs="unbounded">
   <element ref="Recipe"/>
  </sequence>
 </complexType>
</element>
```

A sequence includes one or more element references.

Note that the sequence compositor element contains a maxOccurs attribute that specifies how many times the Recipe element can occur in the document. Because you want the Recipes element to contain any number of Recipe elements, the value is unbounded. The default values for occurrence of an element are a minimum of one and a maximum of one. If you want to specify a different value, you need to use a minOccurs and/or maxOccurs attributes.

The preceding example also includes an element reference:

```
<element ref="Recipe"/>
```

When you use a sequence compositor, you specify child elements using a ref attribute with a value equal to the value of the name attribute in each child element's element declaration. The ref attribute must refer to an actual element declaration, though, and is not sufficient markup just by itself.

Add a complex type definition for the Recipe element, as shown in the following:

```
<element name="Recipe">
 <complexType>
  <sequence>
   <element ref="Title"/>
   <element ref="Category"/>
   <element ref="Ingredients"/>
   <element ref="CookingInstructions"/>
   <element ref="ServingInstructions"/>
  </sequence>
 </complexType>
</element>
<element name="Title"/>
```

The Title element uses a simple element declaration that is included immediately after the complex type definition for the Recipe element. The other elements referenced in the Recipe definition need complex type definitions.

Add a complex type definition for the Category element. This element includes the Name attribute, so you can add the markup you created for this attribute in the previous section of this chapter.

```
<element name="Category">
 <complexType>
  <attribute name="Name" use="required">
   <simpleType>
    <restriction>
     <enumeration value="chinese"/>
     <enumeration value="japanese"/>
     <enumeration value="home-cooking"/>
     <enumeration value="tex-mex"/>
     <enumeration value="continental"/>
     <enumeration value="haute-cuisine"/>
     <enumeration value="other"/>
    </restriction>
   </simpleType>
  </attribute>
 </complexType>
</element>
```

You need to create three more complex type definitions for your schema. The following markup shows the complex type definitions for the `Ingredients`, `CookingInstructions`, and `ServingInstructions` elements:

```
<element name="Ingredients">
 <complexType>
  <sequence maxOccurs="unbounded">
   <element ref="Item"/>
  </sequence>
 </complexType>
</element>
<element name="Item"/>

<element name="CookingInstructions">
 <complexType>
  <sequence maxOccurs="unbounded">
   <element ref="Cinst"/>
  </sequence>
 </complexType>
</element>
<element name="Cinst"/>

<element name="ServingInstructions">
 <complexType>
  <sequence maxOccurs="unbounded">
   <element ref="Sinst"/>
  </sequence>
 </complexType>
</element>
<element name="Sinst"/>
```

Note that the simple element declarations for the `Item`, `Cinst`, and `Sinst` elements are included right after the complex type definitions that reference them.

Congratulations! You've now created all the element declarations and complex type definitions that you need for your schema. All that's left is to add attributes, define datatypes, and put all the pieces together!

Step 4: Using Attributes to Shed Some Light on Data Structure

An *attribute declaration* is a declaration that describes an attribute for that element. Attribute declarations are always *simple* type definitions because they can't contain elements or other attributes. However, attribute declarations are *always* contained within a complex type definition.

Properly built schemas must declare attributes at the very end of the complex type definition, after all the other components of the complex type have been specified.

Our bean burrito document contains two attributes: cook and name. The first attribute, cook, only requires a simple declaration, as shown in the following markup because it's an optional element and we don't want to restrict or more closely define its value. After all, who knows what a cook's name will be or how many characters — or what characters — it will include.

```
<attribute name="cook">
```

Creating the markup for the second attribute, name, is more involved because we really want to limit the values it can take rather than letting the document author use just any text content willy-nilly. To build an attribute declaration that specifies exactly what values the attribute can take, you need to add the list of values to the attribute declaration and specify that the value of the attribute is restricted to those on the list.

In other words, make a list of values and say that the attribute should only take values from the list. Because markup often speaks louder than words, take a gander at the following markup:

```
<attribute name="Name" use="required">
 <simpleType>
  <restriction>
   <enumeration value="chinese"/>
   <enumeration value="japanese"/>
   <enumeration value="home-cooking"/>
   <enumeration value="tex-mex"/>
   <enumeration value="continental"/>
   <enumeration value="haute-cuisine"/>
   <enumeration value="other"/>
  </restriction>
 </simpleType>
</attribute>
```

The simpleType element inside of the attribute declaration indicates that you need to add some additional information about this attribute. The restriction element is a flag that says, "Only choose from the values in this list." Each enumeration element lists the possible options to choose from. Even with the many layers of markup involved, it's still pretty simple.

Attributes are always optional unless you specify that they're required. In this case, you want a value to be present for this attribute, so the use attribute with a value of required is included in the attribute declaration.

Any XML Schema datatype can be further restricted to a certain set of valid content values. For example, you might want to restrict the valid content for an attribute to the set of integers that includes the values 23, 25, 27, and 29. This can be easily done using restriction and enumeration.

Step 5: Using Datatype Declarations to Define What's What

When you were in grade school, there was, no doubt, more than one kid named John (or Ted or Mary or Sue) in your class. Your teacher probably tacked on the first letter of each John's last name ("John S., where's your math homework, young man?") to differentiate between Johns. Or, in those cases when two Johns also had the same last name (which is just plain creepy), your teacher may have had to get creative and call one John "John Brown" because he had brown hair and call the other "John Blond." Just like your fifth-grade teacher, a *datatype* says, "Hey, this is John data."

A datatype declaration added to an element or attribute in a schema lets document creators, or validating parsers, know exactly what kind of data you're actually working with when you declare an element or attribute.

You may have noticed that schemas are more complex to create than DTDs, and you may be asking yourself why you would want to bother with the added complexity. For many documents (especially those with text-intensive content that does not need to be in any specific data format), the benefits of using XML Schema may not be worth the extra time and effort. After all, a text string is a text string.

However, for data-intensive content (that is, content such as invoices, financial data, catalogs, and other content where data format matters), the advantage of being able to use the strong datatyping system of XML Schema makes it well worth the time and effort required.

As you build your custom schema, you need to think carefully about the type of data each element and attribute will hold and take advantage of datatype declarations to pass the specifics to document builders and processing applications. After you've created your initial set of elements and attributes, go back and add datatype declarations to them.

As we mention in Chapter 8, XML Schema offers 44 built-in datatypes — from strings to integers, to date and time stamps, and beyond — for you to use. XML Schema also has the unique feature of supporting reusable user-derived datatypes — in other words, you can derive your own datatypes from the built-in datatypes and reuse these datatypes throughout your schema document.

To find all you ever wanted to know about datatypes, including the gory details of every individual datatype and how you can use them, refer to Part II of the XML Schema specification at

```
http://www.w3.org/TR/xmlschema-2
```

To create a simple type element whose data type is string:

1. **Create the element declaration.**

2. **Include an** xsd: **prefix to specify that this is the XML Schema** string **datatype.**

   The following markup is the element declaration for the Item element, with an added type attribute:

   ```
   <element name="Item" type="xsd:string"/>
   ```

In our recipe schema, each simple type element (Title, Item, Cinst, and Sinst) takes a string datatype.

You define datatypes for attributes in the same way. Create the attribute declaration and add the following datatype declaration:

```
<attribute name="cook" type="xsd:string"/>
```

You can also use datatype declarations to lists of possible values for attributes just once, instead of for each possible value, as in the following markup:

```
<element name="Category">
 <complexType>
  <attribute name="name" use="required">
   <simpleType>
    <restriction base="xsd:string">
     <enumeration value="chinese"/>
     ...
     <enumeration value="other"/>
    </restriction>
   </simpleType>
  </attribute>
 </complexType>
</element>
```

In this example, that `base` attribute with the value `xsd:string` works with the `restriction` element to specify that all possible choices for the value of the `name` attribute of the `Category` element must be strings.

Several XML Schema datatypes are derived from the `string` datatype. A `string` datatype can also be used as a base type for creating a user-defined type, such as a specific pattern of text, or text with a specific number of characters.

Even if an XML element describes text-only data, such as a name or a copyright statement, you may want that text to follow a particular pattern. Using a custom datatype, you can specify, for example, that it must consist of six alphabetical characters followed by three numeric digits, as in the following markup:

```
<xsd:element name="part">
 <xsd:simpleType>
  <xsd:restriction base="xsd:string">
   <xsd:pattern value="\D{6}+\d{3}"/>
  </xsd:restriction>
 </xsd:simpleType>
</xsd:element>
```

In this example, an element named `part` is defined using a simple type definition and a restriction of the `string` type to this particular pattern. An XML document based on this schema must include the `part` element content in this format to be valid.

Tricks of the Trade

In this chapter and in Chapter 8, we cover the basics of building schemas. Here are some reminders and additional tips for building and using them:

- ✔ **Use** `annotation` **and** `documentation`**:** The `annotation` and `documentation` elements are similar to comments in HTML documents — they provide additional information for humans reading the schema document. For more information, see Chapter 8.

- ✔ **The** `schema` **element comes first:** The `schema` element is the root element of the schema document and is always the first element to appear after the XML prolog.

- ✔ **Tools do XML Schemas too:** See Chapter 20 for more details on XML editors that can create schemas from DTDs and vice versa.

- ✔ **Review your validation options:** Schemas are designed for data-intensive documents, or text content that includes many additional constraints, such as patterns of content. Otherwise, a DTD may be a better choice for validating your XML document. Visit Chapter 8 for more information on when to use a schema, and visit Chapter 11 for additional details on using schema for data-intensive documents.

Creating a Simple Schema

Now that you've created all the pieces of your schema, it's time to piece them all together to complete your little (or possibly huge) project:

1. **Create an XML prolog and a** schema **element.**

2. **Add an** xsd: **prefix to all the components to identify them as part of the XML Schema namespace.** For example

   ```
   <?xml version="1.0" encoding="UTF-8"?>
   <xsd:schema xmlns:xsd="http://www.w3.org/2001/XMLSchema">
   ```

3. **Add the element and attribute declarations you created in the previous sections.**

   Remember to add an xsd: prefix to all the components:

   ```
   <xsd:element name="Recipes">
    <xsd:complexType>
     <xsd:sequence maxOccurs="unbounded">
      <xsd:element ref="Recipe"/>
     </xsd:sequence>
    </xsd:complexType>
   </xsd:element>
   <xsd:element name="Recipe">
    <xsd:complexType>
     <xsd:sequence>
      <xsd:element ref="Title"/>
      <xsd:element ref="Category"/>
      <xsd:element ref="Ingredients"/>
      <xsd:element ref="CookingInstructions"/>
      <xsd:element ref="ServingInstructions"/>
     </xsd:sequence>
     <xsd:attribute name="cook" type="xsd:string"/>
    </xsd:complexType>
   </xsd:element>
   <xsd:element name="Title" type="xsd:string"/>
   <xsd:element name="Category">
    <xsd:complexType>
     <xsd:attribute name="name" use="required">
      <xsd:simpleType>
       <xsd:restriction base="xsd:string">
        <xsd:enumeration value="chinese"/>
        <xsd:enumeration value="japanese"/>
        <xsd:enumeration value="home-cooking"/>
        <xsd:enumeration value="tex-mex"/>
        <xsd:enumeration value="continental"/>
        <xsd:enumeration value="haute-cuisine"/>
        <xsd:enumeration value="other"/>
       </xsd:restriction>
      </xsd:simpleType>
   ```

```
     </xsd:attribute>
    </xsd:complexType>
  </xsd:element>
  <xsd:element name="Ingredients">
   <xsd:complexType>
    <xsd:sequence maxOccurs="unbounded">
     <xsd:element ref="Item"/>
    </xsd:sequence>
   </xsd:complexType>
  </xsd:element>
  <xsd:element name="Item" type="xsd:string"/>
  <xsd:element name="CookingInstructions">
   <xsd:complexType>
    <xsd:sequence maxOccurs="unbounded">
     <xsd:element ref="Cinst"/>
    </xsd:sequence>
   </xsd:complexType>
  </xsd:element>
  <xsd:element name="Cinst" type="xsd:string"/>
  <xsd:element name="ServingInstructions">
   <xsd:complexType>
    <xsd:sequence maxOccurs="unbounded">
     <xsd:element ref="Sinst"/>
    </xsd:sequence>
   </xsd:complexType>
  </xsd:element>
  <xsd:element name="Sinst" type="xsd:string"/>
</xsd:schema>
```

Except for attribute declarations, which must occur at the end of complex type declarations, the other declarations in your schema can occur in any order. In other words, you can list the declarations in any order you choose as long as they're contained within the `schema` element. The order of elements in your XML document is determined by the structure of the parent-child relationships defined in your schema document. It is, however, often easier to view a document's underlying structure if the declarations are listed in the same order you use the elements in the XML document.

4. **Save your schema document with an** `.xsd` **file extension.**

   You can give your schema any name you like, but descriptive names make it easier to keep track of which schema document validates which XML documents. For example, we decided to name this schema `Recipes.xsd`.

Listing 9-2 shows the full schema document that we created in this chapter.

Listing 9-2: The Recipes Schema Document in All Its Glory

```
<?xml version="1.0" encoding="UTF-8"?>
<xsd:schema xmlns:xsd="http://www.w3.org/2001/XMLSchema">
 <xsd:element name="Recipes">
  <xsd:complexType>
   <xsd:sequence maxOccurs="unbounded">
    <xsd:element ref="Recipe"/>
```

(continued)

Listing 9-2: *(continued)*

```
   </xsd:sequence>
  </xsd:complexType>
 </xsd:element>
 <xsd:element name="Recipe">
  <xsd:complexType>
   <xsd:sequence>
    <xsd:element ref="Title"/>
    <xsd:element ref="Category"/>
    <xsd:element ref="Ingredients"/>
    <xsd:element ref="CookingInstructions"/>
    <xsd:element ref="ServingInstructions"/>
   </xsd:sequence>
   <xsd:attribute name="cook" type="xsd:string"/>
  </xsd:complexType>
 </xsd:element>
 <xsd:element name="Title" type="xsd:string"/>
 <xsd:element name="Category">
  <xsd:complexType>
   <xsd:attribute name="Name" use="required">
    <xsd:simpleType>
     <xsd:restriction base="xsd:string">
      <xsd:enumeration value="chinese"/>
      <xsd:enumeration value="japanese"/>
      <xsd:enumeration value="home-cooking"/>
      <xsd:enumeration value="tex-mex"/>
      <xsd:enumeration value="continental"/>
      <xsd:enumeration value="haute-cuisine"/>
      <xsd:enumeration value="other"/>
     </xsd:restriction>
    </xsd:simpleType>
   </xsd:attribute>
  </xsd:complexType>
 </xsd:element>
 <xsd:element name="Ingredients">
  <xsd:complexType>
   <xsd:sequence maxOccurs="unbounded">
    <xsd:element ref="Item"/>
   </xsd:sequence>
  </xsd:complexType>
 </xsd:element>
 <xsd:element name="Item" type="xsd:string"/>
 <xsd:element name="CookingInstructions">
  <xsd:complexType>
   <xsd:sequence maxOccurs="unbounded">
    <xsd:element ref="Cinst"/>
   </xsd:sequence>
  </xsd:complexType>
 </xsd:element>
 <xsd:element name="Cinst" type="xsd:string"/>
 <xsd:element name="ServingInstructions">
  <xsd:complexType>
   <xsd:sequence maxOccurs="unbounded">
    <xsd:element ref="Sinst"/>
   </xsd:sequence>
  </xsd:complexType>
 </xsd:element>
 <xsd:element name="Sinst" type="xsd:string"/>
</xsd:schema>
```

Part III
Putting XML to Work

The 5th Wave   By Rich Tennant

"Hold your horses. It takes time to build a DTD for someone your size."

In this part . . .

Here, we take the contents of Part II, which describe XML document structures in general and in particular, and explain how to put those particulars to work. In Chapter 10, you find out about how to read a DTD that describes an XML document and how to use that information to build XML documents based on that description. In Chapter 11, you repeat that same exercise, except that an XML Schema drives your work, instead of a DTD.

Chapter 12 explains how to use alternate alphabets, special symbols, and all kinds of character sets in your XML documents. This is especially interesting to those who seek to represent text in languages other than English in their XML documents. It also explains the mechanisms that make specialized character displays possible for XML applications that may require lots of specialized notation to display their content correctly (such as for mathematics, chemistry, genealogy, and other sorts of documents that make use of specialized symbols, operators, equations, and so forth).

Chapter 10

DTDs at Work

*I*n the end, as always, XML content dictates the document structure that you create with a DTD. The more regular the content is (in other words, the more straight forward, simple, and less prone to give you a major migraine), the easier it will be for you to represent the document's structure in a DTD. The less regular the content is (in other words, the less predictable, consistent, and cooperative), the lower the probability that a DTD can enforce meaningful rules for content structure anyway.

So what's the bottom line? A text-oriented database, such as a collection of recipes or an address book, is more likely to present enforceable rules for structure than a free-form work such as a poem or a novel. That's because record-oriented content, such as a catalog entry or an address, has a much more regular and predictable structure than the prose that makes up a poem or a novel. Those guys weren't joking when they said, "Form follows function!" This is especially true for XML.

If you're working with XML, you may sometimes need to modify or update (if not build) a DTD from time to time, especially if you're building documents that adhere to the markup and structure that a DTD already defines. In this chapter, you explore what's involved in working with a DTD as you investigate the process of constructing markup according to a DTD's rules and regulations. In addition, you find out how to use DTDs to help control document structure.

Eliciting Markup from the DTD

Here's the recipe DTD that we introduced in Chapter 7. This DTD shows the nuances of the markup that documents written according to the DTD should use if they need to be valid. (In the following section, we elaborate on that DTD a bit to demonstrate some of the ways that DTDs can help to manage a document's structure.)

```
<!-- Begin Recipes.dtd last updated January 1, 2002 -->
<!ENTITY mmmm "Madeline Margaret Murphy-Morrison">
<!ELEMENT Recipes (Recipe)+>
<!ELEMENT Recipe (Title, Category, Ingredients, CookingInstructions,
 ServingInstructions)>
<!ELEMENT Title (#PCDATA)>
<!ELEMENT Category EMPTY>
<!ELEMENT Ingredients (Item)+>
<!ELEMENT Item (#PCDATA)>
<!ELEMENT CookingInstructions (Cinst)+>
<!ELEMENT Cinst (#PCDATA)>
<!ELEMENT ServingInstructions (Sinst)+>
<!ELEMENT Sinst (#PCDATA)>
<!ATTLIST Recipe cook CDATA #IMPLIED>
<!ATTLIST Category name ENUMERATED (chinese, japanese, home-cooking, tex-mex,
 continental, haute-cuisine, other)>
<!-- End of Recipes.dtd -->
```

The primary element in this DTD is the `Recipes` element. As defined, the `Recipes` element must contain one or more `Recipe` elements because its definition uses the plus sign (+) occurrence indicator:

```
<!ELEMENT Recipes (Recipe)+>
```

A valid `Recipes` document must contain at least one or more `Recipe` elements to be properly constructed.

Defining the structure of the Recipe element

Because the `Recipe` element is the primary data structure in this DTD, its definition is worth some additional exploration and explanation:

```
<!ELEMENT Recipe (Title, Category, Ingredients, CookingInstructions,
 ServingInstructions)>
```

According to this definition, a `Recipe` element must be structured as follows:

✔ **The structure defines the sequence.** The definition of the `Recipe` element precedes a list of element names (separated by commas). This parenthesized list is called *element content* because it consists entirely of element names. The structure of this list defines the sequence for elements that must or may compose a valid `Recipe` element.

✔ **Every item has to have a title.** The content for a `Recipe` element must begin with one and only one `Title` element, as signified by the appearance of the `Title` element in the first position of the element content specification. In plain English, you could understand this to mean that "any recipe must have a title."

✔ **The order child elements appear in is defined.** Following the `Title` element, a `Recipe` element must include one and only one of each of the following elements: `Category`, `Ingredients`, `CookingInstructions`, and `ServingInstructions`, in that order.

✔ **Each child element is defined on its own terms.** Following the `Recipe` element, each element in the element content list is defined along with its child elements, if applicable. The `Title` element contains PCDATA, the `Category` element is empty, and the `Ingredients`, `CookingInstructions`, and `ServingInstructions` elements contain their own child elements.

✔ **The rules for attribute options are clear.** After elements, attributes are defined. The `Recipe` element has a `cook` attribute that's not required. The `Category` element has a selection of attribute values, and you must choose one.

That's it for the recap of the `Recipes.dtd` file. Next, you can chew on its implications. . . .

Understanding the implications: What's valid — and what's not

As element content structures go, the model inherent in the `Recipe` element's declaration isn't that flexible. Based on that single declaration, the following structure is valid:

```
<Recipe>
  <Title> . . . </Title>
  <Category/>
  <Ingredients>
  </Ingredients>
  <CookingInstructions>
  </CookingInstructions>
  <ServingInstructions>
  </ServingInstructions>
</Recipe>
```

You can, however, add as many `Item`, `Cisnt`, and `Sinst` elements as you like within the appropriate elements. Within a `Recipes` element, you can have multiple `Recipes` elements, so in that way the DTD is flexible.

Here's an example that includes a recipe plus other children elements:

```
<Recipes>
 <Recipe cook="The XML Gourmet">
  <Title>Bean Burrito</Title>
  <Category name="tex-mex"/>
  <Ingredients>
   <Item>1 can refried beans</Item>
   <Item>1 cup longhorn colby cheese, shredded</Item>
   <Item>1 small onion, finely chopped</Item>
   <Item>3 flour tortillas</Item>
  </Ingredients>
  <CookingInstructions>
   <Cinst>Empty can of refried beans into medium saucepan.</Cinst>
   <Cinst>Heat over medium-high heat until beans are smooth and bubbly.</Cinst>
   <Cinst>Warm tortillas in microwave for 30 seconds.</Cinst>
  </CookingInstructions>
  <ServingInstructions>
   <Sinst>Spread 1/3 of warm beans on each tortilla.</Sinst>
   <Sinst>Sprinkle with cheese and onions.</Sinst>
   <Sinst>Roll tortillas and serve.</Sinst>
  </ServingInstructions>
 </Recipe>
</Recipes>
```

Valid `Recipes` elements can include one or more `Recipe` elements, but within each `Recipe` element the `Title`, `Category`, `Ingredients`, `Cooking Instructions`, and `ServingInstructions` elements must all occur in order. `CookingInstructions` and `ServingInstructions` elements must include at least one `Cinst` and `Sinst` element, respectively, because the DTD's occurrence indicator specifies that these elements must occur one or more times. We think you should be able to figure this kind of markup out for yourself, so we won't do it for you here.

Instead, we'd like to write about the things this particular structure makes _invalid_. It's as important to understand what a DTD does _not_ allow — especially one with an element as general as the `Recipes` element — as it is to understand what _is_ allowed.

Here's a list of what's invalid, according to the structure of the declaration for the `Recipe` element (we added examples where we thought they fit):

✔ **There can't be more than one title.** Any `Recipe` element can have one and only one `Title` element, and it must occur first within that element. This markup is invalid for reasons noted in its comments:

```
<!--Two Title elements may not occur in a Recipe element -->
<Recipes>
 <Recipe>
  <Title>Bean Burrito</Title>
  <Title>Or, Tubular Mexican Beans</Title>
<!--Assume the rest of the recipe elements appear correctly -->
```

```
  </Recipe>
  <!-- The Title element must always occur first in a Recipe element -->
  <Recipe>
   <Category name="tex-mex"/>
   <Title>Bean Burrito</Title>
  <!--Assume the rest of the recipe elements appear correctly -->
  </Recipe>
  ...
 </Recipes>
```

✔ **Elements can't appear out of order.** Whenever other elements
  follow the Title element in a Recipe element, the elements can appear
  only in the order specified in the Recipe element's content declaration:
  Category follows Title, Ingredients follows Category, Cooking
  Instructions follows Ingredients, and ServingInstructions follows
  CookingInstructions. The following markup is invalid because it breaks
  the element order requirements specified in the DTD's content model:

```
<Recipes>
 <!-- Elements may only appear in the order specified in the element content
          declaration -->
 <Recipe cook="The XML Gourmet">
 <!-- This markup reverses the required order for elements, and is wrong,
          wrong, wrong. -->
  <ServingInstructions>...</ServingInstructions>
  <CookingInstructions>...</CookingInstructions>
  <Ingredients>...</Ingredients>
..<Category name="tex-mex" />
  <Title>Bean Burrito</Title>
  </Recipe>
 ...
 </Recipes>
```

✔ **Attributes not specifically listed in the DTD can't be used in valid
  documents.** Where elements — such as Recipe and Category — take
  attributes, only the attributes declared in the DTD can actually appear.
  The following markup is invalid:

```
<Recipes>
 <!-- Mismatched quotation marks are invalid, as are missing quotation marks
          -->
 <Recipe cook="The XML Gourmet'>
  <Category name=tex-mex>
 <!-- Assume the rest of the first recipe is correct and complete -->
 </Recipe>
 <!-- The name of the correct attribute value is cook, not chef -->
 <Recipe chef="The XML Gourmet">
 <!-- Assume the rest of the second recipe is correct and complete -->
 </Recipe>
 </Recipes>
```

For any XML document to be well formed, all attribute values must be
enclosed in quotation marks. You may use either single or double quotation
marks, but you must be consistent whenever attribute values are quoted.

Although the structure for a Recipe element is somewhat loose in terms
of the number of child elements that can occur in the Ingredients,

`CookingInstructions`, and `ServingInstructions` elements, there's still plenty of structure here to be enforced.

Trading Flexibility for Structure

Despite the rules we've listed in previous sections, DTDs can be written to be quite flexible and accommodate documents whose content isn't 100 percent predictable; you can mix things up in them:

- ✔ Element declarations in DTDs can use parentheses to create multiple levels of structure.
- ✔ DTDs support a way of specifying that one item from a set of possible choices can be chosen to appear.
- ✔ DTDs permit element choices to be combined with open-ended constructs such as `ANY` or `#PCDATA`. This flexibility means DTDs open the door to just about any conceivable kind of content.

To help you understand what this means, we play some games with the `Recipes.dtd` definition for the `Recipe` element, which appears as follows in the master DTD:

```
<!ELEMENT Recipe (Title, Category, Ingredients, CookingInstructions,
        ServingInstructions)>
```

You might decide that sets of `CookingInstructions` and `Serving Instructions` must appear in pairs, where at least one such pair is required in a valid `Recipe`. A second level of parentheses (and corresponding structure) makes this decision easy to note:

```
<!ELEMENT Recipe(Title, Category, Ingredients,
        (CookingInstructions, ServingInstructions)+)>
```

All you have to do is separate the `CookingInstructions` and `ServingInstructions` elements with a comma, enclose them in parentheses, and added a plus sign as an occurrence indicator outside those parentheses.

Translated into English:

- ✔ A `Recipe` must contain one or more paired sets of `Cooking Instructions` and `ServingInstructions` elements.
- ✔ If a `Recipe` contains a `CookingInstructions` element, that element may be associated with one, and only one, `CookingInstructions` element.
- ✔ In any `Recipe`, the `CookingInstructions` element must always precede the `ServingInstructions` element in each such pair.

If your `Recipe` structure allowed individual `CookingInstructions` to be associated with zero or more `ServingInstructions`, you might change the element declaration to read:

```
<!ELEMENT Recipe (Title, Category, Ingredients,
          (CookingInstructions,(ServingInstructions)*)+)>
```

In that case, zero or more `ServingInstructions` elements could follow any particular `CookingInstructions` element. As before, any `Recipe` element could include one or more such pairs of subelements.

DTDs are easier to read if you don't have to try to follow too many levels of structure in any single element declaration. That's why you might choose to create an intermediate-level element, perhaps named `Instructions`, to capture the nuances of how cooking and serving instructions need to be handled. This structure might lead you to create the following DTD:

```
<!ENTITY mmmm "Madeline Margaret Murphy-Morrison">
<!ELEMENT Recipes (Recipe+)>
<!ELEMENT Recipe (Title, Category, Ingredients, Instructions)>
<!ELEMENT Title (#PCDATA)>
<!ELEMENT Category EMPTY>
<!ELEMENT Ingredients (Item)+>
<!ELEMENT Item (#PCDATA)>
<!ELEMENT Instructions (CookingInstructions, ServingInstructions*)+
<!ELEMENT CookingInstructions (Cinst)+>
<!ELEMENT Cinst (#PCDATA)>
<!ELEMENT ServingInstructions (Sinst)+>
<!ELEMENT Sinst (#PCDATA)>
<!ATTLIST Recipe cook CDATA #IMPLIED>
<!ATTLIST Category name ENUMERATED (chinese, japanese, home-cooking, tex-mex,
  continental, haute-cuisine, other)>
```

This approach lets you concentrate on one level of element structure at a time and helps make your DTD easier for others to read and understand.

A Matter of Selection: The Selection Technique

DTDs also support what might be called a selection technique. The selection technique allows DTD designers to define sets of potential elements from which document authors must choose one when they are creating valid XML documents. Think of it as a la cart XML development: Choose the element that you need from a menu of possible options. This technique provides a lot of flexibility for document authors to accurately describe their content in a valid document because they can pick the element that best suits their content. Here's an example of a particularly flexible DTD for describing addresses to show what we mean.

Given the following DTD fragment

```
<!ELEMENT Address (Name, Company*, Street*, City, State?, Code?, Country*)>
<!ATTLIST Address Type (home|office|other) "office">
<!ELEMENT Name (#PCDATA)>
<!ELEMENT Company (#PCDATA)>
<!ELEMENT Street (#PCDATA)>
<!ELEMENT City (#PCDATA)>
<!ELEMENT State (#PCDATA)>
<!ELEMENT Code (Zip|Postal_Code)>
<!ELEMENT Zip (#PCDATA)>
<!ELEMENT Postal_Code (#PCDATA)>
<!ELEMENT Country (#PCDATA)>
```

the following XML markup is all valid. We tell you why in the comments throughout the markup.

```
<Address Type="home">
<!-- This Address element follows U.S. address syntax,
    including Zip, and designates no country -->
 <Name>Ed Tittel</Name>
 <Street>555 Anywhere Dr.</Street>
 <City>Austin</City>
 <State>TX</State>
 <Code>
  <Zip>78728-5480</Zip>
 </Code>
</Address>
<Address>
<!-- This Address element follows U.K. address syntax,
    including Postal Code, multiple street/location
    terms, and a country designation. Also because no
    type attribute appears, the default is office -->
 <Name>George Worst</Name>
 <Street>555 Best Road</Street>
 <Street>Sparkhill</Street>
 <City>Birmingham</City>
 <Code>
  <Postal_Code>B11 3AX</Postal_Code>
 </Code>
 <Country>U.K.</Country>
</Address>
```

The key lines in the DTD that allow you to select among a defined set of values for the `Types` attribute and that allow designation of a `Zip` or `Postal_Code` are as follows:

```
<!ATTLIST Address Type (home|office|other) "office">
```

and

```
<!ELEMENT Code (Zip|Postal_Code)>
```

The first attribute list indicates that for any `Address` element that takes a `Type` attribute, the value of that attribute must be home, office, or other, and the default value for this attribute is office if an explicit assignment is not supplied. The second element declaration indicates that an address may include a Code element of some kind and this Code element will be either a Zip or a Postal_Code element (which corresponds to the difference between U.S.- and U.K.-derived postal coding schemes).

Two good ways to use DTD selection clauses are

✔ To choose one value from a set of possible values for attributes

✔ To choose one element from a set of possible elements when building an element hierarchy

Either way, you can use this syntax to limit an author's choices and yet still provide alternative elements or attribute values to make the DTD more flexible.

Using the Selection Technique to Mix Up the Order

These DTD selection clauses can be used also to permit the definition of alternative orders. To explain how this might come in handy, take a look at these two addresses:

Ed Tittel	George Worst
555 Anywhere Dr.	555 Best Road
Austin, TX 78728-5480	Sparkhill
USA	B11 3AX
	Birmingham
	U.K.

In the U.S. address, the Zip follows the City and State entries. In the U.K. address, the Postal_Code precedes the City and the State seldom appears. If you want to handle data in either order, you could build the following DTD:

```
<!ELEMENT Address (Name,Company*,Street*,Locator,Country*)>
<!ATTLIST Address Type (home|office|other) "office">
<!ELEMENT Name (#PCDATA)>
<!ELEMENT Company (#PCDATA)>
<!ELEMENT Street (#PCDATA)>
<!ELEMENT Locator ((City,State?,Code?) | (Code?,City,State?))>
<!ELEMENT City (#PCDATA)>
<!ELEMENT State (#PCDATA)>
<!ELEMENT Code (Zip|Postal_Code)>
<!ELEMENT Zip (#PCDATA)>
<!ELEMENT Postal_Code (#PCDATA)>
<!ELEMENT Country (#PCDATA)>
```

TIP

Wandering outside XML's boundaries

Although XML documents include mostly XML data as content, you may occasionally want to include other kinds of data (such as graphics, video, streaming multimedia, and programs) in your XML documents as well. Within an XML document, any data that's not explicitly XML is called an *unparsed entity* and can appear only as the value associated with an attribute. Thus, non-XML data can be referenced from within an XML document but isn't really part of that XML document.

Simply put, when an entity is labeled as non-XML data, it's ignored by the XML parser as it chunks its way through the document. When the XML parser identifies non-XML data, the parser returns control over that data back to whatever application called the parser. As with modern Web browsers, this standard operating procedure provides an opportunity to call a helper module or plug-in that knows how to handle this special non-XML data so that the special data can be rendered or displayed within the overall XML document.

To invoke an unparsed entity in an XML document, you have to include an external general entity reference to that data. The inclusion of the NDATA keyword in that declaration, followed by a notation type name, clues the parser into what's going on — and allows the application to invoke the right kind of help. Then, you must also create a <!NOTATION declaration to identify the NDATA type, and provide the application with the necessary identification to call the correct helper or plug-in. A notation declaration represents a set of rules that describes how an identifiable class of non-XML data behaves, which is usually different from how XML data behaves.

For example, if you want to extend our Recipe element to include a reference to a GIF file that contains a digitized photo of the finished recipe,

ready to serve. Here's the DTD markup you would need to use:

```
<!-- This DTD fragment is
     incomplete -->
<!-- It shows only new markup ->
<!NOTATION gif SYSTEM
     "PSP.exe">
<!-- Associates .gif files with
     PaintShop Pro -->
<!ELEMENT Recipe
 (Title, Category, Ingredients,
  CookingInstructions,
  ServingInstructions)>
<!ELEMENT Title (#PCDATA)>
<!ELEMENT Category EMPTY>
<!ELEMENT Ingredients (Item)+>
<!ELEMENT Item (#PCDATA)>
<!ELEMENT CookingInstructions
     (Cinst)+>
<!ELEMENT Cinst (#PCDATA)>
<!ELEMENT ServingInstructions
     (Sinst)+>
<!ELEMENT Sinst (#PCDATA)>
<!ATTLIST Recipe cook CDATA
     #IMPLIED>
<!ATTLIST Category name ENUMER-
     ATED (chinese, japanese,
     home-cooking, tex-mex,
  continental, haute-cuisine,
  other)>
<!ENTITY Photo-bb SYSTEM
     "photo-bb.gif" NDATA gif>
<!-- Include &Photo-bb; in con-
     tent to call image -->
```

The ENTITY definition for Photo-bb ties the NOTATION declaration to the unparsed entity through the value that follows the NDATA attribute.

By creating an intermediate element named Locator, you create a place-holder in the original Address element. Then, when you define the Locator element, you can use a selection clause to stipulate that either of these two orders is valid: (City, State, Code) or (Code, City, State). In either case, the State and Code elements remain optional, where only one instance of each is allowed if those elements appear.

A close look at the Locator syntax, however, shows one of the problems with selection clauses. You have to repeat the occurrence indicators that apply to each instance of the structure when the syntax allows an author to select from multiple orders. You may notice that your workload will increase (not to mention the amount of thinking you'll have to do) that you have to do if you choose this option. Use selection clauses sparingly.

Mixing Up Your Content Models

XML supports several ways for you to use DTD to manage structure to some degree and still have an out if you can't absolutely determine in advance how to structure the elements that go into such DTDs.

In the DTD code throughout this book, we use elements that consist entirely of child elements or that contain parsed character data (#PCDATA). *Parsed character data* is just a fancy term for plain ol' text that gets parsed so that any entities, such as &mmmm;, can be caught and handled. PCDATA doesn't contain any markup other than characters or general entities, and in the end, it's just text. The parser does look at it, but it doesn't impose any validation rules on it because there's no way to predict what your PCDATA will be.

For example, the list of possible recipe ingredients is endless, which is why the Ingredients element in our RML has (#PCDATA) as its content model — so authors can include any text they want in the ingredients element. The parser checks to be sure the Ingredients element exists and that it has some text in it. If so (and assuming that the rest of the document is valid), then the recipe is valid.

To leave yourself an out when you can't define everything in advance, declare elements that contain both child elements *and* parsed character data. In DTD-speak, this content model is called *mixed content*. Mixed content gives you an out because it indicates that an element

 ✔ Might include some text and entities

 ✔ Might also include some child elements thrown in for good measure

Mixed content consists of PCDATA possibly combined with child elements.

Say you think that the `Locator` element that we declared in the address DTD example in the preceding section might have to accommodate other, arbitrary text data. To reflect this, you can create the following `Locator` declaration:

```
<!ELEMENT Locator (#PCDATA|City|State|Code)*>
```

The preceding declaration specifies that the `Locator` element can contain PCDATA (that is, text and entities), mixed with any combination of `City`, `State`, and `Code` elements. However, notice that there's no sequence or number specified for the elements. When you use a mixed content model, you lose the ability to specify the sequence of the child elements and the number of times that they can appear.

Using this content model as a guide, all three of the following elements are valid:

```
<!-- this version of the element only contains PCDATA -->
<Locator> Austin, TX 78728-5480</Locator>

<!-- this version of the element contains some PCDATA and two elements -->
<Locator>
   <City>Austin</City>
   TX
   <Code>78728-5480</Code>
</Locator>

<!-- this version of the element contains PCDATA and multiple child elements
     in any order -->
<Locator>
   <Code>78728</Code>
   <Code>5480</Code>
   <State>TX</State>
   Austin
</Locator>
```

As this example illustrates, using mixed content means giving up most of the controls over sequence and structure that a DTD can provide. In the real world, it doesn't make much sense to use a mixed content model for the `Locator` element because you probably want it to be very predictable. The more flexible selection options we presented in previous sections make more sense. However, for other elements where sequence and structure aren't as crucial, and you're not sure what combination of elements and PCDATA someone will need to use, mixed content is a good option.

Working with General Entity References in DTDs

In a DTD, an entity provides a way to associate a name or identifier with some kind of arbitrary string of characters or other information. The following declaration occurs within the master DTD for the bean burrito recipe and associates the text "Madeline Margaret Murphy-Morrison" with the much shorter entity &mmmm;

```
<!ENTITY mmmm "Madeline Margaret Murphy-Morrison">
```

There's more than one kind of entity, but in this section when we talk about entities we're referring to general entity references. In XML (and SGML) terminology, *general entity references* are like a gigantic = sign. When an XML processor reads a DTD that includes the mmmm entity declaration, the processor knows to replace all occurrences of the string &mmmm; with the stuff that follows: Madeline Margaret Murphy-Morrison. Note the beginning ampersand (&) and concluding semicolon (;) that denote the start and end of the entity reference.

General entity references can be pretty handy, but they are subject to three important limitations:

- **You can't use an entity before you define it.** No general entity reference may occur in a document before it's been declared and defined. To follow good DTD practices, always declare entities at the beginning of the DTD document.

- **Your entity references have to do something.** In other words, *circular entity references* — when an entity declaration mentions a second entity and the second entity declaration mentions the first — just don't work. The following example is an example of a circular reference:

```
<!ENTITY loc "Library of Congress &US;">
<!ENTITY US "loc; United States">
```

The problem with this pair of declarations is that neither one defines a plain, simple string by itself. Each declaration depends on the other, yet neither is completely defined. Avoid this error in your designs by all means possible!

- **The entity has to refer to data that's in the XML document.** In other words, you can't use entities as shortcuts to writing the DTD. General entity references can't handle text that is only part of a DTD (and not used as part of the XML document's content). The reason for this rule is that you might be tempted to abbreviate common DTD-reserved words, such as (#PCDATA), as in this example:

```
<!ENTITY PCD "(#PCDATA)">
<!ELEMENT Title &PCD;>
...
<!ELEMENT Item &PCD;>
```

DTDs do allow the use of another kind of entity, called a *parameter entity*, which can define substitutable text usable inside DTDs themselves, as you'll find in the next section.

Using Parameter Entities in DTDs

General reference entities that take the form &name; become part of a document but can't become part of a DTD's internal structure or markup. A parameter entity is an entity that is created specifically for the purpose of helping you use shortcuts when you write a DTD. They don't refer to content in XML documents at all.

Parameter entities really shine in two special cases:

✔ **To eliminate the need to repeat commonly-used element and attribute declarations:** Like other kinds of entities, the parameter entity works like a gigantic = sign that says "When I use this markup please replace it with that markup."

✔ **To use parts of DTDs with more flexibility:** You can use parameter entities to carve DTDs into significant chunks of declarations, which you save in separate files and link to as needed.

In general, if you know that you need to repeat complex markup more than twice in a DTD, consider taking time out to create a parameter entity so that you can use the entity reference instead of repeating the markup. This option ultimately simplifies document maintenance, not just for you, but for anyone else who uses the DTD after you do.

Using this technique to mix and match chunks of DTD declarations is easy, simple, and powerful. In fact, we think this tip is almost worth the price of admission!

As with general entities, parameter entities must be declared before they can be used. We hope that's intuitive: without a definition, an XML parser can't know what to substitute for the %name; symbol when it appears in a document prolog or in a standalone DTD.

Here's the general syntax for a parameter entity declaration:

```
<!ENTITY % name "replacement text">
```

As with general entity references, *name* represents the name of the entity, and *replacement text* represents the text that replaces that name each time it appears as a parameter entity.

Unlike general entity references, parameter entities take the form %*name*; to reference the entity when you use it in the DTD.

Using parameter entities to save time

When complex collections of markup occur repeatedly in a DTD, you can make the repeated text the subject of a parameter entity declaration. When you get to a point where you'd have to repeat the text, you use the parameter entity instead. Using parameter entities in this capacity not only speeds data entry considerably, but also means that if the declarations that are part of the entity ever have to change, all you have to do is update the parameter entity. All other occurrences are updated automatically. Cool beans (or is that cool bean burritos?)!

Here's an example of how to use parameter entities to replace complex collections of declarations. Consider the following DTD snippet, which recognizes only primary colors of light:

```
<!ENTITY % Colors "(Red|Green|Blue)">
<!ELEMENT Foreground EMPTY>
<!ATTLIST Foreground Color %Colors; #REQUIRED>
<!ELEMENT Background EMPTY>
<!ATTLIST Background Color %Colors; #REQUIRED>
<!ELEMENT Textcolor EMPTY>
<!ATTLIST Textcolor Color %Colors; #REQUIRED>
...
```

Now, what if you wanted to update this code to accommodate the CMYK color model? It's easy to change the `<!ENTITY ...>` declaration as follows:

```
<!ENTITY % Colors "(Cyan|Magenta|Yellow|Black)">
```

This entity declaration replaces the primary colors of light (red, green, and blue) with the richer, more accurate CMYK colors for every attribute list definition for the `Foreground`, `Background`, and `Textcolor` elements. That's a lot easier and less tedious than having to replace each instance of `(Red| Green|Blue)` with `(Cyan|Magenta|Yellow|Black)`.

```
<!ENTITY % PCD "(#PCDATA)">
<!ELEMENT Title %PCD;>
...
<!ELEMENT Item %PCD;>
```

Creating flexible DTDs with parameter entities

You can use parameter entities to carve DTDs into bite-size bits of declarations that are easy to read and manipulate. You can then save each bit in a separate file and create a single parameter entity in the master DTD that points to each individual file. Using parameter entities in this way lets you mix and match meaningful pieces of DTD markup in various XML projects. Just customize the DTDs, changing specific markup as needed.

Say you build a DTD that includes markup to deal with recipe ingredients, cooking instructions, and serving instructions. You might benefit from separating these three disjointed types of markup into separate files and using parameter entities to tie those files into the master DTD for your recipe information. To create a master list of ingredients for a whole set of recipes, you could create other master DTDs where only ingredients markup is invoked.

These kinds of parameter entities are called *external parameter entity references* because they refer to information that's external to the DTD or document prolog in which they appear. Thus, if you created three DTD files for the markup mentioned in the preceding paragraph named `ingred.dtd`, `cookinst.dtd`, and `servinst.dtd`, respectively, you could use the following markup to create a single DTD to combine their contents:

```
<-- Master DTD for recipe ingredients, cooking instructions,
    and serving instructions -->
<!ENTITY % Ingred   SYSTEM "ingred.dtd">
<!ENTITY % Cookinst SYSTEM "cookinst.dtd">
<!ENTITY % Servinst SYSTEM "servinst.dtd">
%Ingred;
%Cookinst;
%Servinst;
```

Calling All DTDs!

By now, you should understand that it's possible to include an entire DTD as the prolog to any XML document. But it's also possible to refer to an external DTD in a prolog, so you can incorporate the same kind of information from one or more external sources. (The "or more" part comes into play if the DTD that's called uses parameter entities to incorporate multiple chunks of DTD markup from multiple files, as we discuss in the preceding section "Creating flexible DTDs with parameter entities.")

Using external DTDs is a great idea because you can then share a single DTD among any group of XML documents. As long as all those documents use the markup described in the DTD, you can manage that markup by operating on a single, common DTD instead of having to change the same prolog information across an entire set of XML documents. We like to think of this as a divide-and-conquer approach — namely, one where you divide the DTD information common to all documents and manage it apart from the content unique to each document (which must be managed separately).

If you're creating a standalone DTD, such as a file that consists of everything from the opening declaration of the root document element — for example, the `Recipes` element in the DTD at the end of Chapter 6 that follows the `<!DOCTYPE Recipes [` in the prolog — through all of the root element's children, grandchildren, and so forth, up to the `]>` markup that closes the prolog. This matches our master DTD discussed earlier in this chapter exactly:

```
<!-- Begin Recipes.dtd last updated January 1, 2002 -->
<!ENTITY mmmm "Madeline Margaret Murphy-Morrison">
<!ELEMENT Recipes (Recipe)+>
<!ELEMENT Recipe (Title, Category, Ingredients, CookingInstructions,
  ServingInstructions)>
<!ELEMENT Title (#PCDATA)>
<!ELEMENT Category EMPTY>
<!ELEMENT Ingredients (Item)+>
<!ELEMENT Item (#PCDATA)>
<!ELEMENT CookingInstructions (Cinst)+>
<!ELEMENT Cinst (#PCDATA)>
<!ELEMENT ServingInstructions (Sinst)+>
<!ELEMENT Sinst (#PCDATA)>
<!ATTLIST Recipe cook CDATA #IMPLIED>
<!ATTLIST Category name ENUMERATED (chinese, japanese, home-cooking, tex-mex,
  continental, haute-cuisine, other)>
<!-- End of Recipes.dtd -->
```

If this were stored in a file named `Recipes.dtd` that resides in the same directory as the XML document itself, the prolog to the original XML document could be condensed into this single line:

```
<!DOCTYPE Recipes SYSTEM "Recipes.dtd">
```

Also, the related XML document must change because it's no longer a standalone document; it now requires access to the external DTD. Thus, the initial line of the document, which reads like this in Chapter 6:

```
<?xml version="1.0" standalone="yes"?>
```

must change to

```
<?xml version="1.0" standalone="no"?>
```

to instruct the XML parser to seek its DTD information from an external source. It's really simple, don't you think?

When DTD Definitions Collide

In computer science jargon, a *name collision* occurs when more than one definition exists for a named object. Speaking generally, resolving such conflicts first requires that a developer — that's you! — understands what it means (and what to do) not if, but *when* such conflicts occur.

Name collisions can occur when multiple definitions of the same markup appear in multiple DTD fragments. They may also occur when there's an inconsistency between internal DTD markup within a document and the references to an external DTD. This might sound like a recipe for chaos, and such collisions can be problematic if you don't watch what you're doing. But understanding how such collisions are resolved in an XML document can sometimes help you control the bleeding. Read on for all the gory — er . . . glorious — details!

Here's how collisions might occur:

✔ Say you break DTD markup into discrete chunks, put each chunk in a file, and assemble those chunks in a single, master DTD. If more than one chunk contains a definition for the same markup, you've got a collision situation on your hands.

✔ Say you combine a reference to an external DTD within a standalone DTD or inside the prolog of an XML document with internal DTD markup. You may face a name collision situation.

The answers are surprisingly simple:

✔ **The best offense is a good defense:** Whenever you assemble multiple DTDs to create a single, master DTD, you're best served if you structure them to avoid name collisions across whatever collection of component DTDs you use. In some cases, you might be able to get away with collisions, but we recommend that you avoid them between external DTDs just like you avoid them on the road!

✔ **Seek validation:** If you're not sure that there are no collisions, try a validating XML parser or editor, and see what kinds of error messages you find. (For example, both XMLSpy and Adept Editor can ferret out this kind of information for you, if properly instructed. See Chapter 20 for more information about these and other XML tools.) When you find errors, you can correct them one by one.

✔ **Internal markup is always the best markup, so let the best markup win:** For the purposes of this discussion, internal markup is "best" merely because if a collision occurs, the processor defers to the internal DTD markup. (In other words, our only criteria for determining what's best is what's going to be less likely to make you cry and tear your hair out.) Well, that's not the only reason. Consider that this rule provides a mechanism that enables you to incorporate standard, external markup into an XML document, *and* customize that markup to your heart's content for special purposes. In other words, it's not *only* a whim; it's also a *good* thing.

Starting accidents *can* be okay

Because we want you to avoid collisions between external DTDs, we're trying to avoid explaining how to make them happen. But because adding internal DTD markup after an external DTD reference is a valuable customization tool, we're willing to show you how to start a collision, as long as you're willing to use the information responsibly (no starting DTD collisions in school zones or we'll be forced to revoke your Markup License):

1. **Start your document with a <!DOCTYPE declaration that invokes your external DTD.**

   For example:

   ```
   <!DOCTYPE Recipes SYSTEM
      "Recipes.dtd"
   ```

   Don't close this declaration just yet!

2. **Follow this with standard internal DTD markup.**

For this example, we assume that you want to redefine the order of elements in the Recipe element so that Category precedes Title:

```
[ <!-- This bracket opens
    internal DTD code -->
<!ELEMENT Recipe
(Category, Title, Ingredients,
    CookingInstructions,
    ServingInstructions)>
]> <!-- This bracket closes
    internal DTD code -->
```

Although this is a trivial example of customization, as long as you remember that you can redefine any entity or attribute declarations that appear in the external DTD (or any DTDs that it references in turn), you have the right idea. Because internal markup trumps the markup in the external DTD, customization is possible. Change the order, add new entities, or redefine old attributes — it's all up to you!

Turning DTD Content On or Off: IGNORE

When documents can take multiple forms of display, or when they're under construction, it's sometimes necessary to turn parts of a DTD on or off to enable or disable particular types of markup. To turn DTD content off, manually wrap DTD text in comment tags (<!− and −>). To turn text on, remove the unwanted comment wrapper.

Another way to perform the same trick is to use the XML IGNORE directive to turn text off, which works like this:

```
<![IGNORE[
 All text is ignored up to closing brackets on the next line.
]]>
```

As with most other XML markup, white space is not significant. But if you keep the opening <![IGNORE[and closing]]> text on separate lines, the ignore references will be easy to find and remove as necessary.

You can use this directive to skip over any text in a DTD (either a standalone DTD or an internal DTD in a document's prolog), but be sure that you bracket entire chunks of markup inside the directive. Otherwise, the DTD becomes nonsense. In other words, make sure that you ignore complete declarations, and don't leave incomplete bits of markup outside the brackets.

Likewise, an INCLUDE directive for XML lets you explicitly include text in a DTD as well. The syntax is the same as for IGNORE, but uses the keyword INCLUDE instead.

If an INCLUDE directive occurs inside an IGNORE directive, it's ignored because the parser always ignores everything it sees until the IGNORE directive is closed.

An even better way to use the INCLUDE and IGNORE directives is to use one or more parameter entities in your DTDs to control what gets included or ignored in those DTDs. If you use the parameter entity name around a section of markup, whatever value you assign to that entity as you parse the document determines whether the markup is included or ignored. For example, editing the %Case1; entity definition as follows

```
<!ENTITY % Case1 "IGNORE">
```

causes any markup bracketed like the following to be ignored:

```
<![%Case1;[
Any complete section of DTD markup.
]]>
```

To include that markup in a subsequent pass through the document, you'd only need to edit the DTD to read

```
<!ENTITY % Case1 "INCLUDE">
```

Not only can you flip-flop the values for %Case1; references as you like, you can also create as many such ignore/include case values as you like (Case2, Case3, and so on), so that you can arbitrarily include and ignore related sections of your DTD at will. (Ah, the power!) This function is especially helpful if you happen to be using a modular design to create DTDs (for example, if you're building the DTDs piecewise for inclusion in master DTDs). You can use the master DTD to control the behavior of its component DTDs by adding include/exclude parameter entities. This capability is not yet available in XML Schema, either, so here's something that you can do with SGML DTDs that XML Schema cannot match!

Chapter 11

XML Schema at Work

*I*n Chapter 8, you learn the basic structure of an XML Schema document. In addition, in Chapter 9, you build a custom schema step by step according to the rules of the XML Schema specification. In this chapter, you continue to explore the capabilities of schemas built using XML Schema (simply called a schema for the rest of this chapter).

If you're using a schema to guide the development of your XML documents, you can work with an existing schema, create your own schema from scratch, or strike a happy medium between the two and customize an existing schema to fit your content like a glove. You can also convert a DTD to a schema if you want to take advantage of the XML Schema specification's strong datatyping capabilities. In this chapter, you explore what's involved in working with the XML Schema specification and how to construct a schema in different ways depending on the type of data you're working with. In addition, you discover how to convert a DTD to a schema.

Trading Control for Flexibility

Schemas offer much tighter control of your content format than DTDs. This is a major advantage of using schemas to drive document creation and for validation when the documents are pulled into a processing system.

Of course, decisions about control and flexibility are best made at the beginning of the document design process. Examine your content closely and make decisions about the most effective way to obtain and share the information in your XML document. After reviewing the content that you want to include in your content, you can make choices about how that content needs to be structured to meet your requirements. Making these decisions at the beginning of the document design cycle saves time in the end, and reduces time spent revising and rewriting your documents.

The basic structure of the content determines the flexibility of the document. Flexibility in schemas can be added through the use of the `choice` compositor and enumerated lists of attributes. Add flexibility with care, though — the price of this flexibility may be a much more complex schema design.

Eliciting Markup from an XML Schema

Following is the schema for the Recipe Markup Language (RML) that we introduce in Chapter 9. If you're unfamiliar with the basic rules of schemas, check out Chapter 9 because this section expands the basic rules to use more of the XML Schema specification features, including designing reusable custom datatypes for data and for text content. Listing 11-1 shows the RML schema.

Listing 11-1: Recipe XML Schema

```
<?xml version="1.0" encoding="UTF-8"?>
<xsd:schema xmlns:xsd="http://www.w3.org/2001/XMLSchema">
 <xsd:element name="Recipes">
  <xsd:complexType>
   <xsd:sequence maxOccurs="unbounded">
    <xsd:element ref="Recipe"/>
   </xsd:sequence>
  </xsd:complexType>
 </xsd:element>
 <xsd:element name="Recipe">
  <xsd:complexType>
   <xsd:sequence>
    <xsd:element ref="Title"/>
    <xsd:element ref="Category"/>
    <xsd:element ref="Ingredients"/>
    <xsd:element ref="CookingInstructions"/>
    <xsd:element ref="ServingInstructions"/>
   </xsd:sequence>
   <xsd:attribute name="cook" type="xsd:string"/>
  </xsd:complexType>
 </xsd:element>
 <xsd:element name="Title" type="xsd:string"/>
 <xsd:element name="Category">
  <xsd:complexType>
   <xsd:attribute name="name" use="required">
    <xsd:simpleType>
     <xsd:restriction base="xsd:string">
      <xsd:enumeration value="chinese"/>
      <xsd:enumeration value="japanese"/>
```

```
      <xsd:enumeration value="home-cooking"/>
      <xsd:enumeration value="tex-mex"/>
      <xsd:enumeration value="continental"/>
      <xsd:enumeration value="haute-cuisine"/>
      <xsd:enumeration value="other"/>
    </xsd:restriction>
   </xsd:simpleType>
  </xsd:attribute>
 </xsd:complexType>
</xsd:element>
<xsd:element name="Ingredients">
 <xsd:complexType>
  <xsd:sequence maxOccurs="unbounded">
   <xsd:element ref="Item"/>
  </xsd:sequence>
 </xsd:complexType>
</xsd:element>
<xsd:element name="Item" type="xsd:string"/>
<xsd:element name="CookingInstructions">
 <xsd:complexType>
  <xsd:sequence maxOccurs="unbounded">
   <xsd:element ref="Cinst"/>
  </xsd:sequence>
 </xsd:complexType>
</xsd:element>
<xsd:element name="Cinst" type="xsd:string"/>
<xsd:element name="ServingInstructions">
 <xsd:complexType>
  <xsd:sequence maxOccurs="unbounded">
   <xsd:element ref="Sinst"/>
  </xsd:sequence>
 </xsd:complexType>
</xsd:element>
<xsd:element name="Sinst" type="xsd:string"/>
</xsd:schema>
```

Modifying a Schema

The first step in creating or modifying a schema is to look at the content you want to describe with the structures defined in the schema. The basic structure of your XML document is specified by the complex type definitions in the schema; in other words, which elements contain other elements and attributes. You need to have a good understanding of the pieces and parts of your content before you can create a set of structural components to accurately describe them.

Look back at the RML schema in Listing 11-1 and you have all the information you need to create a valid XML document according to this schema. Because the schema explicitly states exactly what can appear in the document, and in what order and described with what markup, you also know that any content or markup not described in the schema will be invalid if you include it in a RML document.

Listing 11-2 shows a recipe that can be validated against the RML schema.

Listing 11-2: Creating a Valid Document from Schema

```
<Recipes>
<Recipe>
 <Title>Lucinda's Guacamole</Title>
 <Category name="tex-mex"/>
 <Ingredients>
  <Item>4 large ripe avocados</Item>
  <Item>1/2 tsp salt</Item>
  <Item>1/2 tsp lemon juice</Item>
  <Item>dash of cumin powder</Item>
  <Item>2 tsp finely chopped white onion</Item>
  <Item>1/2 cup chopped tomato</Item>
  <Item>salsa</Item>
 </Ingredients>
 <CookingInstructions>
  <Cinst>Peel the avocados and remove the pits.</Cinst>
  <Cinst>Mash the avocados well with a fork.</Cinst>
  <Cinst>Mix in all the other ingredients.</Cinst>
  <Cinst>Adjust to taste.</Cinst>
 </CookingInstructions>
 <ServingInstructions>
  <Sinst>Serve with tortilla chips.</Sinst>
 </ServingInstructions>
</Recipe>
</Recipes>
```

Listing 11-2 is a valid document because it follows all of these structural rules:

✔ **The** Recipes **element must contain one or more** Recipe **elements.** At least one Recipe element is required. Of course, without a Recipe element, both our schema document and XML document would only be a few lines long because the Recipe element contains all the other elements in the document!

✔ **The** Recipe **element must contain the** Title, Category, Ingredients, CookingInstructions, **and** ServingInstructions **elements, and in that specific order.** The following markup is invalid because the Category element occurs before the Title element.

```
<Recipes>
 <Recipe>
  <Category name="tex-mex"/>
  <Title>Lucinda's Guacamole</Title>
  . . .
```

✔ **The** Recipe **element can contain a** cook **attribute.** Attributes are optional unless otherwise specified with a use attribute with a value of required. Because this is an optional attribute, both of the following markup examples are valid:

```
<Recipe>
  <Title>Lucinda's Guacamole</Title>
```

```
<Recipe cook="Wali">
  <Title>Lucinda's Guacamole</Title>
```

✔ **The** `Category` **element must include a required** `name` **attribute.** The value of `name` can be any one of the values defined in the enumeration statements. The first two examples are valid because they include a `name` attribute with one of the values specified in the enumeration statements. The third example isn't valid because it doesn't contain a `name` attribute.

```
<Category name="tex-mex"/>
<Category name="chinese"/>
<Category/>
```

✔ **The** `Ingredients` **element must contain one or more** `Item` **elements.** The following markup is invalid because the Item elements occur outside the Ingredients element:

```
<Ingredients/>
<Item>4 large ripe avocados</Item>
<Item>1/2 tsp salt</Item>
<Item>1/2 tsp lemon juice</Item>
```

✔ **The** `CookingInstructions` **element must contain one or more** `Cinst` **elements.** This example is invalid markup because the `CookingInstructions` element has no content; it's empty!

```
<CookingInstructions/>
```

✔ **The** `ServingInstructions` **element must contain one or more** `Sinst` **elements.** The following markup is invalid because the `Cinst` elements should not be contained in the `ServingInstructions` element, and also because no `Sinst` elements are included within the `ServingInstructions` element.

```
<ServingInstructions>
<Cinst>Peel the avocados and remove the pits</Cinst>
<Cinst>Mash the avocados well with a fork</Cinst>
<Cinst>Mix in all the other ingredients</Cinst>
<Cinst>Adjust to taste</Cinst>
</ServingInstructions>
```

The RML schema that drives the markup description of the recipe in Listing 11-2 is not very flexible, but you do have some choice regarding how many elements you include in your XML document. For example, you could include one serving instruction or twenty. Both instances are valid according to our RML schema. In addition, because our recipe and schema have very simple structures at this point, they're easy to extend by adding additional elements, attributes, and datatypes.

Using Datatypes Effectively

You can use XML Schema datatypes in your schemas whether your document content is data intensive or text intensive.

Data-intensive content (such as numerical data) includes many additional constraints, such as patterns of content. *Text-intensive* content does not need to be in any specific format — other than text strings, of course.

Using datatypes with data-intensive content

For data-intensive content, XML Schema offers built-in datatypes for most of the datatypes used in common database programming languages such as the Structured Query Language (SQL). In addition, XML Schema offers the ability to further customize these datatypes by defining new ones. For example, numeric data of any type can be restricted to

✔ A minimum value, either exclusive or inclusive

✔ A maximum value, either exclusive or inclusive

You don't have to use minimum values and maximum values together. You can use one or the other or both. For example, if you want to be sure that a telephone number has at least 10 digits (the seven-digit number plus the area code), you can set the minimum value to 10.

If you want to leave the maximum size of the phone number open so folks can include an extension or even an international number, just don't set the maximum size. Or, if you want to be safe, you can cap the phone number at 50 characters or so, just so you don't get a thousand-digit phone number.

There may be a time when your minimum value and maximum value are the same. Huh? What's that you ask? If you want to be sure a value is made up of a specific number of digits, 9 for a Social Security number, for example, you'd set both the minimum value and maximum value to 9. A Social Security number has to be at least 9 digits but no more than 9 characters, and setting the minimum and maximum values to the same number ensures that you'll get exactly 9 digits.

You can also further restrict numeric data that includes a decimal point. You can specify

✔ The total number of digits in the data (includes digits on both sides of the decimal point)

✔ The number of digits to the right of the decimal point

For example, to include a price for the recipe, you could require that it include four total digits and two digits after the decimal place like this:

```
<xsd:element name="price">
 <xsd:simpleType>
  <xsd:restriction base="xsd:decimal">
```

```
    <xsd:totalDigits value="4"/>
    <xsd:fractionDigits value="2"/>
  </xsd:restriction>
 </xsd:simpleType>
</xsd:element>
```

Using datatypes with text-intensive content

For text-intensive content, XML Schema offers the `string` datatype and other built-in datatypes for text content, including time and date formats. String content can also be extensively customized by creating a custom datatype. Through custom datatypes, valid string content can be further detailed to contain

- Specific patterns of alphanumeric characters
- A minimum and/or a maximum length (number of characters)
- One of a list of valid values
- Instructions for preserving or converting white space in content

Making Elements Work Wisely and Well

One of the first steps in designing an effective schema is defining elements and attributes. Your XML document will include elements and attributes in a particular pattern and all of these elements and attributes must be specified in the schema for the document to be valid.

The basic structure of your schema is based on the structure of the content you want to describe in an XML document. The content itself will tell you which elements are complex types (contain other elements and/or attributes) and which elements are simple types (contain only text content).

When it's clear which elements are complex types and which are simple types, you can create the schema type definitions to specify these elements and attributes.

Creating crafty content models

Content models define what type of content can be contained in an element. The four types of content are

- **Element:** The element can contain child elements.
- **Text:** The element can contain only text.

✔ **Mixed:** The element can contain child elements and text.

✔ **Empty:** The element can't contain child elements or text — that is, the content of the element must be empty.

See Chapters 8 and 9 for detailed examples of each content model.

Both element content and text content are straightforward. An element content model requires a complex type definition. A text content model can be defined with a simple element declaration, for example:

```
<xsd:element name="Sinst" type="xsd:string"/>
```

If your content lends itself to elements that can contain both other elements as well as text content, you want to use a mixed content model. This model would be very useful for fixed text content with variable data content; for example, you could use the following markup to include specific elements for quantities of ingredients in recipes:

```
<xsd:element name="Item">
<xsd:complexType mixed="true">
 <xsd:sequence>
  <xsd:element ref="amount"/>
  <xsd:element ref="measurement"/>
 </xsd:sequence>
</xsd:complexType>
</xsd:element>
<xsd:element name="amount" type="xsd:integer"/>
<xsd:element name="measurement" type="xsd:string"/>
```

You could include the preceding element definitions in a schema to validate this XML document:

```
<Ingredients>
<Item>
 Include<amount>3</amount> <measurement>cups</measurement>
 of local honey for the best flavor.
</Item>
</Ingredients>
```

Using an empty content model is a useful way to include attributes without specifying any element content. Basically, the empty element acts as a container for attribute content. There's room for an empty content model in the RML schema. For example, rather than including the cook attribute in the Recipe element, the name of the cook could be included within an empty element named Cook, as shown in the following markup:

```
<xsd:element name="Cook" ID="The XML Gourmet"/>
```

A matter of selection

You can include two different ways of selecting what attributes work with an element or which elements make up the content model for an element. The `choice` compositor is used for elements and the `enumeration` compositor is used for attributes. Selections help you create a schema that fits a wider collection of content by adding flexibility to the schema and the content it can describe. If you aren't sure exactly what the content model for an element will be, down to the last element, or you want to allow some flexibility in the attributes and values an element takes, use a selection.

The `choice` compositor element is used for making a choice between child elements. For example, to include a choice of ingredients in the recipe, you could specify that in the XML Schema document, as shown in the following:

```
<xsd:element name="Ingredients">
<xsd:complexType>
  <xsd:choice maxOccurs="unbounded">
   <xsd:element ref="Item1"/>
   <xsd:element ref="Item2"/>
  </xsd:choice>
</xsd:complexType>
</xsd:element>
<xsd:element name="Item1" type="xsd:string"/>
<xsd:element name="Item2" type="xsd:string"/>
```

The `choice` compositor element in the preceding example includes a `maxOccurs` attribute with the value `unbounded`. The `unbounded` occurrence constraint means that this choice can occur an unlimited number of times in the XML document. The unbounded occurrence allows you to include any number of `Item1` elements and also any number of `Item2` elements. This is a very useful way to include some flexibility in your document structure.

The following components are required to make a choice between attribute values possible:

- ✔ A complex type definition for the element containing the attribute
- ✔ An attribute declaration
- ✔ A simple type definition
- ✔ A restriction on the simple type definition
- ✔ A series of enumeration elements to define the possible attribute values

Although creating attribute choices might seem complex, it's actually quite simple. For example, to include a choice of values for the `cook` attribute, you could use this markup:

```
<xsd:element name="Recipe">
<xsd:complexType>
  <xsd:attribute name="cook" use="required">
   <xsd:simpleType>
    <xsd:restriction base="xsd:string">
     <xsd:enumeration value="Ed"/>
     <xsd:enumeration value="Mary"/>
     <xsd:enumeration value="Lucinda"/>
    </xsd:restriction>
```

```
    </xsd:simpleType>
   </xsd:attribute>
  </xsd:complexType>
 </xsd:element>
```

Next you add the `sequence` compositor and its element references before the attribute declaration to complete the complex type definition:

```
<xsd:element name="Recipe">
 <xsd:complexType>
  <xsd:sequence>
   <xsd:element ref="Title"/>
 . . .
   <xsd:element ref="ServingInstructions"/>
  </xsd:sequence>
  <xsd:attribute name="cook" use="required">
   <xsd:simpleType>
    <xsd:restriction base="xsd:string">
     <xsd:enumeration value="Ed"/>
     <xsd:enumeration value="Mary"/>
     <xsd:enumeration value="Lucinda"/>
    </xsd:restriction>
   </xsd:simpleType>
  </xsd:attribute>
 </xsd:complexType>
</xsd:element>
<xsd:element name="Title" type="xsd:string"/>
 . . .
```

Mixing up the order

You can also make your schema more flexible by using a `choice` compositor to include a selection of elements that contain different child elements or that contain different sequences of the same child elements.

For example, to include an option to specify metric measurements for ingredients to make your documents usable internationally, you could include a choice for the amount and measurement elements you defined earlier in this chapter, as shown in the following:

```
<xsd:element name="Item">
 <xsd:complexType mixed="true">
  <xsd:choice>
   <xsd:element ref="nonmetric"/>
   <xsd:element ref="metric"/>
  </xsd:choice>
 </xsd:complexType>
</xsd:element>
<xsd:element name="nonmetric">
 <xsd:complexType>
  <xsd:sequence>
   <xsd:element ref="amount1"/>
   <xsd:element ref="measurement1"/>
  </xsd:sequence>
 </xsd:complexType>
</xsd:element>
```

```
<xsd:element name="amount1" type="xsd:integer"/>
<xsd:element name="measurement1" type="xsd:string"/>
<xsd:element name="metric">
 <xsd:complexType>
  <xsd:sequence>
   <xsd:element ref="amount2"/>
   <xsd:element ref="measurement2"/>
  </xsd:sequence>
 </xsd:complexType>
</xsd:element>
<xsd:element name="amount2" type="xsd:integer"/>
<xsd:element name="measurement2" type="xsd:string"/>
```

The preceding example specifies a choice of metric and nonmetric measurement for ingredients. The choice is followed by the specification for the two alternate sets of elements. It's certainly possible to include flexibility in your schemas by using selections of elements and attributes. As you can see in this example, though, your schema can quickly become complex.

Using Complex Datatypes

XML Schema offers extensive support for custom (user-derived) datatypes. These custom datatypes can be used to tightly control the structure of the content in your XML document.

Both simple and complex types can be used for custom datatypes. Simple types are used to put further restrictions on a datatype. You could, for example, put further restrictions on the content (no more than 50 characters total) of the Ingredients element in the recipes schema, as in the following:

```
<xsd:element name="Item">
 <xsd:simpleType>
  <xsd:restriction base="xsd:string">
   <xsd:maxLength value="50"/>
  </xsd:restriction>
 </xsd:simpleType>
</xsd:element>
```

Complex datatypes can be named, which allows you to reuse the datatype in your schema. As a result, you can write more efficient (and less complex!) schemas. Take another look at the first part of the recipes schema:

```
<xsd:element name="Recipes">
 <xsd:complexType>
  <xsd:sequence maxOccurs="unbounded">
   <xsd:element ref="Recipe"/>
  </xsd:sequence>
 </xsd:complexType>
</xsd:element>
<xsd:element name="Recipe">
 <xsd:complexType>
  <xsd:sequence>
   <xsd:element ref="Title"/>
```

```
      <xsd:element ref="Category"/>
      <xsd:element ref="Ingredients"/>
      <xsd:element ref="CookingInstructions"/>
      <xsd:element ref="ServingInstructions"/>
     </xsd:sequence>
     <xsd:attribute name="cook" type="xsd:string"/>
    </xsd:complexType>
   </xsd:element>
```

In this portion of the schema document, a Recipe element is used with a complex type definition, but the type is not named. Although you can include as many Recipe elements as your heart desires, you can't reuse the structure of the Recipe element for another element without rewriting the complex type definition. D'oh!

In the following example, a complex type definition is used to create a complex datatype named Recipe:

```
 <xsd:element name="Recipes">
  <xsd:complexType>
   <xsd:sequence maxOccurs="unbounded">
    <xsd:element ref="Recipe1"/>
   </xsd:sequence>
  </xsd:complexType>
 </xsd:element>
 <xsd:element name="Recipe1" type="Recipe"/>
 <xsd:complexType name="Recipe">
  <xsd:sequence>
   <xsd:element ref="Title"/>
   <xsd:element ref="Category"/>
   <xsd:element ref="Ingredients"/>
   <xsd:element ref="CookingInstructions"/>
   <xsd:element ref="ServingInstructions"/>
  </xsd:sequence>
  <xsd:attribute name="cook" type="xsd:string"/>
 </xsd:complexType>
```

The Recipe element has been renamed Recipe1, and the complex datatype is named Recipe. Otherwise, these schemas are exactly the same. The advantage of using a complex datatype is that it can be reused an unlimited number of times. This datatype definition is not limited to any particular element. You could, for instance, include a new element named LunchRecipe with the Recipe datatype with just an element declaration:

```
 <xsd:element name="LunchRecipe" type="Recipe"/>
```

When XML Schemas Collide: Namespaces

You can use namespaces to include multiple references to schemas written according to the XML specification from within one master schema document. Doing so enables you to use elements and attributes from other schemas within your XML document.

Because you can use components from multiple schemas in your schema document, it's inevitable that conflicts may arise. These conflicts are mainly a result of namespace issues. Collisions can occur, for example, if an element in one schema has the same name as an element in another schema.

A *namespace* is a collection of names of attributes, types, and elements. Namespaces enable you to associate prefixes with a different schema (schema A) in your schema (schema B), and then reference the elements, types, and attributes from schema A in schema B quickly and easily.

For example, you could include components from other recipe schemas in your XML document by identifying the namespaces and defining prefixes for that namespace in the schema element of your schema document, as in the following:

```
<?xml version="1.0" encoding="UTF-8"?>
<xsd:schema xmlns:xsd="http://www.w3.org/2001/XMLSchema"
            xmlns:lc="http://www.lacantina.com/dessert.xsd"
            xmlns:bis="http://www.bistro.net/appetizer.xsd"
            xmlns:soup="http://www.soupsrus.com/soup.xsd">
<xsd:element name="Recipes">
. . .
```

To access elements from other namespaces, you create components that include the prefix you assigned to that namespace. You could, for example, create new elements to include in the Ingredients element in the following way:

```
<xsd:element name="Ingredients">
<xsd:complexType>
  <xsd:sequence maxOccurs="unbounded">
    <xsd:element ref="Item"/>
    <xsd:element ref="lc:DessertItem"/>
    <xsd:element ref="soup:SoupItem"/>
    <xsd:element ref="bis:AppetizerItem"/>
  </xsd:sequence>
</xsd:complexType>
</xsd:element>
<xsd:element name="Item" type="xsd:string"/>
<xsd:element name="lc:DessertItem" type="xsd:string"/>
<xsd:element name="soup:SoupItem" type="xsd:string"/>
<xsd:element name="bis:AppetizerItem" type="xsd:string"/>
```

Namespaces are one of the most complex areas in XML, and especially in XML Schema. For more details on using namespaces, see "The XML Namespaces FAQ" at www.rpbourret.com/xml/NamespacesFAQ.htm#q4_1.

Including External Data

If you're using a DTD to drive the creation of your XML documents, it's easy to include external data by using entities and notations. A major weakness of XML Schema is its very limited support (so far!) for entities and notations.

Although notations and entities can be used in your schemas, they can only be used in very specific and limited ways.

If your XML document includes references to external non-XML data or external entities (any non-text file, like a picture or an XML file), consider using a DTD rather than a schema, and check out Chapter 10.

XML Schema only provides for entities and notations to be used as attribute values. This severely limits the use of external data in your schemas. Better support for entities and notations in XML Schema is at the top of the wish list for improvements in the next version of the XML Schema specification.

Including/Excluding Document Content

XML Schema includes two methods for including or excluding content in an XML document. The first method is using a choice group, which allows you to use either/or choices between two elements as well as choices between several elements. For example, you could extend the recipes schema to include a choice between child elements of the CookingInstructions element. In this example, the choice is between the lunch and the dinner elements:

```
<xsd:element name="CookingInstructions">
<xsd:complexType>
  <xsd:choice>
   <xsd:element ref="lunch"/>
   <xsd:element ref="dinner"/>
  </xsd:choice>
</xsd:complexType>
</xsd:element>
<xsd:element name="lunch" type="xsd:string"/>
<xsd:element name="dinner" type="xsd:string"/>
```

The second method uses a substitution group, which allows you to substitute one element for another element of the same type (or derived from the same type). One element acts as the head of the substitution group. This element can be replaced by other elements in the group.

If the recipes schema included a Menu element, and you wanted to replace it with a more specific element (BreakfastMenu, LunchMenu, or DinnerMenu), you could create a substitution group so that you could use one of these more specific elements.

To create a substitution group in the recipes schema, follow these steps:

1. **Add a Menu element.**

   ```
   <xsd:element name="Menu" type="MenuType" abstract="true"/>
   ```

   The Menu element declaration includes an abstract attribute with the value true. Because the Menu element is abstract, it can't appear in an

XML document, but instead it's represented in the document by a member of the substitution group. The Menu element is the head element of the substitution group.

2. **Include a** substituionGroup **that consists of three other elements:** BreakfastMenu, LunchMenu, **and** DinnerMenu.

   All of them use the same datatype: MenuType.

   ```
   <xsd:element name="BreakfastMenu" type="MenuType"
    substitutionGroup="Menu"/>
   <xsd:element name="LunchMenu" type="MenuType"
    substitutionGroup="Menu"/>
   <xsd:element name="DinnerMenu" type="MenuType"
    substitutionGroup="Menu"/>
   ```

   Each of these element declarations includes a substitutionGroup attribute with the value Menu to identify them as members of this group.

3. **Define the** MenuType **datatype.**

   It includes a sequence of four elements: Appetizer, Soup, Entree, and Dessert.

   ```
   <xsd:complexType name="MenuType">
   <xsd:sequence>
    <xsd:element name="Appetizer" type="xsd:string"/
    <xsd:element name="Soup" type="xsd:string"/>
    <xsd:element name="Entree" type="xsd:string"/>
    <xsd:element name="Dessert" type="xsd:string"/>
   </xsd:sequence>
   </xsd:complexType>
   ```

Your XML document can now use a BreakfastMenu, LunchMenu, or DinnerMenu element in place of a Menu element.

Converting DTDs to Schemas

If you've been using DTDs to drive the development of your XML documents, you may want to convert a DTD to a schema to provide tighter control of your document content.

Tools for DTD to schema conversion are available both separately and as part of XML editor packages, such as XML Spy and Turbo XML. Doing the conversion yourself, however, without any additional software is easy. Just keep in mind as you do the conversion that a DTD is usually a less specific structure than a schema. You will definitely need to make some modifications to the DTD structure to change it from a general document description tool to a much more specific datatype-focused tool that utilizes the features of XML Schema. No instant transformation here.

Take another look at the RML DTD (Listing 11-3), and then we'll look more closely at how to transform a DTD into a schema.

Listing 11-3:   The Recipes DTD

```
<!ENTITY mmmm "Madeline Margaret Murphy-Morrison">
<!ELEMENT Recipes (Recipe+)>
<!ELEMENT Recipe (Title,Category,Ingredients,
  CookingInstructions,ServingInstructions)>
<!ELEMENT Title (#PCDATA)>
<!ELEMENT Category EMPTY>
<!ELEMENT Ingredients (Item)+>
<!ELEMENT Item (#PCDATA)>
<!ELEMENT CookingInstructions (Cinst)+>
<!ELEMENT Cinst (#PCDATA)>
<!ELEMENT ServingInstructions (Sinst)+>
<!ELEMENT Sinst (#PCDATA)>
<!ATTLIST Recipe cook CDATA #IMPLIED>
<!ATTLIST Category name ENUMERATED (chinese, japanese, home-cooking, tex-mex,
  continental, haute-cuisine, other)>
```

The first line of our DTD is an entity reference. There's no equivalent in XML Schema at the present time, so you can't include this entity reference as part of your schema.

```
<!ENTITY mmmm "Madeline Margaret Murphy-Morrison">
```

The next line specifies that the `Recipes` element includes one or more `Recipe` elements:

```
<!ELEMENT Recipes (Recipe+)>
```

To create the same specification in an XML Schema, use a complex type definition and a sequence compositor with unlimited occurrence:

```
<xsd:element name="Recipes">
 <xsd:complexType>
  <xsd:sequence maxOccurs="unbounded">
   <xsd:element ref="Recipe"/>
  </xsd:sequence>
 </xsd:complexType>
```

These lines of the DTD are transformed into a schema in a similar fashion, using complex type definitions and sequence compositors:

```
<!ELEMENT Ingredients (Item)+>
<!ELEMENT CookingInstructions (Cinst)+>
<!ELEMENT ServingInstructions (Sinst)+>
```

This line indicates that the `Recipe` element contains five other elements in a specific order:

```
<!ELEMENT Recipe (Title,Category,Ingredients,
  CookingInstructions,ServingInstructions)>
```

To convert this DTD element declaration into a schema declaration, we create a complex type definition and a sequence, as follows:

```
<xsd:element name="Recipe">
 <xsd:complexType>
  <xsd:sequence>
   <xsd:element ref="Title"/>
   <xsd:element ref="Category"/>
   <xsd:element ref="Ingredients"/>
   <xsd:element ref="CookingInstructions"/>
   <xsd:element ref="ServingInstructions"/>
  </xsd:sequence>
  <xsd:attribute name="cook" type="xsd:string"/>
 </xsd:complexType>
```

The attribute declaration for the `cook` attribute is included at the end of the complex type definition for this element. In the DTD, attribute declarations occur at the end of the DTD. The DTD uses CDATA to specify that the content is any combination of characters, whereas the schema invokes the XML Schema `string` datatype.

```
<!ATTLIST Recipe cook CDATA #IMPLIED>
```

`#IMPLIED` specifies that the attribute has no default value, and can be omitted if desired. Default values for attributes can be included in DTDs, but are not supported in the current XML Schema recommendation.

These lines of the DTD declare elements with PCDATA content. PCDATA content can include numbers, letters, symbols, and entities.

```
<!ELEMENT Title (#PCDATA)>
<!ELEMENT Item (#PCDATA)>
<!ELEMENT Cinst (#PCDATA)>
<!ELEMENT Sinst (#PCDATA)>
```

In this case, the schema uses the `string` datatype for these elements:

```
<xsd:element name="Title" type="xsd:string"/>
<xsd:element name="Item" type="xsd:string"/>
<xsd:element name="Cinst" type="xsd:string"/>
<xsd:element name="Sinst" type="xsd:string"/>
```

More specific XML Schema datatypes could be used for PCDATA content, such as date and time formats. XML Schema also allows you to further restrict the `string` datatype if you want to control other attributes, such as the pattern of the characters, minimum and maximum length, and instructions for dealing with white space.

The only remaining part of the DTD is the `Category` element and its required attribute, `name`. In the DTD, the element is declared separately from the attribute:

```
<!ELEMENT Category EMPTY>
. . .
<!ATTLIST Category name ENUMERATED (chinese, japanese, home-cooking, tex-mex,
 continental, haute-cuisine, other)>
```

To convert this data to a schema, the empty element and the attribute choices are both included in a complex type definition that contains a simple type definition with a restriction and a list of enumerations of valid values for the attribute. The use attribute with the value required is used to indicate that the name attribute is required.

```
<xsd:element name="Category">
 <xsd:complexType>
  <xsd:attribute name="name" use="required">
   <xsd:simpleType>
    <xsd:restriction base="xsd:string">
     <xsd:enumeration value="chinese"/>
     <xsd:enumeration value="japanese"/>
     <xsd:enumeration value="home-cooking"/>
     <xsd:enumeration value="tex-mex"/>
     <xsd:enumeration value="continental"/>
     <xsd:enumeration value="haute-cuisine"/>
     <xsd:enumeration value="other"/>
    </xsd:restriction>
   </xsd:simpleType>
  </xsd:attribute>
 </xsd:complexType>
</xsd:element>
```

Schemas are designed to be more specific than DTDs. If you convert a DTD to a schema, convert the general DTD markup to specific XML Schema markup whenever possible. Both built-in and user-derived XML Schema datatypes make this possible.

Chapter 12

Adding Character to XML

• •

• •

*A*lthough experts estimate that about 80 percent of the Web's current content is in English, that doesn't mean English is the only language that the Web supports. As Web technology becomes increasingly global in scope, the ability to use character sets beyond the traditional Roman alphabet will help you reach a truly global audience in their native languages.

As you've probably noticed by now, all markup and syntax related to XML uses Roman characters — ASCII text to be specific. Although that's all well and good for those of us in the Western world, it doesn't get you very far when you want to create localized sites or application for deployment in Asia with content available in both Mandarin and Cantonese. To expand the scope of your content to encompass the whole world and all of its character sets, you need to have a good understanding of how XML works with characters (letters) and how you can use XML's character conventions (called *encoding*) to make your XML content available in any language. Armed with knowledge about character encoding, you can take further advantage of XML's extensibility by making content available to multiple applications as well as across spoken languages.

When you get right down to it, computers think in *binary* — 1s and 0s. Those 1s and 0s are called *bits* and they're the most basic unit of storage in a computer. To give you some perspective, a byte is made up of 8 bits, even if you're only using 4 of them (the other 4 are sad and get ignored). When you put 1,000 bytes together, you have a kilobyte (the *k* in 64K). Early computers used 7-bit strings to represent simple alphabetical characters; modern computers use a mix of 8- and 16-bit strings to represent a broad range of characters, depending on the application and the location. To put it simply, the more bits you have in your string, the more characters you can use (more about this in a minute). You usually don't use 16-bit character strings unless you want to work with non-Roman alphabets, such as those for Hebrew or Japanese.

In keeping with its intent to be friendly to all Web users, XML is designed to support 16-bit character encoding. *Encoding* is the technical term for how many bits you use to describe your characters. 16-bit character encoding uses 16-bit strings to represent characters in XML documents. This encoding already includes character strings for most of the world's known alphabets, plus all kinds of symbols for disciplines from genetics to mathematics. It even has room left over to accommodate more character sets and symbols as need for them arises.

This chapter is full of a bunch of technical stuff. We apologize in advance for the pounding "huh?" headache that may accompany this chapter.

About Character Encodings

Clearly, the trend is toward longer bit strings to encode character data, so size does matter when representing character data:

- A 7-bit string can represent a maximum of 2^7, or 128, different characters. This is enough for the 26-character basic Roman alphabet in uppercase and lowercase (*A–Z* and *a–z*), plus a modicum of symbols, punctuation characters, and so on. In short, a 7-bit string works fine for simple Roman alphabets and related characters, but just barely.

- An 8-bit string can represent a maximum of 2^8, or 256, different characters, including everything a 7-bit encoding can handle and leaves room for what some experts call higher-order characters (accented letters, trademark symbols, and so forth). An 8-bit string permits computer character sets to add all kinds of control characters and a modest set of diacritical marks not frequently used in English but frequently used in German (with its umlauts), French (with its diacritical marks), and other European languages.

- A 16-bit string can represent a maximum of 2^{16}, or 65,536, different characters. This captures everything an 8-bit encoding can handle and allows for another 65,280 character codes (or more than 99.6 percent of the available character space). This leaves room for all the major human alphabets, from ancient Aramaic and Greek to modern Mandarin and Hangul (Korean), plus all kinds of symbols and other special characters.

In short, where international representation is concerned, 16-bit character encodings provide the space necessary to cover a full range of known character sets, with room left over for future expansion. That's why XML supports 16-bit character encodings. It's also why experts expect XML to enable universal access to online character data to any human being who can read almost any language!

Many modern computers still use 8-bit encodings to represent most character data, especially in English. The bottom line is that it's faster to process 8-bit characters than it is 16-bit characters. Because most Western language characters fit with 8-bit encoding, there's no reason to use 16-bit unless you're going to work with the characters only supported in 16-bit encoding. Most global solutions, however, do use 16-bit encoding to support all possible languages and characters. The one you use will depend entirely on what characters you need to represent.

Introducing Unicode

An industry group called the Unicode Consortium was formed in January 1991 to promote an open, standard, fully international, 16-bit character encoding technology. Not surprisingly, this encoding is also known as Unicode. Today, Unicode 3.0 (the current, standard version of Unicode) represents the third generation of the consortium's work in defining a single character encoding technology to accommodate nearly every known human character set under a single representational scheme. Pretty amazing stuff! Note that Unicode 3.2 is due for release in March 2002.

In addition, the Unicode Consortium has maintained an ongoing relationship with the International Organization for Standardization (ISO). This produced an organized, international ISO standard (how's that for redundant?), known as ISO 10646, that represents the same information as the Unicode standard. By 1993, the ISO working group responsible for incorporating Unicode as an official ISO standard had completed its initial work, and ISO 10646-1:1993 came into being. The *-1* after the number indicates that it is the first draft of the standard; *1993* indicates that it was approved in 1993. ISO has updated 10646 to stay synchronized with the most current Unicode standards.

Today, Unicode defines just over 40,000 different character codes. Of this range, 20,000 characters are defined for the Han ideographs used for Mandarin and other Chinese languages, whereas over 11,000 characters are defined for Hangul (Korean). The nearly 9,000 remaining characters represent most other written languages. For convenience, the Unicode character code for 0 through 255 (8-bit character codes, in other words) match the character set defined for ISO-8859-1, also known as the ISO-Latin-1 character set. This is the default character set that's used to encode HTML documents on the Web.

Many people — including numerous XML experts — refer to the XML character set as "Unicode" (and we think there's good reason to do so). However, if you ever spend any time perusing the W3C XML specifications, you'll observe that *they* refer to character sets by their ISO designations. Thus, you'll see plenty of references to ISO 10646 but only scant mention of Unicode. Go figure!

Note that XML 1.0, 2nd Edition (www.w3.org/TR/2000/REC-xml-20001006) references Unicode 2.0 and 3.0, whereas the 1st Edition only references Unicode 2.0.

For more information about Unicode characters, symbols, history, and the current standard, you can find a plethora of information at the Unicode consortium's Web site at `www.unicode.org`.

You can even join a Unicode-oriented mailing list that operates at `unicode@unicode.org` by sending an add request in the Subject field of an e-mail message to `unicode-request@unicode.org`. For those seeking a definitive reference to Unicode, the Unicode Consortium has authored a book entitled *The Unicode Standard, Version 3.0* (published by Addison-Wesley Developers Press). Although it lists for $50, it's a worthwhile reference if you want to be able to check that what your browser is showing for a character matches its correct representation.

Of Character Sets, Fonts, Scripts, and Glyphs

Although XML can represent just about any kind of character data imaginable, that's just the beginning of what's involved to make exotic character data appear on a computer's display. The raw character data — which XML can handle just fine, thank you very much — represents a set of written characters, called a *script*, which may or may not use a conventional Roman alphabet.

To see what's in XML scripts that 7- or 8-bit character encodings can't cover — which means special symbols or non-Roman alphabets — you'll need a few extra local ingredients:

- **A character set that matches the script you're trying to read and display.** For the purposes of this discussion, a *character set* represents a collection of 16-bit values that maps to some specific symbol set or alphabet.

- **Software that understands the character set for the script (or at least the general encoding type).** Such software includes the underlying operating system on your computer. Fortunately, most modern operating systems — including various flavors of UNIX, Linux, and Windows 9*x*, NT, 2000, and .NET — can handle 16-bit character codes. The Mac OS has some minor problems, but conversion tools are readily available. Likewise, that character set must be interpreted as an application (such as your Web browser or a word processor; some browsers can handle 16-bit character codes, others can't).

- **An electronic font that allows the character set to be displayed on screen (and in print, and so forth).** A *font* contains graphical bitmaps that correspond to character codes that appear in a character set, so that each character has its own unique bitmap. These bitmaps are scaled (to create font sizes) and styled (to create font appearances, such as bold and italic) to create bitmaps for display on-screen or in print image files. Each individual bitmap in a font is known as a *glyph*.

All these ingredients are necessary to work with alternate character sets because humans understand scripts, computers understand numbers (or bit patterns, if you prefer), and displays require images. Character sets represent a mapping from a script to a set of corresponding numeric character codes. Fonts represent a collection of glyphs for the numeric character codes in a character set. All three elements are necessary to represent and render characters on-screen.

Finally, to create text to match the alphabet used in a script, you need an input tool — such as a text or XML editor — that can work with the character set and its corresponding font to create additional text that uses that character set so that you can use the alternate alphabet in your document (and to see what you're doing).

For Each Character, a Code

In the ISO 10646 character set, individual characters correspond to specific 16-bit numbers. For convenience, most character sets occur in the form of sequential ranges of such numbers, where uppercase and lowercase characters as well as characters for the digits 0 through 9 are in sequence. To determine the code that represents a character, you have to look it up in the Unicode or ISO 10646 specification. (This is where the Unicode book we mentioned earlier in this chapter comes in handy.)

Even if you don't have access to an editor or text entry tool that understands a particular character set, you can always use numeric entities to represent its characters. In general, numeric entities take one of two forms (explanations are indicated in comments below the code):

```
&#4096;
<!-- &# id is a decimal number -->
&#x0F00;
<!-- &#x id is a hexadecimal number-->
```

Each of these two entities represents the first character in Tibetan script; 4096 in decimal is the same as 0F00 in hexadecimal (base 16) notation.

Key Character Sets

Around the world, computers use a variety of character sets, depending on the languages (or scripts, if you prefer) that their users employ to represent text. Most computers today use some variant of American Standard Code for Information Interchange (ASCII), an 8-bit character set that handles the basic Roman alphabet used for English, along with punctuation, numbers, and simple symbols. To augment this meager character set, extensions to support additional characters or diacritical marks are added on a per-language basis.

Most European languages match standard ASCII values from 0 to 127 and define alternate mappings between character codes and local script characters for the code from 128 to 255.

Non-Roman alphabets, such as Hebrew, Japanese, and Thai, depend on special character sets that include basic ASCII (0-127, or 0-255, depending on the implementation) plus the character sets for the script that corresponds to the "other alphabet" in use. The number of bits in such character encodings depends on the size of the other alphabet. It's not uncommon for such encodings to use 16-bit values to accommodate a second character and symbol set along with the ASCII set. A listing of character sets built around the ASCII framework appears in Table 12-1.

Table 12-1		ISO 8859 Character Sets
Charset	*Script*	*Languages*
ISO-8859-1	Latin-1	ASCII plus most Western European languages, including Albanian, Afrikaans, Basque, Catalan, Danish, Dutch, English, Faroese, Finnish, Flemish, Galician, German, Icelandic, Irish, Italian, Norwegian, Portuguese, Scottish, Spanish, and Swedish. Omits certain Dutch, French, and German characters
ISO-8859-2	Latin-2	ASCII plus most Central European languages, including Czech, English, German, Hungarian, Polish, Romanian, Croatian, Slovak, Slovene, and Serbian
ISO-8859-3	Latin-3	ASCII plus characters required for English, Esperanto, German, Maltese, and Galician
ISO-8859-4	Latin-4	ASCII plus most Baltic languages, including Latvian, Lithuanian, German, Greenlandic, and Lappish; now superseded by ISO-Latin-6
ISO-8859-5		ASCII plus Cyrillic characters for Slavic languages, including Byelorussian, Bulgarian, Macedonian, Russian, Serbian, and Ukrainian
ISO-8859-6		ASCII plus Arabic characters
ISO-8859-7		ASCII plus Greek characters
ISO-8859-8		ASCII plus Hebrew
ISO-8859-9	Latin-5	Latin-1 except that some Turkish symbols replace Icelandic ones
ISO-8859-10	Latin-6	ASCII plus most Nordic languages, including Inuit, non-Skolt Sami, and Icelandic

Charset	Script	Languages
ISO-8859-11		ASCII plus Thai
ISO-8859-12	Latin-7	ASCII plus Celtic
ISO-8859-13	Latin-8	ASCII plus the Baltic Rim characters
ISO-8859-14	Latin-9	ASCII plus Sami (Finnish)
ISO-8859-15	Latin-10	Variation on Latin-1, including Euro currency sign, plus extra accented Finnish and French characters

A careful reading of Table 12-1 shows that most character sets can render English and German, plus a collection of other, sometimes related languages. When choosing a variant of ISO-8859, remember that all the languages you want to include must be part of that variant; otherwise, you must use Unicode.

XML goes beyond such idiosyncratic or customized character sets and uses Unicode because it can house character codes for the vast majority of known human scripts in a single encoding. Even if an XML processor can't display certain character codes — because necessary fonts are not present, for instance — such processors must be capable of handling any valid character code in the Unicode range from 0 to 65,535.

In fact, each text entity in XML has an associated text encoding. If some specific encoding is not defined in a text entity's definition, the default is an encoding called UTF-8, which stands for Unicode Transformation Format, 8-bit form. UTF-8 matches all 7-bit ASCII code values for character encodings 0 through 127, and matches ISO-8859-1 for values 128 through 255. But even though UTF-8 represents code in 8-bit chunks, a single character code can be as long as three such chunks. UTF-8 uses a mathematical formula to convert standard Unicode encodings into more compact forms; please consult www.unicode.org for details. For our discussion, the important thing to remember is that UTF-8 represents the Roman alphabet efficiently, requiring only a single byte for common characters.

Unicode itself has been dinged because it fails to represent the Han ideographs fully. Unicode defines encodings for 20,000 such ideographs out of a possible lexicon of 80,000 needed to completely represent Chinese, Japanese, Korean, and historical Vietnamese. For that reason, ISO-10646 specifies a character encoding called Universal Character System (UCS) that combines four 8-bit values for each character encoding. 31 bits of this total string may be used to represent characters for over 2.1 billion unique codes. In addition to providing space for every character in every known written language, UCS permits complete and distinct character sets to be assigned to each language. At this point, UCS is mostly of theoretical interest because its only defined encodings match Unicode's. But UCS certainly leaves plenty of room for more characters in everyone's future!

Using Unicode Characters

Any software that supports XML files directly, including the XML tools and editors included on the CD-ROM that accompanies this book, supports Unicode or UTF-8 formats. So do many modern word processors — for instance, Word 97 and later versions support a format called encoded text that uses Unicode encoding.

If you don't have ready access to such tools and want to save XML files in Unicode format, you must use a conversion tool, probably to convert ASCII to Unicode or to UTF-8. Sun Microsystem's free Java Development Kit (JDK) is available at `http://java.sun.com/products/jdk/1.2/`.

This material includes a command-line utility named `native2ascii` that converts between numerous localized character sets and Unicode. Please consult the associated help file to understand the syntax for and options that work with this utility or go to `http://java.sun.com/j2se/1.3/docs/tooldocs/win32/native2ascii.html`.

If you can't convert your XML text into UTF-8 or straight Unicode encodings, you can tell the XML processor what kind of character encoding you're using. If you do this, however, you're taking a chance because not all XML processors can handle arbitrary encodings. However, widely used tools such as Netscape Navigator (Version 4.1 or newer) and Internet Explorer (Version 5.0 or newer) can handle most ISO-8859 variants. To use an alternate character encoding, you must identify that encoding in your XML document's prolog as follows:

```
<?xml version="1.0" encoding="ISO-8859-9"?>
```

In addition to the encoding names that appear in Table 12-1, you can use other encoding names as well. For other possible encodings, check the official Internet Assigned Numbers Authority (IANA) list at

```
www.isi.edu/in-notes/iana/assignments/character-sets
```

Please note that XML parsers are required to support only UTF-8 and UTF-16 (native Unicode) encodings, so the `encoding` attribute in an XML document prolog might not work with all such tools. If you try using an ISO-8859 variant or some other character set and don't get the results you want, you might have to figure out how to translate the document into Unicode. Ouch!

Finding Character Entity Information

Elsewhere in this chapter, we mention one excellent source for obtaining information about character entity assignments for Unicode — namely, the

Unicode Consortium's book entitled *The Unicode Standard, Version 3.0*. You can also find plenty of encoding information online. For example, here's the site of the Unicode Character Database:

```
ftp://ftp.unicode.org/Public/UNIDATA/UnicodeCharacterDatabase.html
```

Likewise, the W3C has information about Unicode character ranges and encodings in Appendix B "Character Classes," for the XML 1.0 Recommended Specification, at

```
www.w3.org/TR/REC-xml#CharClasses
```

You'll also find the XHTML entity lists useful in this context:

- ✔ **Latin-1:** www.w3.org/TR/xhtml11/DTD/xhtml-lat1.ent
- ✔ **Special:** www.w3.org/TR/xhtml11/DTD/xhtml-special.ent
- ✔ **Symbols:** www.w3.org/TR/xhtml11/DTD/xhtml-symbol.ent

The previous URLs will open the File Download box of your browser.

A bit of judicious poking around in your favorite search engine, using search strings such as "Unicode encodings" or "XML character encodings" can turn up other interesting sources of this information online. Happy hunting!

Part IV

Using and Delivering XML Content

The 5th Wave   By Rich Tennant

"With style sheets, I understand properties and values, and I get inheritance. But that darn "cluttermorphism" stumps me."

In this part . . .

By itself, XML doesn't look like much in a Web browser. But there's a lot more to XML than making it look pretty for human reading or consumption. Part IV delves into the mysteries of packaging and delivering XML content for all kinds of uses. Chapter 13 tackles what's involved in using XML to create solutions for information delivery, including data exchange, the important roles that turning XML into other forms for data (called transformation) can play, and about the strange and friendly relationship between XML and databases. Chapter 14 covers how the eXtensible Stylesheet Language (XSL) works with XML not only to turn XML into HTML, but also to turn it into just about any format you might need.

Chapter 15 talks about what's involved in handling XML for data delivery, as it explains how XML processors read and internalize XML content, and other aspects of internalizing and handling XML content for reuse, delivery, or transformation. Chapter 16 covers the specifics involved in viewing XML content on the Web, for those who seek to marry modern XML content with Web browsers that sometimes seem behind the times. (They're soooo 20th century, if you know what we mean . . . .) We also explain how we use XML, XSLT, CSS, and XHTML to create a more positive viewing experience for our XML examples from this book as you look at them on the CD.

Chapter 13

Inside an XML Solution

● ●

In This Chapter

▶ Doing something meaningful with your XML

▶ Examining common uses for XML

▶ Integrating XML with databases

▶ Styling and transforming your XML

▶ Identifying the pieces and parts of an XML solution

● ●

*P*erhaps by the time you read this chapter, you've already whipped up an XML document, and maybe even a DTD or XML Schema document as well. After all your hard work, slaving over an XML editor all day, you might not have much to show for your efforts except for a bunch of, frankly, plain and boring-looking text. Perhaps you're thinking, "There has to be more to XML than this."

You're right. XML is more than just text, elements, and DTDs. In Parts I through III, we hammer home the importance of separating content from formatting, and we concentrate entirely on how to describe your content.

In this, the first of four chapters devoted to using and delivering XML, we look at exactly what it takes to make your XML work for you in a total solution. Although these chapters don't tell you absolutely everything you need to know to design and implement a complete XML solution, they give you a good idea of what's involved. You'll walk away from these chapters with a good understanding of how XML fits in the larger context of a complete solution, and what you need to do to make your XML work as hard for you as you did to create it.

So You Have Some XML . . . Now What?

In previous chapters, we've insinuated — if not outright said — that by itself, XML can't do much more for you than define the structure of a document. Doing something useful and meaningful with those documents is a whole other ball of wax.

192 Part IV: Using and Delivering XML Content

Generally, XML documents (and their related DTDs or schemas) are put together as part of a total solution to a specific problem. Online stores use XML to describe the contents of their catalogs. Banks exchange financial data in XML. Mobile phones with wireless connections to the Internet use XML to otore content that people can view on their phones' little LED displays. The list goes on and on.

The point is that XML doesn't act alone, and it's up to you to figure out how XML fits into your overall solution. You may already have a project in mind that you know XML can be a part of, or you might be wondering exactly what XML can do for you. Either way, it's good to have a solid understanding of how XML fits into a bigger picture — and that's what this chapter is all about.

In general, most XML solutions fall into one of these four categories:

- ✔ Solutions that use XML to exchange data, the way banks exchange financial data.

- ✔ Solutions that focus on displaying the content you've described with XML, the way online vendors display their catalog wares online.

- ✔ Solutions built on programming frameworks, such as ASP.Net and ColdFusion, that use XML to help programmers define how an application can work.

- ✔ Solutions that use XML as a neutral format for data storage, so that archived data can be used later, the way wireless and Web technologies are now used seamlessly with XML applications.

Notice that our introduction to the preceding list includes the words "in general" and "most." We didn't say "all" or "every single one." We've left ourselves some wiggle room because these four categories are very broad and aren't catchalls for the endless uses of XML. It's been our experience that these categories cover a good percentage of the XML solutions at work in the world today, and they will help you to figure out how XML can best work for you. If your ideas about XML don't seem to fit into one of these categories, or they seem to span more than one (we know of several solutions that do), don't worry. XML is so flexible and so useful that you can come up with new and creative uses for it that we don't cover here.

Data exchange with XML

You're probably very tired of hearing that XML is platform and application independent, and even more tired of hearing that XML's freedom from those traditional constraints makes it such a useful method for describing content. We can't talk about data exchange — a very common use for XML — without restating what we hope is indelibly ingrained in your head by now: XML is just text and works on any platform and with just about any application that can read a text file.

These days, data exchange makes the world go 'round. Online billing systems can receive electronic bills and send out electronic statements. Colleges and universities can exchange student data without the hassle of printouts or data entry. Loan underwriters can receive credit reports electronically instead of by fax and incorporate that information directly into their systems. If one business needs to share data with another — for any reason — it can be done electronically with XML.

The ins and outs of data exchange

One of the greatest things about the information and computing worlds is that there's a flavor of everything — from operating systems to applications — to suit just about anyone. Although this variety is great for the individual, it makes a programmer's life just a *little* difficult.

Traditionally, creating processes for data exchange between systems (computers running applications) was a chore because each system had its own particular data format. Exchange involved complex conversions from one format to another, and data loss was a common side effect. With the advent of XML, data exchange has become one of the easiest parts of building any solution that requires it.

In an XML-based data exchange solution, two or more systems (it's hard to exchange data with yourself — kind of like clapping with one hand) agree on XML as the best way to send and receive data. Both systems know what kind of data to create and what kind of data to expect.

One of the more interesting aspects of an XML-based data exchange solution is what kind of DTD or schema you decide to use in the exchange. Two (or more) systems may agree

  ✔ **To use the schema or DTD that one system already has in place.** In this case, the other system agrees to send data in the same format.

  ✔ **To use a new DTD or schema that each has accepted as the best XML format.** The systems may work together to create the new DTD or schema, or they may agree to use a pre-existing DTD or schema that fits their mutual needs.

  ✔ **To each use different DTDs or schemas.** This decision means that every time data is sent and received, each system must convert the data from the foreign schema or DTD into the native DTD or schema.

For the last option to work successfully, the solution needs to incorporate another facet of XML — the eXtensible Stylesheet Language (XSL). XSL makes it possible to convert data described with one DTD or schema to data described with a different DTD or schema. If your system requires a particular XML vocabulary to work, but you receive data described with a different vocabulary, you need XSL's help to make it all come out in the wash. A section later in this chapter, "The Role of Style and Transformation," digs into this issue a little deeper. See Chapter 14 for more on XSL.

One of the traits of an XML data exchange solution is that people may very well never see the actual data being exchanged, even though they're using a solution that relies on that data. In a data-exchange solution, most of the XML work goes on behind the scenes, but the effects of the data are seen throughout the system.

Data exchange in the real world

A good example of an XML-based data exchange system is a loan refinancing system that accepts applications from everyday people. The system's job is to connect the loan applicants with the lender that's the best match. This particular system uses XML-based data exchange in several stages of the process, one of which is the stage where credit information is exchanged between the refinancing system and a particular lender.

As you might expect, part of the application process is a credit report review. The credit report becomes part of the refinancing system so that the employees trying to make the loan happen have access to the report in the same system that holds loan application data. Employees are very thankful that they don't have to bounce from the company's internal refinancing system to the external credit reporting bureau's system to find the information they need to work on an application.

The refinancing system can also use the credit report to preprocess applications based on a person's credit report. The system knows that certain lenders approve applications only when credit is good, and that others are more flexible about working with people whose credit needs a little help. Based on the XML data in the credit report, the system can begin to sort applications into virtual piles before a human being ever sees them.

If data exchange is a significant part of your solution — as it is for the refinancing system — one of the key roles XML can play is as a format for the data you need to exchange. Part of the work you do when you set up your system is to find out if the other systems you want to exchange data with are capable of handling XML (most are), and whether they have an XML format they like to use. If it turns out that you need to do some data conversion along the way, XSL will play a role in your solution as well. See Chapter 4 to find out more about data analysis and planning.

Displaying your XML content

When you use XML to exchange and display content, the audience is usually a human. A good example of a content-display solution is a repository that makes recipes available for viewing online, for download to a recipe application on a Personal Digital Assistant (PDA), and for printing via the Adobe Acrobat PDF reader. The end goal of the system is to make the recipes available for human consumption (literally), but in any of three different media: online, in the palm, and on paper. In this scenario, XML describes the structure of the recipes, but the display of the recipes is a separate issue.

One of the benefits of using XML to describe data is that you get a true representation of the data's structure. On the other hand, data structure doesn't include display instructions — content can't be system independent if it does. That means that display systems, such as Web browsers, PDAs, and printers, all need instructions on how to display your content.

Think about our recipe repository solution. A Web browser needs to know that we want the title to be displayed in 24-point Times New Roman font, and a printer needs to know (via the PDF file) that we want each recipe to fit on a single 4-x-6-inch recipe card, but that information isn't part of the RML.

Solutions that intend to display data described with XML must have a way to make that data, well, display. The display instructions live outside of the XML document that includes your content and as a group are called *style sheets*.

Chapters 14, 15, and 16 give you the complete rundown on how to use style sheets with your documents for all kinds of things. When you read the chapters on style, remember what you've read in this chapter about all the pieces in a solution.

Programming frameworks

At the intersection of machine readability and human readability are solutions that use XML to define a set of instructions that a programming framework, such as ASP.NET, uses to make an application tick. Computer programmers have to use an XML DTD or schema to create applications that run in the framework. That means that the DTD or schema has to be intelligible and useful to people. At the same time, the instructions that the developers put down in XML have to be intelligible and useful to the framework.

In this case, the schema or DTD usually provides a complex set of markup for describing standard programming devices, such as variables, loops, database connections, and more. Programmers learn the XML syntax that the solution works with and use it to create applications in that framework.

More and more programming frameworks, from Active Server Pages (ASP) to ColdFusion, are adopting XML as the data format of choice. XML is particularly attractive to developers of Internet- or Web-based programming frameworks because it's platform independent; the issues associated with porting code from one platform to another don't apply with XML. Sometimes it's a little more cumbersome to create programs with XML, but the flexibility and extensibility this approach offers down the line more than makes up for the inconveniences you face during the programming process.

Data storage

An often unexpected but supremely practical use for XML is to use it to describe data that you simply want to tuck away for later. (A good example of this is log files or data an application generates that you want to report on later.) By choosing XML as a format for archived data, you don't commit to any specific platform or proprietary data format. Content is stored as text, along with detailed information about its structure. When you need it, just grab it, with its structural information intact.

This data is supremely flexible because when you need to import it into a system, you can write a simple import program that reads your XML and converts it to whatever format the system requires — whether it's a database or some other information management system.

Although XML-based data storage systems aren't as prevalent as some of the other kinds of solutions we describe, it's a good example of the ways you can use XML that you may have never really considered before. In general, if you need a flexible and platform-independent format for your data for any reason, XML is an excellent candidate for the job.

XML and Databases

Taking a short trip down the road to database land, you see how XML can work with the databases in your solutions. Looking back on the four general kinds of XML solutions that we discuss in the "So You Have Some XML . . . Now What?" section, notice that we mention databases more than once.

The connection between databases and XML is a logical one: Both store data in a structured manner. A very common use for XML, particularly in a data-exchange solution, is to take data stored in XML documents and move it into a database so that the data can be accessed and manipulated by an application. All the major database systems — from Oracle to Microsoft Server and beyond — have XML utilities that help you work with XML in the context of the database.

Think back to the financial data exchange solution that we mention earlier in the chapter, and you'll find a good example of moving data from XML documents into databases. When the refinancing system gets a credit report in the form of an XML file, it moves the data from the XML file to a collection of fields in the database. In addition, you can extract data from the database and put it into an XML document for exchange with another system.

Another common use of databases with XML is to let the database serve as an index to the content described with XML. For example, an online article archive uses XML as the format for describing articles. When a new article comes into the system, the tool that pulls the article into the archiving system populates a database with some basic data about the article, such as the author, date, title, and topic. The rest of the article is stored as a flat text file on the system's hard disk for access later on when someone wants to see it. You can then use the database, which will likely be Standard Query Language (SQL), to search for articles by the information stored in the database: author, date, title, and topic.

This particular solution, an online article archive, takes advantage of the individual strengths of both XML and databases:

✔ XML provides detailed structural information about the articles that a database can't handle very well.

✔ The data about the articles (the article metadata) stored in the database can be searched and filtered according to all manner of criteria — something XML isn't particularly suited to do.

For example, if you want to find all articles written by John Doe between January and February of 2001 that include *XML* in the subject line, this system helps you find them and then make their content available to you (or a display system) for further manipulation.

If your solution includes a database, you need to think about how, if at all, your XML documents will interface with the database.

The Role of Style and Transformation

Earlier in this chapter, we introduce the concept of style sheets as a tool to help you manipulate your XML files, whether it be to convert them from one set of markup to another or to help a particular display device show content. This section takes a closer look at the role style and transformation play in an XML solution.

Using XSLT for data transformation

In the earlier section "The ins and outs of data exchange," we say that it's entirely possible that two (or more) systems exchanging data don't use the same exact schema or DTD. One possible solution to this quandary is for one system to change its internal programming to work with the other's DTD or schema. As much as this fosters a cooperative spirit, often it simply isn't practical. If a system is built around a particular DTD or schema, you can't just come along and rebuild it.

A more practical solution is for each system to support data transformation so that each can continue to use the format it needs. Here's how that solution works:

1. When My Business, Inc gets data from Your Company, Ltd, described with markup based on Your Company's schema or DTD, My Business simply transforms that data into its data described with markup based on My Business's schema or DTD before pulling it in.

2. Alternatively, Your Company, Ltd may be nice enough to transform its data to My Business's XML format before sending it along to My Business.

    Either way, a data transformation has to take place.

The mechanism XML uses for defining how data should be transformed from one flavor of XML markup to another is XSL, and specifically the transformation functionality of XSL known as XSL Transformations (XSLT). Chapter 14 provides much greater detail on how XSLT works and how you use it.

Using style sheets

When you use XML as part of a solution with the end goal of displaying the content that the XML describes, some mechanism has to provide display information. That mechanism is a display style sheet (not to be confused with a set of transformation instructions written in XSLT).

Style sheets for display are designed to provide complete information to a display device about how to show the content described with XML. Style sheets provide information about page breaks, font sizes, text color, line spacing, and more.

When you create a style sheet for an XML document, you have a couple of choices:

✔ **XSL-FO (XSL Formatting Objects),** the display mechanism of XSL

✔ **CSS (Cascading Style Sheets),** the style sheet language created for HTML

Of the two, XSL-FO is more robust because it was designed to work specifi-cally with XML. However, XSL-FO is a fairly new specification, and it isn't as completely supported as CSS, especially in Web browsers. CSS is also easier to learn than XSL-FO. Chapters 14 and 16 delve deeper into the inner work-ings and syntax of XSL-FO and CSS.

One of the great things about XSL — both the XSLT and XSL-FO mechanisms — is that XSL style sheets are nothing more than XML documents. XSLT and XSL-FO are really just XML vocabularies that define rules for creating style sheets. This means you don't have to learn a whole new syntax to use XSL, just the ins and outs of the DTDs behind XSLT and XSL-FO.

Transformation for style?

To make things more interesting, you can use XSLT to convert your XML into formats for different types of displays. For example, an online recipe reposi-tory makes recipes available on the Web, in a format for a PDA, and for print.

To ensure that the online display works in as many browsers as possible (many older browsers don't support XML), the best way to make our recipes available online is to convert them from RML (Recipe Markup Language) to XHTML. The best way to do this would be to use XSLT to do the conversion. We cover RML-to-XHTML conversions with XSLT in Chapter 14.

Adobe Portable Document Format (PDF) is the best format for printing recipes because it retains original formatting. You can use XSLT to convert your XML document (like our RML) into a version of XML that Adobe Acrobat can take in and turn into a PDF. Once again, transformation leads to style.

In both of these scenarios, you would only be using the transformation side of XSL to ensure the display of content. In the Web scenario, you might add a CSS style sheet to the final XHTML to more closely control its display in a browser, but you wouldn't have to apply CSS style sheets to the original XML document.

To help you get a better handle on what the best uses for the various style sheet languages are, we've put together two chapters to bring you up to speed on the basics of each. Chapter 14 gives you a good overview of XSL, both the transformation and formatting object mechanisms. Chapter 16 shows you how you can use CSS with XML, and even HTML generated from XML, to display data in a Web browser. When you've read these two chapters, you should have enough information to make an informed decision about which style sheet mechanism, or mechanisms, best fit your solution.

Chapter 14

Using XSL with XML

XSL (eXtensible Stylesheet Language) helps you do something meaningful with your XML. Though XSL is the style sheet language that was created specifically for XML, it's more than just a tool for creating display templates. XSL provides you with a powerful tool for converting XML described with one set of markup to another. Translation from one XML vocabulary to another is a key component of many solutions that use XML for data exchange, and is equally important if you want to turn your XML into a format that a display device can understand — such as the eXtensible HyperText Markup Language (XHTML) or Portable Document Format (PDF).

The great thing about XSL is that it's really just XML. XSL documents are XML documents written according to a particular set of rules. The really good news is that you don't have to learn a new language to learn XSL, just the particular rules of creating transformation or display style sheets. Learning to use XSL is just like learning to use any other XML vocabulary. Neat, huh?

In this chapter, we look at XML's style needs and how the solution to them has morphed over time. You also find out how XSL's two sides, transformation and display, make it a powerful tool for manipulating your XML for a variety of purposes. XSL has many facets and moving parts, so bear with us as we take a look at each one in turn and then bring them together into one big picture in the end.

The Two Faces of XSL

XML's style needs are extensive. Clean XML document structures are rarely in the form you need for presentation, and you may need to present the same XML document in several ways: in print, on the screen, or even in a multimedia presentation. In addition, to truly take advantage of XML's power as a tool for sharing data across systems, there should be an easy way to convert documents from one Document Type Definition (DTD) to another.

The architects of XML decided that the responsibility for display and for document conversion should be handled by a separate mechanism from XML proper, so they developed XSL as a vocabulary of XML that's specifically designed to describe style sheets for XML documents. During development, these same architects realized that creating one mechanism for both display and conversion was a Herculean task. So they split the style and conversion mechanisms of XSL into two different but related mechanisms:

- ✔ **XSL Transformations (XSLT)** to handle the conversion from one set of markup to another
- ✔ **XSL Formatting Objects (XSL-FO)** to help devices that want to display XML

Before diving into the inner workings of these two sides of XSL, take a look at the following section, which shows how XSL got two faces and what each is especially designed to do.

How We Got Here . . . The Long Road to XSL

The development of the style specifications for XML has been a roller coaster ride — and we're not talking about a kiddie roller coaster either. We're talking about a big, scary, inverted, looping roller coaster. Of all the XML-related specifications, style sheets have had the hardest time. Originally, there was only going to be one style sheet mechanism, and its goal in life was to drive the display of XML documents. But as the architects of XML style sheets got further along with their task, they discovered that there's much more to styling XML than they originally imagined.

Transformation is at the heart of displaying an XML document. Most display devices — like a PDF viewer, for instance — have a preferred method of describing display rules. Before any XML document described with any set of elements can be displayed, it may very well have to be converted to the display device's preferred format. Over time, of course, more and more display devices will accept straight XML with a traditional style sheet to guide display, but we're not quite there yet, so this issue is still one that many XML solutions have to tackle.

Knowing which XSL you're dealing with

If you're just getting into XSL, figuring out which version of XSL a particular book or article is really talking about can be difficult. Generally, information about XSLT involves the word *transformation,* and anything that involves the word *formatting* probably refers to XSL-FO. If you see the word *Microsoft,* you can figure that the information is about Microsoft XSL; but you can't assume that what you read applies outside of the Microsoft domain. The W3C uses the term XSL to mean the general XML style sheet standard that includes both XSLT and XSL-FO. In this book, when we use the term XSL, we're also using the W3C definition. But if we're talking about XSLT or XSL-FO specifically, we use their proper names.

That means a lot of people are converting documents from one DTD or schema to another — especially if the end goal is data exchange. After all, two companies may need to share the same data and both may use XML to describe it, but who says they use the *same* XML?

To make a long story short, the original XSL specification morphed into XSL Transformations (XSLT) — an XML vocabulary for defining the transformation from one set of markup to another. Nowhere in this mix was a scheme for driving display. At the time, most display devices required their native data and style sheet formats (such as XHTML and CSS) and weren't able to accept XML and a style sheet for display anyway.

Somewhere along the way — around 1998 or so — Microsoft came out with a very early version of XSLT called Microsoft XSL. For a while, XSL, XSLT, and Microsoft XSL all floated around with no clear indication of which would emerge as the standard and which would be useful for real-world development.

Because the initial XSL focus was on transformation, the W3C's XSLT emerged as a very stable specification. The specifics of formatting for display with XSL (XSL-FO) were debated for a long time, and only recently has XSL-FO also emerged as a stable recommendation.

When you go looking for information about XSL — whether it be in books, magazines, or online — look for the most recent information. Although XML itself has been stable for quite a while now, XSL is only just now starting to slow down. The more recent your information is, the more likely it refers to the latest developments of XSL.

For a complete history of XSL, XSLT, and XSL-FO, as well as links to the current XSL recommendation that includes both XSLT and XSL-FO, visit the W3C's XSL page at

www.w3.org/Style/XSL

Though the basic concepts behind XSL are fairly straightforward, the syntax for building XSL style sheets is complex. First, you have to get a handle on XSLT, and then you need to learn a new XML vocabulary. Although it's definitely something you can do, it's not something we can cover in detail in this chapter. The "Introducing XSL-FO" section, later in this chapter, gets you started, but the rest is up to you.

XSLT

The first and most well-developed face of XSL is a conversion tool known as XSLT. The *T* stands for *transformation*, and that's exactly what this part of XSL is designed to do. XSLT provides a set of rules to convert documents described by one set of elements into documents described by another set of elements. The two sets of elements don't even have to look anything alike.

You can use XSLT

- ✔ To transform data exchanged between two or more systems that aren't using a common XML vocabulary. (See Chapter 13 for more information on data exchange with XML.)

- ✔ To transform documents described using XML elements into XHTML for display in a Web browser. This nifty trick overcomes the dilemma created by the overall lack of consistency in browser support for XML and its friends, such as XSL-FO and even CSS. One day, browsers will all be XML savvy, but until then, XSLT lets us have our cake and eat it too — with XSLT, you can describe data with XML for storage and manipulation and transform it into XHTML to display it on the Web for all the world to see.

- ✔ In XML-based data exchange systems. Systems need to exchange data regularly, and many use XML for that exchange. More often than not, the two systems don't use the same XML internally, so they have to spit out and receive data written in an XML vocabulary they aren't ready to work with. These systems use XSLT to convert data from their internal XML vocabulary to one that another system can work with, and vice versa.

To write an XSLT style sheet, you simply identify an element in one document and specify how it should be described using a different element or set of elements in the new document. You can grab entire elements or just an element's content. You can even reference attribute values and turn them into element content (or turn element content into attribute values). All in all, XSLT is really cool.

The role of XPath

Without XPath, XSLT simply wouldn't work. Before you can transform an element, attribute, or even a chunk of content using XSLT, you have to be able to identify it. For example, if you want to do something special to every third instance of a list item, you have to be able to point to it — and that's what XPath makes possible. XPath is the mechanism XSLT uses to point to a piece of an XML document so that it can be transformed. If you can't find it, you can't change it.

XPath is a very sophisticated set of rules — *syntax* in geek speak — for identifying the most specific pieces of an XML document. You can not only specify particular elements or attributes or

their content, but you can also find individual pieces of content — *strings* in geek speak — based on the elements and letters around them.

XPath is such a helpful specification that it's not only used by XSLT to guide transformations, but it's also used by the XML Linking (XLink) specification to make very specific pieces of XML document into links. Because XPath is so sophisticated, we've devoted Chapter 18 to it. As you read along and wonder, "But how do I point to the third instance of the Item element that begins with 'part# - 4'..." fear not, XPath makes it possible.

XSL-FO

XSL-FO is the content-formatting vocabulary of the XSL style. To use XSL-FO, you use XSLT to convert a document from its original XML into the XSL-FO vocabulary. Take a look at Figure 14-1 to see how this process works for a document described with the Recipe Markup Language (RML).

Figure 14-1:
Using XSLT to convert an RML document to XSL-FO.

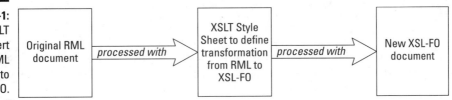

Original RML document → *processed with* → XSLT Style Sheet to define transformation from RML to XSL-FO → *processed with* → New XSL-FO document

The idea behind XSL-FO is that display devices of all types, from printers to Web browsers, will (someday) standardize on XSL-FO as a syntax for defining formatting. Of course, it may take a while for the idea to become a reality, but everyone remains hopeful.

The key to an XSL style sheet is a critter known as a formatting object. A *formatting object* represents a piece of a document. These pieces can be as large as a page or as small as a list item. When you build an XSL-FO style sheet, you take each part of a document that you want to display, fit it into a formatting object, and then describe how that formatting object should appear.

After you've converted your XML documents to XSL-FO documents with XSLT, the display device has to interpret the XSL-FO content in the right way. A Web browser might display the entire document, while a presentation application such as PowerPoint might only show the titles and section headings. The final display is based on the device's interpretation of the XSL-FO.

Just like Cascading Style Sheets (CSS), XSL-FO has a host of formatting properties to help you control every aspect of a formatting object's display — from its text color to the amount of space between letters and words — much of which comes directly from CSS2. And just like CSS, after you find out how to build style rules — as well as what properties you have at your disposal when you're building style rules — you're well on your way to building XSL-FO style sheets.

Although XSL is a recommendation, with both XSLT and XSL-FO included, XSL-FO is still relatively new. Support for it in software is limited, as is information about it. We're convinced the XSL architects have finally settled on how XSL-FO should work, but don't be surprised if they continue to tweak it over time. What you learn about it now will serve you well in the future. Keep an eye on the XSL recommendation to see how it evolves at the W3C's XSL page:

```
www.w3.org/TR/xsl
```

Why XSL Style Sheets Are XML Documents

The good news is that XSL style sheets (XSLT or XSL-FO) are really just XML documents. They use elements, attributes, and all the other standard XML syntax tools. This means that when you master XSL, you're really just mastering two more DTDs.

Because XSL style sheets are just XML documents, technically, any system that can process XML can process an XSL style sheet. For a style sheet to be useful, however, the system has to know what to do with the results of the processed style sheet.

Specialized XSL tools are under development and some already exist. But beware: XSL processing tools that have been around for a while may have been written before the current XSL working draft was released and may not support style sheets written using the most current XSL syntax.

The best way to keep up with new XSL tools is to visit the W3C's XSL Web page (www.w3.org/Style/XSL). Another great XSL resource on the Web is XSL Info, which you can find at www.xslinfo.com. This site is a sibling site to www.xmlinfo.com, www.schema.net, and www.xmlsoftware.com — all run by James Tauber, a knowledgeable and well-respected member of the Web community.

A Simple Transformation Using XSLT

An XSLT style sheet is made up of a set of instructions to convert documents described using one DTD or schema into documents described using a second, different DTD. Each instruction focuses on one element in the source document and specifies how it should be changed to fit the second DTD or schema. The style sheet doesn't replace or change the elements in the source file, but instead builds a new file to hold the results of the transformation.

An XSLT style sheet is an XML document. When you're working with XSLT, all you're really doing is using XSLT elements to transform a document using one set of elements into a document that uses another set of elements. XSLT is nothing more than elements for changing elements to elements. Whew!

The best way to show you how XSLT works is by example. In the following section, "The bean burrito recipe," we look at an XML document we want to transform into XHTML. In the "Describing the bean burrito recipe with XHTML" section, we show the transformed XHTML document. In the "An XSL style sheet for converting XML to XHTML" section, we show the XSLT style sheet that manages the transformation. We then break that XSLT style sheet into its component parts so that you can see what's really going on and how the transformation occurred in that section.

The bean burrito recipe

If you've read previous chapters in this book, you may have heartburn from all the references to the bean burrito recipe. If you read the entire book, by the time you're finished, you'll want to go on a non-Mexican food diet. Trust us, we have chosen this example because it's the best way to show you what XSLT can really do.

Listing 14-1 shows the now-classic bean burrito recipe, described with Recipe Markup Language (RML).

Listing 14-1:   The Bean Burrito Recipe — Again

```
<?xml version="1.0"?>
<Recipes>
 <Recipe cook="The XML Gourmet">
  <Title>Bean Burrito</Title>
  <Category name="tex-mex"/>
  <Ingredients>
   <Item>1 can refried beans</Item>
   <Item>1 cup longhorn colby cheese, shredded</Item>
   <Item>1 small onion, finely chopped</Item>
   <Item>3 flour tortillas</Item>
  </Ingredients>
  <CookingInstructions>
   <Cinst>Empty can of refried beans into medium saucepan.</Cinst>
   <Cinst>Heat over medium-high heat until beans are smooth and bubbly.</Cinst>
   <Cinst>Warm tortillas in microwave for 30 seconds.</Cinst>
  </CookingInstructions>
  <ServingInstructions>
   <Sinst>Spread 1/3 of warm beans on each tortilla.</Sinst>
   <Sinst>Sprinkle with cheese and onions.</Sinst>
   <Sinst>Roll tortillas and serve.</Sinst>
  </ServingInstructions>
 </Recipe>
</Recipes>
```

If we feed this file into Internet Explorer, it ignores all the elements it doesn't recognize — which is all of them — and simply displays the text within the markup, as shown in Figure 14-2.

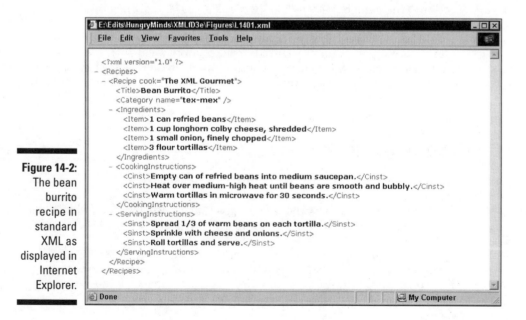

Figure 14-2:
The bean burrito recipe in standard XML as displayed in Internet Explorer.

If you want people to see the bean burrito recipe in a useful and meaningful way with a Web browser, you have to describe it with something that the Web browser can work with — namely XHTML.

Describing the bean burrito recipe with XHTML

Although XHTML markup doesn't describe the pieces and parts of the bean burrito recipe as well as RML (our Recipe Markup Language) does, Web browsers speak XHTML and display XHTML-described content in a nice, pretty way (while it doesn't have a clue about what to do with RML-described content). Based on the different roles each bit of content in our XML document plays, we can build XHTML markup to display the content that looks something like Listing 14-2.

Listing 14-2:   The Bean Burrito Recipe Represented in XHTML

```
<html>
 <head>
  <title>Bean Burrito</title>
 </head>
 <body>
  <h1>Bean Burrito</h1>
   <h2>Ingredients</h2>
    <ul>
     <li>1 can refried beans</li>
     <li>1 cup longhorn colby cheese, shredded</li>
     <li>1 small onion, finely chopped</li>
     <li>3 flour tortillas</li>
    </ul>
   <h2>Cooking Instructions</h2>
    <ol>
     <li>Empty can of refried beans into medium saucepan.</li>
     <li>Heat over medium-high heat until beans are smooth and bubbly.</li>
     <li>Warm tortillas in microwave for 30 seconds.</li>
    </ol>
   <h2>Serving Instructions</h2>
    <ol>
     <li>Spread 1/3 of warm beans on each tortilla.</li>
     <li>Sprinkle with cheese and onions.</li>
     <li>Roll tortillas and serve.</li>
    </ol>
  </body>
</html>
```

Simple and to the point, Figure 14-3 shows what this XHTML looks like displayed in a Web browser.

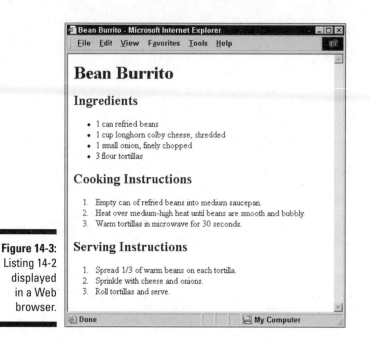

Figure 14-3:
Listing 14-2
displayed
in a Web
browser.

An XSL style sheet for converting XML to XHTML

A fairly simple XSLT style sheet manages the conversion of the bean burrito recipe from XML to XHTML, as shown in Listing 14-3.

For the sake of simplicity, we wrote this XSLT style sheet for a document that contains one recipe only. There's nothing that says the style sheet couldn't be modified to loop through several recipes in a single document — we just stuck with one to make the whole thing easier to digest.

Listing 14-3:   A Style Sheet Used to Convert the Bean Burrito Recipe

```
<xsl:stylesheet version="2.0"
 xmlns:xsl="http://www.w3.org/1999/XSL/Transform"
 xmlns="http://www.w3.org/TR/xhtml1/strict">
<xsl:output
     method="xml"
     encoding="iso-8859-1"/>
<xsl:template match="Recipes">
 <html>
  <head>
   <title>
```

```
    My Favorite Recipes
  </title>
  </head>


  <body>
  <xsl:apply-templates/>
  </body>
  </html>
</xsl:template>
<xsl:template match="Recipes/Recipe/Title">
 <h1>
  <xsl:apply-templates/>
 </h1>
</xsl:template>
<xsl:template match="Recipes/Recipe/Ingredients">
 <h2>Ingredients</h2>
 <ul>
   <xsl:for-each select="Item">
    <li>
     <xsl:apply-templates/>
    </li>
   </xsl:for-each>
  </ul>
</xsl:template>
<xsl:template match="Recipes/Recipe/CookingInstructions">
 <h2>Cooking Instructions</h2>
 <ol>
   <xsl:for-each select="Cinst">
    <li>
     <xsl:apply-templates/>
    </li>
   </xsl:for-each>
  </ol>
</xsl:template>
<xsl:template match="Recipes/Recipe/ServingInstructions">
 <h2>Serving Instructions</h2>
 <ol>
   <xsl:for-each select="Sinst">
    <li>
     <xsl:apply-templates/>
    </li>
   </xsl:for-each>
  </ol>
</xsl:template>
</xsl:stylesheet>
```

In a nutshell, this style sheet specifies how each element in RML should be
changed to XHTML. Each style rule identifies one element from RML and provides instructions on how to convert it to a similar or equivalent XHTML element or set of elements. We discuss how the style sheet does this in more
detail in the "Creating and Using Templates" section.

When style takes a name, it's not in vain

Looking at the XSLT style sheet that converts our bean burrito recipe from XML to XHTML in Listing 14-3, you probably noticed that it does indeed look like a good ol' XML document — elements and all. You probably also noticed a strange addition to each and every element — `xsl:`. The `template` element in this style sheet is expressed as `xsl:template`. So what's that all about?

The use of the `xsl:` identifier is part of an addition to XML called namespaces. A *namespace* is a unique identifier that links an XML markup element to a specific DTD or schema. So the `xsl:` portion of `xsl:template` indicates that the template element is defined by the XSL specification.

Namespaces prevent conflicts in markup by identifying which DTD or schema an element comes from. Before you can use a namespace marker such as `xsl:` or `xhtml:` — or `rml:` — you have to identify it, like this:

```
<html:ul
    xmlns:html="http://www.w3.o
    rg/TR/REC-html40">
<html:li>List item</html:li>
```

```
<html:li>List item</html:li>
</html:ul>
```

In this example, the DTD the namespace references is the DTD for the HTML 4.0 specification. The `xmlns` attribute, which stands for XML namespace, indicates that the element (`ul` in this case) belongs to a namespace other than the one that belongs to the current DTD. The value for `xmlns` — `http://www.w3.org/TR/REC-html40` — points to the DTD that defines the namespace.

If you want to know more about namespaces, check out the XML Namespaces recommendation at

www.w3.org/TR/REC-xml-names

and check out Chapter 17, which describes them in depth.

In addition, James Clark, the developer of one of the more popular XML parsers, provides a good explanation of how namespaces work and why you might want to use them to put together a Web page. Check out

www.jclark.com/xml/xmlns.htm

Creating and Using Templates

In this section, we break an XSLT style sheet into its component parts to see what makes it go. XSLT is a robust conversion tool and has many facets. We don't attempt to describe them all here. Instead, we focus on the most basic structures that make up an XSLT style sheet.

The instructions in an XSLT style sheet that control how an element and its content should be converted are called templates. A *template* identifies which element in a document should be changed and then specifies how the element should be changed. The template element is `xsl:template`.

Looking back at the XSLT style sheet in Listing 14-3, notice that it's comprised of a series of template elements, shown in Listing 14-4.

Listing 14-4:   A Close-up of Template Elements

```
<xsl:template match="Recipes">
 <html>
  <head>
   <title>
    My Favorite Recipes
   </title>
  </head>
. . .
</xsl:template>
```

Using patterns

A template in an XSLT style sheet focuses on a single element in a document. To identify the element to which the template applies, XSLT uses the `match` attribute with the `xsl:template` element to point to a specific element. The value of `match` is called a *pattern*. The XSLT processor looks at the pattern, works its way through the source document to find the pattern, and applies the template to every element that matches the pattern. In Listing 14-4, the pattern to match is the `Recipes` element.

In the following slightly more complex example, the pattern to match is any instance of the `Title` element found nested in the `Recipe` element:

```
<xsl:template match="Recipes/Recipe/Title">
 <h1>
  <xsl:apply-templates/>
 </h1>
</xsl:template>
```

Using instructions to get results

In addition to using a pattern to identify which element in the source document to transform, the template also specifies how to transform the element itself. These transformation instructions guide the XSLT processor through content transformation. As shown in Listing 14-5, this template looks for the `Recipes` element and creates a standard XHTML document structure — with a title that reads *My Favorite Recipes* attached for good measure.

Listing 14-5:   My Favorite Recipes

```
<xsl:template match="Recipes">
 <html>
  <head>
   <title>
    My Favorite Recipes
   </title>
  </head>
```

(continued)

Listing 14-5 *(continued)*

```
  <body>
   <xsl:apply-templates/>
   </body>
 </html>
</xsl:template>
```

Processing element content

When you create a template for an element, you also have to think about how you want all its child elements treated. If you have other templates you want applied to the children of an element, you need to include an `xsl:apply-templates` element within your template. In the following example, because the `Title` element doesn't have any other content that matches any template patterns in the style sheet, the XSLT processor simply moves the content within `<Title>. . .</Title>` as-is from the source document to the results document, which locates this XML:

```
<xsl:template match="Recipes/Recipe/Title">
 <h1>
  <xsl:apply-templates/>
 </h1>
</xsl:template>
```

The template specifies that the XML should be transformed to

```
  <h1>Bean Burrito</h1>
```

You see the `xsl:apply-templates` element used frequently in XSLT style sheets.

The `apply-templates` element doesn't always move text from one document to another. In many cases, there are other templates to apply to the content of an element. Look at the first template in our sample XSLT style sheet (refer to Listing 14-5).

This template looks for the recipe's document element (`Recipes`) and replaces it with the basic building blocks of an XHTML document (`html`, `head`, `title`, and `body`). Notice the `xsl:apply-templates` element within the `body` element. The placement of the `apply-templates` element here tells the XSLT processor to apply all the remaining style sheet templates to all the content within the `Recipes` element — that's the rest of the recipe — and places the results within the `body` tags of the resulting document.

So when you create style rules, you have to think not only about how you're transforming an individual element, but also about how you're dealing with its content. Does the content from the source document need its own transforming? Does it need to be nested in a particular set of markup in the new document? Or do you even want to transform the content at all? If you don't specify `xsl:apply-templates`, the results document won't include any of the content from within an element — text, markup, or otherwise.

Dealing with Repeating Elements

A single list might have 50 items, and you want each of those items to be transformed the same way. You can write a template that loops through each item and applies the same transformation to each instance of the element, as in the following style rule:

```
<xsl:template match="Recipes/Recipe/Ingredients">
 <h2>Ingredients</h2>
 <ul>
  <xsl:for-each select="Item">
   <li>
    <xsl:apply-templates/>
   </li>
</xsl:for-each>
  </ul>
</xsl:template>
```

The `xsl:for-each` element points at a specific element that is repeated and applies the same transformation to each instance of that element. In this template, every `Item` element nested within `<Recipes><Recipe>` `<Ingredients>` . . . `</Ingredients></Recipe></Recipes>` is changed to an XHTML list item (`li`) within an unordered list (`ul`). The style rule points to this portion of the recipe:

```
<Ingredients>
 <Item>1 can refried beans</Item>
 <Item>1 cup longhorn colby cheese, shredded</Item>
 <Item>1 small onion, finely chopped</Item>
 <Item>3 flour tortillas</Item>
</Ingredients>
```

The transformation to XHTML looks like this:

```
<h2>Ingredients</h2>
 <ul>
  <li>1 can refried beans</li>
  <li>1 cup longhorn colby cheese, shredded</li>
  <li>1 small onion, finely chopped</li>
  <li>3 flour tortillas</li>
 </ul>
```

The XSLT elements we discuss are only a few of the XSL elements that you can use to transform an XML document from one DTD to another. You can sort through elements, point to attribute values, create attributes, and assign attributes values in the results document — and that's only the beginning.

To take total advantage of XSLT, you need to be familiar with the XSLT 2.0 recommendation, which you can find at `www.w3.org/TR/xslt20`.

Using a Different Approach: Abbreviated Syntax

You can create XSLT style rules for transforming documents in multiple ways. You can write a separate style sheet, or you can use the XSLT abbreviated syntax and build the conversion style rules right into the results document, as shown in Listing 14-6.

Listing 14-6:   Building Conversion Rules into the Results Document

```
<html xsl:version="2.0"
      xmlns:xsl="http://www.w3.org/1999/XSL/Transform"
      lang="en">
 <head>
  <title>
   My Favorite Recipes
  </title>
 </head>
 <body>
  <h1>
   <xsl:value-of select="Recipes/Recipe/Title"/>
  </h1>
  <h2>Ingredients</h2>
   <ul>
    <xsl:for-each select="Recipes/Recipe/Ingredients/Item">
    <li>
     <xsl:value-of select=" /"/>
    </li>
    </xsl:for-each>
   </ul>
  <h2>Cooking Instructions</h2>
   <ol>
    <xsl:for-each select="Recipes/Recipe/CookingInstructions/Cinst">
    <li>
     <xsl:value-of select=" /"/>
    </li>
    </xsl:for-each>
   </ol>
   <ol>
    <xsl:for-each select="Recipes/Recipe/ServingInstructions/Sinst">
    <li>
     <xsl:value-of select=" /"/>
    </li>
    </xsl:for-each>
   </ol>
 </body>
</html>
```

This XHTML document with XSLT style rules built in (let's hear it for namespaces) converts our recipe using techniques similar to those we used to create the series of templates. Instead of creating a template that converts the `Title` element to a paragraph with a first-level heading attached, this document simply extracts the title content and places it between the first-level tags already in place in the document.

In some ways, this method is much easier than creating an entire set of templates for converting a document from one DTD to the other. The downside to this method is that you can't process the content of an element as you can with the `xsl:apply-templates` element in an XSLT style sheet.

When you use this method, you also *hard-code* the results document (enter the markup into the document by hand instead of using a program to dynamically generate it). That means that if someday you want to change the results document, you must change the hard coded markup. That's not a big deal if you only have one document to convert, but what if you have 500?

Introducing XSL-FO

Earlier in this chapter, we show XSLT at work: You create XSLT documents (which are really XML documents) to convert all your XML content to one set of markup. XSL-FO works the same way, except the markup you're converting your original XML content into is defined by the XSL-FO recommendation.

As you might imagine, the key to working with XSL-FO is becoming familiar with the elements and attributes of the XSL-FO specification. We expect that entire books will be devoted to the subject, so we don't try to give you an in-depth discussion here, but give you just enough information to be dangerous — and motivated to find out more.

Getting comfortable with formatting objects

As XSL-FO's name indicates, formatting objects are the key to making your XML ready for display. Before you jump right into mastering the syntax of XSL-FO, it helps if you understand what the different formatting objects are and what you use each one for.

If you're familiar with CSS2 and CSS3, many of these formatting objects will be very familiar, as will the general concepts of formatting. Also, if you're new to formatting objects and are dismayed at the scarce resources for learning XSL-FO, look for a good advanced CSS2 or CSS3 tutorial like the one at `http://glish.com/css/`. Although CSS2 isn't exactly like XSL-FO (or we wouldn't need both), they both make extensive use of formatting objects.

The different XSL-FO formatting objects are organized into these eight categories:

- **Declaration, Pagination,** and **Layout** formatting objects include all the things you need to set up the basic layout of a document, including pages, master pages, and a title.

- **Block** formatting objects create paragraphs, blockquotes, and other document building blocks.

- **Inline** formatting objects to apply styles such as boldface, italics, color specifics, and more to individual characters or strings inside of a block.

- **Table** formatting objects to create and control tables.

- **List** formatting objects create and control lists of all kinds.

- **Links and Multi** formatting objects handle and style links and multi-media components.

- **Out-of-line** formatting objects create and style floating areas and footnotes.

- **Other** formatting objects are catch-alls for the objects that don't fit in other categories.

Every formatting object has properties that can be applied to it. For example, the object that creates a table (`fo:table`) can take properties that specify how thick its borders are, what color they are, and so on. With properties, you can control just about every aspect of a particular object.

Not every property works with every object. Part of learning the ins and outs of XSL-FO is figuring out which objects and properties you can use together to describe a particular layout.

Formatting objects and the bean burrito recipe

Even if you don't know much more about XSL-FO than this, you can guess which formatting objects we may want to use to describe the content in the bean burrito RML document:

- A **pagination** formatting object can specify a recipe should always start on a new page. The properties for these objects may specify the new page's margins, background color, and default fonts for text as well as the font size and color. We may also want a title object to set the title for the document and the different recipes in the document (if there's more than one recipe in the document).

✔ Several **block** formatting objects can create the section titles in the recipe: Ingredients, Cooking Instructions, and Serving Instructions. The properties for these objects might include font size and color, margins, and the amount of space before and after the heading.

✔ **List** formatting objects for the different lists (ingredients, cooking instructions, and serving instructions) in the recipe. The properties for these objects may specify the kind of bullets or numbers to use for each list, as well as margin information.

✔ **Inline** formatting objects can style specific characters or strings in the document — to make the ingredient names or cooking techniques appear in italics, for example.

Imaging a skeleton of the bean burrito document with the formatting objects in place (leaving out the content), and you can begin to see how the formatting objects work together to drive the display of a page. Figure 14-4 illustrates this.

Figure 14-4:
An illustration of the formatting objects we might use to describe the bean burrito recipe.

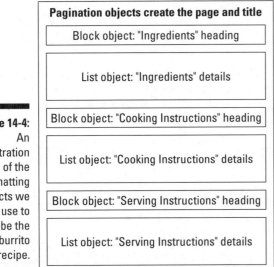

Pagination objects create the page and title

Block object: "Ingredients" heading

List object: "Ingredients" details

Block object: "Cooking Instructions" heading

List object: "Cooking Instructions" details

Block object: "Serving Instructions" heading

List object: "Serving Instructions" details

Understanding XSL-FO Syntax

XSL-FO documents are created by applying XSLT style sheets to XML documents, so the style templates you're about to see look suspiciously like those shown previously in this chapter.

The document for an XSL-FO style sheet is the same as any other XSL style sheet:

```
<?xml version="1.0" encoding="utf-8"?>
<xsl:stylesheet
    xmlns:xsl="http://www.w3.org/1999/XSL/Transform"
    xmlns:fo="http://www.w3.org/1999/XSL/Format">
. . .
</xsl:stylesheet>
```

A particular DTD's namespace isn't based on when a recommendation was created for it, but rather when the namespace was assigned. The xsl and fo namespaces were assigned to the W3C in 1999, which is reflected in the namespace declaration.

Thinking back to the bean burrito recipe and the general way we might want to display recipes on a Web site or even in print, we can use this style rule to add a page break before each recipe:

```
<xsl:template match="Recipes/Recipe">
 <fo:block break-before="page">
  <xsl:apply-templates/>
 </fo:block>
</xsl:template>
```

The following template uses the block formatting object and a set of properties to create a heading for the list of ingredients and to specify that the heading should be displayed in a 14 point Arial font with a space before of 18 points and a space after of 9 points.

```
<xsl:template match="Recipes/Recipe/Ingredients">
 <fo:block text-align="left" space-after="9pt"
          space-before="18pt" font-size="14pt"
          font-family="Arial">
 <xsl:apply-templates/>
 </fo:block>
</xsl:template>
```

Because the ingredients list has list items under it that need to have list formatting objects created for them, we include <xsl:apply-templates> element so the list items are processed.

Believe it or not, lists are right up there with tables in complexity in the XSL-FO syntax, simply because you have so much control over them: spacing between them, what markers to use, and more. For the details of lists, tables, all the other formatting objects, and the complete details on XSL-FO syntax, be sure to visit the XSL specification online at www.w3.org/TR/xsl/.

XSL-FO isn't intended just to specify how XML documents should display; it's also designed to make them easier for computers to read content aloud. The aural part of the XSL-FO specification focuses on how to make XML content accessible to everyone, including those who can't see the content.

Chapter 15

Processing XML

*P*rocessing XML means putting your document to work so that an application, regardless of its function, can do something with your XML document.

The key to the "something" that an application can do with your XML is the Document Object Model (DOM) — a breakdown of your XML document into a form an application can get at and work with. This chapter explains how applications use the DOM to work with the content in your XML documents.

To process your XML documents, you need an XML processor. An *XML processor* sucks in XML text files — along with any style sheets — and makes their structure and content available in a format that's useful to a programming language so that the XML document can be used in an application. In this chapter, we take an in-depth look at what's involved in processing XML, and we give you some insight into how a program can access and work with the data in an XML document.

Frankly My Dear, 1 Don't Give a DOM

A *Document Object Model (DOM)* is a programming interface that allows other programs and programming languages to access and update the content, structure, and style of XML documents in a standard way. The DOM does this by using a standard syntax to describe a document as a series of objects. When an XML document is passed through an XML processor, the processor creates a DOM for that document. Programming languages, such as JavaScript, VBScript,

C++, and Java, can access the DOM, reach out and grab a particular object, and manipulate it. We take a different view of the bean burrito recipe to show its DOM.

To really understand what a DOM is, you need to get a mental picture of how XML documents actually work with the DOM. This Zen approach to understanding may be a little, um Zenlike (After all, how can you know how a DOM works without knowing what it is?), but trust us on this one. You'll feel much more balanced. Keep in mind that although there's a sense of hierarchy to how a DOM works, you shouldn't confuse it with the hierarchy of a filing system (such as Windows Explorer or another filing cabinet application) because the DOM is *not* a filing system or data-storage hierarchy. It's a programming hierarchy and a method for exposing data for manipulation.

Throughout this book, we use an example bean burrito recipe described with the Recipe Markup Language (RML). In case you've managed to avoid it, you can check it out in Listing 15-1.

Listing 15-1:   The Famous Bean Burrito Recipe

```
<?xml version="1.0"?>
<Recipes>
 <Recipe cook="The XML Gourmet">
  <Title>Bean Burrito</Title>
  <Category name="tex-mex"/>
  <Ingredients>
   <Item>1 can refried beans</Item>
   <Item>1 cup longhorn colby cheese, shredded</Item>
   <Item>1 small onion, finely chopped</Item>
   <Item>3 flour tortillas</Item>
  </Ingredients>
  <CookingInstructions>
   <Cinst>Empty can of refried beans into medium saucepan.</Cinst>
   <Cinst>Heat over medium-high heat until beans are smooth and bubbly.</Cinst>
   <Cinst>Warm tortillas in microwave for 30 seconds.</Cinst>
  </CookingInstructions>
  <ServingInstructions>
   <Sinst>Spread 1/3 of warm beans on each tortilla.</Sinst>
   <Sinst>Sprinkle with cheese and onions.</Sinst>
   <Sinst>Roll tortillas and serve.</Sinst>
  </ServingInstructions>
 </Recipe>
</Recipes>
```

You can describe this document as a series of elements and their content. You can also describe the document as a series of objects — each element in the document is an individual object. The following piece of the recipe includes five different objects:

```
<Ingredients>
 <Item>1 can refried beans</Item>
 <Item>1 cup longhorn colby cheese, shredded </Item>
 <Item>1 small onion, finely chopped</Item>
 <Item>3 flour tortillas</Item>
</Ingredients>
```

The five objects are:

- ✔ The `Ingredients` element
- ✔ The `Item` element that contains the content "1 can refried beans"
- ✔ The `Item` element that contains the content "1 cup longhorn colby cheese, shredded"
- ✔ The `Item` element that contains the content "1 small onion, finely chopped"
- ✔ The `Item` element that contains the content "3 flour tortillas"

Even though the individual `Item` elements use the same markup tags, they're all individual objects in the document.

All of these individual objects are part of the DOM for the bean burrito recipe document. In addition to identifying each element in an XML document as an individual object, a DOM also shows how each element relates to the others hierarchically. In fact, the DOM identifies each unique object in a document based on its position in the document's hierarchy.

As in any hierarchy, the DOM consists of a fairly complex system of relationships that must be adhered to. We introduce these relationships in Chapter 7. See "Keeping in touch with the family" (the section coming up) to get a better picture of siblings, parents, and the rest of the gang.

A *processor* is an application that makes your documents do something. XML processors create a DOM each time they process an XML document so that the programming code can get and work with the content in the document. Figure 15-1 illustrates how the DOM for the bean burrito recipe might look to an XML processor. See "What Goes In Must Come Out: Processing XML" for more information about how processing works.

Keeping in touch with the family

To understand how the DOM works and how applications use programming commands to access individual objects in a document, you need to have a good grasp of how the document's elements relate to each other. The terms *parent, child,* and *sibling* are all used to describe element relationships. These relationships have to do with how the elements are nested: For example, in the following bit of the bean burrito recipe, the `Title` and `Category` elements are nested within (and children of) the `Recipe` element:

```
<Recipes>
 <Recipe cook="XML Gourmet">
  <Title>Bean Burrito</Title>
  <Category name="tex-mex"/>
. . .
 </Recipe>
</Recipes>
```

Title and Category are also siblings of each other, and Recipe is their parent. The concept of parents and siblings doesn't extend past one level of nesting in this collection of objects. The Recipe element is considered the child of Recipes but Title isn't called a grandchild of Recipes, just the child of Recipe.

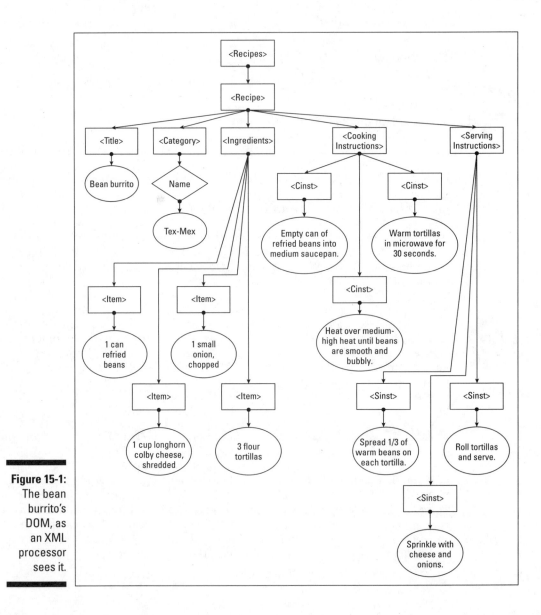

Figure 15-1:
The bean burrito's DOM, as an XML processor sees it.

Finding your way through the forest

The following discussion of trees and nodes is a bit on the techie side (it can't be helped). If you don't plan to program an application that reads and processes XML documents, you can probably live the remainder of your life happily without knowing the first thing about trees and nodes. However, many XML resources — especially the more technical ones — tend to assume that you at least understand the basics of trees and nodes. So, although you can skip this section if you're not planning on programming applications for XML, you might want to revisit it later as you encounter more technical XML resources.

A *tree* is a diagram of an XML document's structure that shows the order of elements and illustrates the relationships between elements, in exactly the same way that a family tree illustrates genealogy. A tree is a visual representation of

the DOM. If you refer to Figure 15-1, you can see the tree (an upside down tree, but a tree none the less). The tree's root is the `Recipes` element. The `Recipe` element is a branch under the `Recipes` element and all the other elements are children of the `Recipe` element.

The `Ingredients`, `CookingInstructions`, and `ServingInstructions` elements each branch out one step further with the `Item`, `Cinst`, and `Sinst` children, respectively. Also notice that the tree includes things other than the elements in the document, such as attributes and element content. The objects included in a DOM are more than just the elements and are called *nodes* when displayed on the DOM tree. Think of nodes as the tree's leaves. We use the terms parents, children, and siblings to talk about the way all the branches and leaves relate to one another.

Understanding DOM structure

Ultimately this whole discussion comes down to a common terminology that explains how this relates to that. If you take the family metaphor to the extreme, elements would have grandchildren, second and third cousins, and so on. We stick with simple parent, child, and sibling relationships for discussion so that you don't have to trudge through a tangle of elements to figure out complex relationships. Besides, those relationships are all you'll usually need to understand for your own XML documents.

Because the bean burrito recipe is such a simple document, we can't use it to illustrate all the parts a DOM tree can include. For that, you need to turn to Figure 15-2.

A *tree* is the visual representation of the DOM structure, and a *node* is like a leaf dangling from one of a tree's branches. See the sidebar "Finding your way through the forest" for a more detailed discussion of what nodes and trees are.

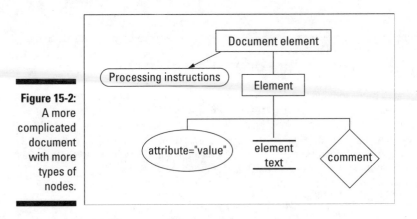

Figure 15-2:
A more
complicated
document
with more
types of
nodes.

Each of the nodes you see in Figure 15-2 represents a type of node that a DOM's tree can include. If you're familiar with basic XML structures, you probably recognize the majority of node types because they're common XML elements. The ones in our bean burrito recipe are

- ✔ **The document's root element:** `Recipes`
- ✔ **Elements:** `Recipe`, `Title`, `Category`, `Ingredients`, `Item`, `CookingInstructions`, `Cinst`, `ServingInstructions`, and `Sinst`
- ✔ **Text:** `Title`, `Item`, `Cinst`, and `Sinst`
- ✔ **Attributes:** `name`
- ✔ **Attribute values:** `tex-mex`

Node types that aren't included in the bean burrito recipe, but are discussed in other chapters of the book, are

- ✔ **Namespaces** (Chapters 14 and 17)
- ✔ **Processing instructions** (Chapter 6)
- ✔ **Comments** (Chapter 6)

As you can see, there's not much in any given XML document that you can't access using the DOM. Not surprisingly, that's what the members of the W3C had in mind when they created the DOM specification.

Introducing XSL-FO and XSLT

The reality is that today XSL-FO (eXtensible Stylesheet Language Formatting Objects) is a long ways away from creating real-world solutions because most of the world uses a 4.0 or 5.0 browser, not a 6.0 browser. That means that HTML is still the standard for Web page display.

We cover transforming documents with XSL-FO and XSLT in more depth in Chapter 14, but here's a taste of how DOMs work with these technologies

✔ **Using DOM and style sheets:** XSL-FO and XSLT style sheets are really just XML documents. When an application uses a style sheet, it processes the style sheet like any other XML document. The only difference is that the application applies the style sheet to the XML document. Both the style sheet and the XML document have their own DOMs, and the final transformation or display guided by the style sheet takes information in both DOMs into account.

✔ **Web browsers and the DOM:** A good example of an application that uses XSLT style sheets and the DOM to process XML documents is a Web browser — Internet Explorer in particular. To display XML documents in Internet Explorer as something other than a list of elements, attributes, and content, you actually have to apply an XSLT style sheet to the XML document for conversion to HTML, XHTML, or an XSL-FO style sheet for display in the browser (versions 6.0 and later). For example, when a browser displays content using an XSL-FO style sheet, the browser accesses the DOM that's created when the Internet Explorer processor, Microsoft XML (MSXML), reads and processes both the XML document and the related XSL-FO style sheet, and uses the two together to drive the final display of the document content.

Before you can use the DOM, XSLT, XSL-FO, and XML to do interesting things in Web pages, you must have a solid understanding of not only XML and its related technologies, but also a scripting language. The Microsoft Developer Network Web site has extensive resources that provide detailed instructions for converting XML documents to HTML using the DOM and scripting languages. Visit
`http://msdn.microsoft.com/library/default.asp?url=/library/en-us/xmlsdk/htm/xsl_intro_7yw5.asp`.

The DOM recommendation

As you might have guessed, the way a DOM is laid out adheres to a specific syntax, and that syntax is defined in a W3C recommendation. To find out all there is to know about the DOM 1.0 recommendation, visit `www.w3.org/DOM`.

Note that the DOM Level 2 is a recommendation. The DOM Level 2 adds more features without adding lots of detail. The DOM Level 3 was issued as a working draft in January 2002, so it may be 2003 before it's actually a recommendation. As always, keep your eye on the W3C Web site to keep up with the latest versions of all specifications.

The DOM recommendation is divided into two different parts: Core DOM and HTML DOM. The Core portion of the recommendation specifies how to create DOMs for XML documents. The HTML portion specifies — yep, you guessed it — how to create DOMs for HTML documents. When you look for and study DOM references, be sure to identify which portion of the DOM the reference covers.

What Goes In Must Come Out: Processing XML

In Chapters 13 and 14, we look closely at what you have to do to make your XML do something for you. XML DTDs, schemas, and documents are almost always part of a larger solution, such as the XML solution used by an online loan refinancing system or by a recipe repository. Style sheets can be important tools, both for the transformation of data from one set of markup to another and to drive the display of data in an XML document.

For all the different pieces in a solution to work together, you need programming code of some kind, and that programming code needs a way to access the content you've described with XML and any style sheets you've written to go with it. Enter the XML processor. A processor takes the code and makes it do something. A processor may be part of a simple Web browser, such as Internet Explorer or Mozilla, or it can be another kind of program, such as a utility that takes in an XML document and populates an Oracle database.

The DOM and XML processors go hand in hand. The processor creates the DOM; without the DOM, you can't use programming code to get your XML content and do something with it. All things considered, the XML processor is a really, really important tool in your XML arsenal.

All Web browsers have HTML processors built into them, and those that can work with XML also have XML processors built into them. Because a browser is really designed for display, when you view an XML document in a browser, the browser uses the information the processor feeds it to drive the display of your document.

If you create a style sheet in either XSL or CSS, an XML-enabled browser can also open and process that style sheet. It then uses the processed XML and processed style sheet to present a final display. The browser is programmed to look for information provided by the processed document and do something with it.

Although we use a display-driven solution (to display XML documents in a browser) as an example, remember that display is just *one* use for XML. All XML solutions have processors involved in them; the programming code behind the solution's XML processor just does something different — whatever the solution calls for — with the processed XML. For example, if the solution takes data from a document and plugs it into a database, the document is processed, and then the processor uses the processed data to insert the document's content into the database.

Many different processors are available for you to choose from. This is a Good Thing because it means you don't have to write your own processor; you can use one that someone else wrote. You probably don't want to pick the first processor you trip over on a Web page — it helps to know a little bit about your processor options so that you can find the processor that's right for you.

Although the job of every XML processor is approximately the same — to expose the structure and content of the document to a program for manipulation — processors are written in a variety of languages. Processors may also be validating or non-validating (more about these in just a bit). Throughout the rest of this section, we take a look at different kinds of processors and give you the information you need to find the processor that best meets your requirements.

We use the terms *processor* and *processing* in our discussions of making your XML do something useful. You often see the words *parser* and *parsing* used in the same context. An XML parser and processor are really the same thing — a tool you use to make your XML content and structure available to programming code for manipulation. We stick with processor. As you check out other sources of information, keep in mind that parsers and processors do the same thing.

So many processors, so little time

Browse the XML Parsers/Processors section of xmlsoftware.com (www.xml software.com/parsers), and you see more than two dozen processors listed (and this isn't even a complete listing, just a good start). So what makes all these processors different from one another? Each processor has four distinct characteristics:

- ✔ **The programming language it was written in:** For each of the many different programming languages, there's at least one processor. Each language needs its own processor because the processor has to be programmed to work seamlessly with that language and to run on the same system as the code written in that language. For example, if you're creating a C++ application, it doesn't make sense to use a processor written in Java. You would waste a lot of time trying to get the two to communicate, when you can get a C++ processor that's designed to play nice with your C++ code.

- ✔ **Whether or not it validates documents:** A key difference among processors is whether they validate your XML documents. Every XML document needs to be well formed, and if it isn't, any processor (validating or not) spits it (or an error message) right back at you. No DOM, no content, no nothing. On the other hand, some processors also validate your documents against a DTD or schema. Invalid documents are spit out just like malformed ones.

The benefit of a validating processor is that you know the data coming into your system adheres to a DTD or schema, so you can be sure that you get the data you need for the system to work properly. The downside to a validating processor is that it takes longer to process the XML document because the document must first be checked for well-formedness and then for validity. In the next section, we talk a little more about whether you need a validating processor.

✔ **The version of the different specifications (DTD, schema, and so on) that it supports:** For example, most processors support XML 1.0 DTDs, but many don't support XML Schemas yet. When you read the description of a processor, be sure that it supports the standards you're using.

✔ **If it was written to accompany a particular software or database application:** Some processors are built specifically to work with different applications or databases. MSXML is the processor built by Microsoft for Microsoft solutions. Oracle has a collection of processors out, written in different programming languages, specifically designed to work with Oracle database applications. Processors built specifically for different applications or databases usually have utilities or functionality designed to work with that application or database.

Which processor is right for you?

When you're tying to pick a processor, you should ask yourself the following questions to help narrow your search:

✔ **What programming language is the rest of your solution using?**

Generally, you want to go with a processor that's written in the same language.

✔ **Do your documents need to be validated during processing?**

If you created a solution that revolves around a particular DTD or schema, you want valid documents coming into that system. You don't necessarily have to validate during processing though. If you control the document creation process, you can set up standards for valid documents. If you don't control that process (data is submitted via a Web page or from someone else's system, for example), you may want to think about validating during processing. You can do some testing to find out which is the greater tradeoff: the slower processing time you get with a validating processor, or the number of errors you have to handle when invalid data gets into your system.

✔ **Which XML versions and standards are you using?**

If you're using schemas, be sure that your processor supports them. Usually, you want the most up-to-date processor you can lay your hands on.

✔ **Does the application framework or database you're using have a processor?**

If you're working with an Oracle database, it pays to look into the Oracle processor. If you're working with any of Microsoft's products, look into MSXML. Read the documentation for your database or application and find out what kind of processor it offers. Be sure the processor meets your other criteria: proper programming language support, validating if necessary, and proper standards support.

The best person to help you pick out your processor is probably an experienced programmer who can help you answer the preceding questions. Good programmers have worked with XML, know the pitfalls of the various processors for each language, and can help you work through validation issues.

Chapter 16

Viewing XML on the Web

· ·

· ·

Most of the cool things you can do with XML don't involve the Web. But many of you *do* want to use XML to contribute to or to drive a Web-based solution, so that's what this chapter is all about.

In previous chapters, you find out how you can use XSLT to convert XML to XHTML for display on the Web. You also examine the future of XML styling, XSL-FO, which gives you an XML-based way to drive the display of a document without converting it into XHTML first. Another option is somewhere in between: Using XML and Cascading Style Sheets (CSS) to put your documents on the Web.

CSS is a topic too big to cover thoroughly in this book — we leave that to *Cascading Style Sheets For Dummies,* by Damon Dean, published by Hungry Minds, Inc.

Not Letting the Realities of the Web Intrude: CSS

Although XML is a great tool for storing data for all kinds of stuff, it's not completely Web-compatible yet. But because the Web is hot, hot, hot, content developers — like you — want to deliver their data through the Web. So if you want to transmit XML through the Web, CSS provides a mechanism to display XML documents directly.

If you want to see how a simple CSS document can affect the look and feel of a Web page, visit the W3C's CSS page, at `www.w3.org/Style/css`, also shown in Figure 16-1. Notice how the text overlaps at the top of the page and how whole chunks of text are indented beneath headings. What you see is a good style sheet at work, not a trick made possible by convoluted XHTML. In the end, a good style sheet is a lot easier to build (after you get the hang of the underlying markup conventions) because it's designed to drive complex displays. You will be using the right tool for the right job.

CSS is really, really easy to use — even if you're building style sheets from scratch. This is a huge plus when you're trying to get a solution of any kind up and running quickly. We don't dispute that XSLT is more powerful than CSS and robust enough to support many uses for XML. But XSLT is more work and may be overkill in some simple situations.

Using CSS to style your XML documents only works with Netscape 5.0 and later and Internet Explorer 5.0 and later. Results on Windows are better than those on a Mac, so you need to test your pages carefully before you put them out there for the world to see.

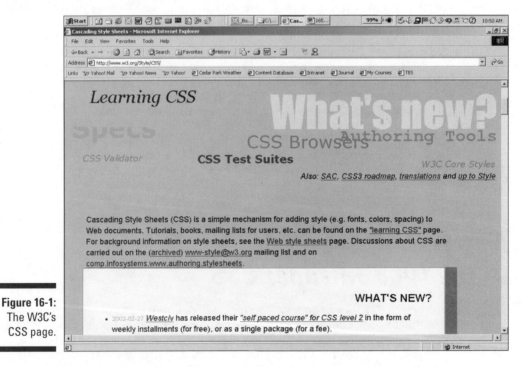

Figure 16-1:
The W3C's
CSS page.

That said, you may be wondering why you'd use this approach at all. Wouldn't plain ol' XHTML be better? If you know for sure that people will access your site with everything from a 2.0 browser to a beta version of the newest Microsoft browser, the answer is probably yes. However, if you're working on an "experimental" part of your site, or you know for sure that the browsers people are using to access your site are XML and CSS compliant (an intranet is a good example), then go for it. Given that rationale, the following sections explain why CSS may be worth using anyway.

We like CSS because it's human-readable and uses a simple but flexible syntax. To understand CSS, you only need to remember this magic formula:

```
selector {property: value}
```

Tasting Cascading Style Sheets Flavors

To use CSS with XML (or XHTML), you need to know a bit about how to create CSS style sheets. To start, CSS is simply a set of rules that you use to create style sheets that Web browsers know how to work with. CSS documents are just plain text, so you don't have to buy special software to use them or do something special to your browser to make it work with them. All you need to do to use CSS is to learn its syntax.

CSS1: The original master of Web style

Cascading Style Sheets 1 (CSS1) was the first version of CSS developed for use with HTML. Support for CSS1 in Web browsers was limited to Internet Explorer 3.0 and Netscape Navigator 4.0.

Now, however, the newest versions of the big browsers (namely, Internet Explorer 6.0 and Netscape Navigator 6.0) support all elements in CSS1. Can we hear a big *woo hoo?* CSS1 deserves a cheer; it took a long time for this support to happen.

With CSS1, you can control the format and display of

- Colors and backgrounds
- Fonts and text
- Spacing
- Element positioning and sizing
- Element visibility

As you find out in the next section, CSS1 has been supplanted by CSS2. However, most CSS style sheets that you see at work on the Web today use the CSS1 specification simply to make them backward compatible with older browsers.

CSS2: The current style master

Cascading Style Sheets 2 (CSS2) was published as a W3C recommendation in 1998. Unfortunately, developers and browser vendors have been slow to adopt CSS2, even though it provides more page layout controls. The latest big browsers support parts of the CSS2 specification, but not quite all of it. So you must use CSS2 markup with care (and test your work carefully on your target browsers).

Additions to CSS1 in CSS2 include the following:

- ✔ Support for specifying page breaks
- ✔ Tables
- ✔ Aural style sheets
- ✔ Support for system colors and fonts
- ✔ Counters and automatic numbering

Building a Style Sheet with CSS

In this section, you lift the hood on CSS and poke into some of the details involved in using CSS markup to create style sheets. Here, the primary focus is understanding and using CSS markup and understanding its capabilities and limitations.

Although a judicious mixture of XML and CSS creates a positive presentation, be aware that the combination may not always work the way you want or the way you think it should. You must also understand that not all Web browsers treat CSS definitions exactly the same, so experimentation and testing to achieve the right looks may be required.

You're probably wondering what the *C* in CSS is about. What does cascading mean in the context of a style sheet? *Cascading* refers to the capability to apply multiple style sheets to any document in a way that handles conflicting style definitions gracefully. Each CSS style sheet attached to any document carries a weight that identifies how important it is in the overall scheme of style. If one style sheet conflicts with another, the style sheet with the heavier weight — the one that's higher on the style sheet food chain — takes precedence.

For example, if an individual Web page implements CSS, three style sheets apply to it: The CSS style sheet that you created, the browser's built-in style sheet (if any), and the individual user's preference settings, such as font sizes, styles, and colors. These three style sheets cascade, or are applied to, the Web page in the following priority order:

1. User's preferences
2. Your style sheet
3. Browser's style sheet

If your style sheet indicates that the font size should be 10-point Times, but the user has set his or her preferences so that all text is displayed in 12-point Garamond, the user's style sheet wins. More often than not, your style sheets override a browser's default settings.

User preferences are uppermost in the hierarchy because they enable the visually impaired to be sure their user preferences trump any and all other style sheet settings.

The Basics of CSS

See Listing 16-1 to see an XML document that may be a familiar classic to you by now.

Listing 16-1: The Recipe XML Document

```
<?xml version="1.0"?>
<Recipes>
 <Recipe cook="The XML Gourmet">
  <Title>Bean Burrito</Title>
  <Category name="tex-mex" />
  <Ingredients>
   <Item>1 can refried beans</Item>
   <Item>1 cup longhorn colby cheese, shredded</Item>
   <Item>1 small onion, finely chopped</Item>
   <Item>3 flour tortillas</Item>
  </Ingredients>
  <CookingInstructions>
   <Cinst>Empty can of refried beans into medium saucepan.</Cinst>
   <Cinst>Heat over medium-high heat until beans are smooth and bubbly.</Cinst>
   <Cinst>Warm tortillas in microwave for 30 seconds.</Cinst>
  </CookingInstructions>
  <ServingInstructions>
   <Sinst>Spread 1/3 of warm beans on each tortilla.</Sinst>
   <Sinst>Sprinkle with cheese and onions.</Sinst>
   <Sinst>Roll tortillas and serve.</Sinst>
  </ServingInstructions>
 </Recipe>
</Recipes>
```

This recipe includes the following elements (we list our ideas on display as well so that you know what we're planning when we build the style sheet):

- ✔ Recipes holds everything in the document (much like the html element in an XHTML document). Its style rule should include margin information for the entire document as well as background color and base font information.

- ✔ Title should use colored text in a sans-serif font that's centered on the page and a bit larger than the text around it.

- ✔ Ingredients works with the Item element to create a bulleted list.

- ✔ CookingInstructions works with the Cinst element to make a numbered list.

- ✔ ServingInstructions works with the Sinst element to create a numbered list.

We could do quite a bit more with a style sheet to create an impressive layout and design, but that only adds more lines of markup to our examples. For demonstration purposes, simple is beautiful. Feel free to enhance and build on this style sheet, however, as you find out more about CSS.

A simple CSS style sheet for XML

Listing 16-2 shows a truly simple CSS style sheet for an XML recipe.

Listing 16-2: CSS Style Sheet for the XML Recipe

```
Recipes Recipe {font-family: serif;
                margin-top: 0.5in;
                margin-bottom: 0.5in;
                margin-left: 1.5in;
                margin-right: 1in;
                color: navy;
                background-color: white;
                display: block;
               }
Title {text-align: center;
       font-size: 120%;
       font-family: sans-serif;
       color: maroon;
       display: block;
      }
Ingredients Item {margin-left: 2in;
                  display: list-item;
                  list-style-type: circle;
                  color: black;
                  font-size: 12pt;
                 }
```

```
CookingInstructions, ServingInstructions
   {display: block;
    color: black;
    font-family: serif;
    font-size: 12pt;
   }
Cinst, Sinst {margin-left: 2in;
              display: list-item;
              list-style-type: decimal;
              color: black;
              font-size: 12pt;
              }
```

Dissecting a simple CSS style sheet

A style sheet is nothing more than a collection of style rules that governs the formatting of the various elements in an XML document. All style rules use the same syntax, so even if you've never seen a CSS style sheet, you can probably guess how to build a basic style rule.

The magic formula for building CSS style rules

All style rules in a CSS style sheet follow the same syntax — or magic formula if you prefer:

```
selector {declaration}
```

The *selector* identifies the element to which the style rule applies. The *declaration* holds all the specifics that the style rule applies to the selector.

We can even break this basic syntax down a bit further:

```
selector {property: value}
```

All declarations consist of *property*: *value* pairs. Some of the ones from our RML style sheet include

 ✔ {font-family: sans-serif} to display the Title element content using a sans-serif font, such as Arial or Geneva

 ✔ {margin-left: 1.5in} to set the left margin to 1.5 inches for element content

 ✔ {color: navy} to display element content in navy

All specific CSS properties — and the values they can take — are predefined in the CSS1 and CSS2 specifications. The hardest part of learning CSS is remembering specific property names and their values.

A quick note about another important CSS term: *inheritance*. When you set style rules (as we did for the `Recipes` and `Recipe` elements) and specify margins, background color, font, and text color, you don't have to set them again for every other document element. When you create a style rule for an element, any other elements it contains are also subject to that style rule. Cool, eh? Just put together a whole bunch of selectors and declarations and poof! — you have a style sheet.

In our example, the `Recipes` element is the document element and contains all other elements inside it, so the style rule is *inherited* by all other elements it contains.

Variations on the magic: Selector specifications

Not all the selectors in our truly simple style sheet look the same. What about space between `Recipes` and `Recipe` and `Ingredients` and `Item`? That extra space between the element names tells the application processing the style sheet to look for `Ingredients` and `Recipes` tags followed by `Item` and `Recipe` tags, respectively. If those tags don't appear in that specific order, the style rule doesn't apply to the `Item` or `Recipe` elements.

The example in the previous paragraph is just one of the many variations on the selector portion of the magic formula. You can link selectors to different elements based on attribute values, context, type, parent-child relationships, and a variety of other options.

The specifics of selectors are too detailed to discuss here, but they are covered brilliantly in the CSS1 specification at

```
www.w3.org/TR/REC-CSS1
```

and the CSS2 specification at

```
www.w3.org/TR/REC-CSS2
```

Efficiency is good: Combining selectors and declarations

What if you want to assign the same style rule to two different elements? You could retype the declaration or cut and paste it. But then, if you change one instance of that declaration, you must change it in each and every selector where that declaration appears. It's much easier to simply apply one declaration to several selectors. To do so, simply list all your selectors separated by commas, as in:

```
selector, selector . . . {declaration}
```

Our sample style sheet combines selectors this way in its last two style rules:

```
CookingInstructions, ServingInstructions
   {display: block;
    color: black;
    font-family: serif;
    font-size: 12pt;}
Cinst, Sinst {margin-left: 2in;
             display: list-item;
             list-style-type: decimal;
             color: black;
             font-size: 12pt;
             }
```

Along these same lines, you can also combine declarations in a style rule to include a collection of property/value combinations in a single selector. The syntax for this neat trick is to separate your *property: value* combinations with semicolons, as we did in most of our style rules, including this one:

```
Title {text-align: center;
       font-size: 120%;
       font-family: sans-serif;
       color: maroon;
       display: block;
       }
```

Punctuating CSS rules

Punctuation plays a large role when creating CSS style rules. If you accidentally use a colon instead of a semicolon to separate *property: value* pairs in a declaration, your style sheet will break. Table 16-1 provides a short, but helpful, guide to punctuating CSS properly.

Table 16-1		Punctuation in CSS
Character	*Name*	*What It Does*
	Space	Specifies that an element must appear after the other element for the rule to apply
,	Comma	Separates multiple selectors in a style rule
;	Semicolon	Separates multiple property/value combinations in a style rule
:	Colon	Separates a property and its value in a declaration

Linking CSS to XML

So you've built some style sheets and now you want to use them with XML. This process is pretty easy, but the method varies between XML and XHTML.

To reference a CSS style sheet in an XML document, use a processing instruction that takes this format:

```
<?xml-stylesheet href="url" type="text/css"?>
```

Listings 16-1 (the XML document) and 16-2 (the CSS document) are on the CD that comes with this book. To see the CSS style sheet from Listing 16-2 applied to the bean burrito XML document, save both listings in the same directory. Add the following line of markup to Listing 16-1 (the bean burrito XML document) to reference the style sheet:

```
<?xml-stylesheet href="16ex01.css" type="text/css"?>
```

You can then view the styled burrito recipe in your Web browser.

An entire W3C recommendation governs how style sheets link to XML documents. The recommendation is updated frequently, so it always includes the most current information about this topic. Check it out at

```
www.w3.org/TR/xml-stylesheet
```

XSL and CSS Pack a 1-2 Punch

Just because CSS and XSL (including XSLT and XSL-FO) are competing technologies doesn't mean that you must choose one or the other. CSS and XSL play well together — so much that one of the most powerful uses for both style mechanisms involves using them in tandem.

XSL has two primary purposes: As XSL-FO, to apply style to XML documents, and as XSLT, to convert documents written according to one DTD or schema into documents that use another DTD or schema. Many XML developers use the transformation side of XSL, XSLT, to transform documents written using any XML vocabulary (even our own made-up RML) into XHTML documents.

If you take this approach, you can style your newly transformed XHTML documents with CSS for display on the Web. By using XSLT to convert XML documents to XHTML and then using CSS to control the display of the resulting XHTML, you can use the power of XML for data storage yet still deliver content to users through standard Web browsers.

Part V
XML's Lovely Linking Languages

The 5th Wave   By Rich Tennant

"You show a lot of promise in ePublishing.
Your first novel was rich with gripping
XLL, breathtaking in its XPath hyperlinks,
and visionary in its cross-browser platform."

In this part . . .

Some of XML's enduring appeal is that it can support all kinds of advanced capabilities that HTML can only dream of. XML's linking languages make a good case in point — they make it possible to create hyperlinks with multiple targets, reference points inside other XML documents without changing those document's innards, and control access to external resources of many kinds.

In Chapter 17, we explore and explain the XML Linking Language (XLink), which permits construction of all kinds of complex links. Chapter 18 covers the XML Path Language (XPath), which makes it possible to locate remote resources of many kinds, and explains the complex harmonies that XLink, XPointer, and XPath can deliver to those in the know. Finally, Chapter 19 tackles the XML Pointer Language (XPointer), which enables anchors and targets of many kinds and allows documents to point to specific locations without having to alter the destination's markup one whit.

Chapter 17

The XML Linking Language

*U*sing the XML Linking Language (XLink) enables you to bring the wonders of hyperlinking into your XML documents. In this chapter, you find out how to link in XLink and declare simple eXtensible HyperText Markup Language (XHTML) by using namespaces. In addition, you gain an understanding of extended and out-of-line XLinks. Finally, you find out how to declare linking elements in a Document Type Definition (DTD). Sounds like more fun than a barrel of monkeys. (Although we do like monkeys, bananas are not included.)

Discovering XLink

XLink is another one of XML's companions (like XSL) that brings the magic of hyperlinking to your XML documents. XLink, however, not only allows for hyperlinking in the same ways that HTML delivers, but also allows all kinds of wonderful new types of links, such as groups of links and links that let you include content from one document in another (you'll find out all about these a little later).

Before we get down to the nitty-gritty of XLink, master these basic definitions. If you have some knowledge of HTML or markup, most of these will be familiar:

- **Resource:** A *resource* is anything that can be retrieved over the Internet, such as a document, an image, a sound file, or even a list generated automatically in response to a query.

- **Link:** You may tend to think of a link as something that you click to go somewhere else in cyberspace, but that's not necessarily what a link really is. A *link* represents a relationship between two or more objects.

- **Hyperlink:** A *hyperlink* is an object (that you do click!) that usually causes a fresh display or presentation on-screen.

- **Linking element:** A *linking element* is one that contains a link. In HTML, `img` and `a` elements are examples of linking elements. In XLink, the `simple` element is an example of a linking element. See the "Types of Linking Elements" section later in this chapter for more details.

- **Locator:** A *locator* is data that identifies a resource to which you can link.

- **Traversal:** A *traversal* is the act of using a link. By following a link, you traverse from one resource to another.

- **Arc:** An *arc* is a symbolic representation of traversal behavior, containing information about both ends of a link, as well as the direction and the timing of the traversal. XLink uses an `arc` element to capture such data. See the "Types of Linking Elements" section later in this chapter for more details.

Using Namespaces

If you follow the news and discussions about the development of XML, you may have seen XML gurus arguing about namespaces in much the same way medieval pundits argued over how many angels could dance on the head of a pin. There's no getting around it — you need to know about namespaces if you're going to get serious with your XML.

For one thing, you can't get more than a superficial understanding of XLink without some knowledge of the XML namespace specification.

In XML, a *namespace* is a reference to a collection of elements. You can borrow markup from a namespace for use in your XML documents. Big deal, you say. Ah, but here's where namespaces become a godsend: They enable you to do this borrowing without going through the rigamarole of defining and declaring the markup in a DTD. How do you do that? Magic. Nah, just kidding.

Think of it this way. Namespaces prevent you from having to reinvent the wheel. Do you like the way XHTML defines tables and want to incorporate table markup in your custom DTD? Have at it! You don't have to redefine all the table elements and attributes in your DTD; you can just use the XHTML namespace.

Behind the scenes with namespaces

Many namespaces are already in existence. XHTML is a namespace that encompasses all the structures in the XHTML DTD. All XHTML elements and attributes are contained in the XHTML namespace. This namespace requires a unique name to identify it — a name that won't be used for anything else. That unique name is a Uniform Resource Locator (URL), of course. Therefore, a namespace usually has a URL as part of its name.

URLs are designed to each have unique names — just like people. No two are alike, and that's the reason you use a URL to identify a namespace. In other words, don't worry if you don't have a source or page at the URL you choose to identify your namespace. The URL is nothing more than a unique identifier for your namespace.

You should choose a URL that you control. For example, `www.lanw.com` is a domain that happens to be under our control, so we can make up a unique name for use as a namespace, such as `www.lanw.com.xml.mynamespace`, and be absolutely sure that no one else can (legally) use the same name. If we were to choose `www.w3c.com.xml.mynamespace`, the World Wide Web Consortium (W3C) probably wouldn't be too happy with us. Also, we wouldn't have any way of controlling what URLs they create on their site, so the fate of our unique namespace identifier would be out of our hands.

This does mean that you must have a domain name under your control to use namespaces. You'll have to register for one (visit `www.networksolutions.com` or your ISP's Web site for information on how to do this) so that you can set up your unique name. If you rent space on someone else's server and your Web site's address is something like `http://www.isp.com/~yourname/`, you can also set up a namespace under your name, like this: `www.isp.com/~yourname/yournamespace`.

In XML, namespaces help you reuse elements and attributes from a variety of markup collections (usually DTDs) and help you avoid yucky naming conflicts when two sets of markup that have the same name are used within the same document. For example, say that you want to create a document that includes information about a book and all the reviews you've found for it. You include elements from a book DTD that includes the `title` element to define the book's title. You also use a book review DTD that includes the `title` element to define the review's catchy title. Namespaces help you use these two elements that have the same name in your document but still keep them separate.

Every namespace has its own unique URL, but not every URL actually has to lead somewhere. That's because you can use a general URL, like `http://www.mysite.com/namespace` to create a link to your namespace that's easy to use and remember. The real DTD that holds the element and attributes for the namespace may actually be `http://mysite.com/public/namespaces/namespace.dtd`. Your can set up your server to redirect computers that ask for the short and easy URL to the longer, and less friendly, actual URL.

Building XML documents with namespaces

A namespace is really nothing more than a URL that points to a collection of markup, usually a DTD. When you want to use the markup in a namespace in your document, you have to do two things:

- ✔ Specify in your XML document that you are using markup from a specific namespace (so the system processing it isn't taken by surprise by elements in your document that don't come from your DTD or schema).

- ✔ Identify elements and attributes that you use from the namespace in your document as coming from the namespace.

The W3C says that you need to follow a two-part naming system when you specify a namespace that you want to reference in your document. That said, here are the parts that make up a namespace:

- ✔ **Prefix:** The identifier you'll use in your documents to specify that an element or attribute is part of the namespace

- ✔ **URL:** The URL that's the unique identifier for your namespace

You can use this naming system to raise the namespace flag for all systems to see. The simplest way is to use the `xmlns:somename` attribute in the root element. The `somename` is the prefix. The prefix can be anything that you care to call it. (You could call the XHTML namespace `broccoli` if you really wanted to.) It's usually a good idea, however, to use a name that reflects the namespace so that others can work with your documents, too.

See that colon (`:`) in the syntax? The colon is reserved for use by the W3C, and it tells software that it's dealing with a special attribute (like a namespace). Pretty slick, huh?

After the clever name you've chosen as the prefix in the attributes, you need to add the URL that identifies the namespace for the external elements. For example

```
<Clients xmlns:xhtml="http://www.w3.org/1999/xhtml">
```

tells the processing system that you use the markup defined in the XHTML namespace in your document. (The name of the XHTML namespace is `http://www.w3.org/1999/xhtml`.)

The prefix we added after the colon (but preceding the URL) tells processors that whenever they come across an element or attribute prefixed with that name, that the markup belongs to the `http://www.w3.org/1999/xhtml` namespace. You can use any name that you want after the colon; such as `xmlns:junk` or `xmlns:myprefix`, but using a descriptive name (like `xmlns:xhtml`) is a good habit to get into. You can't, however, make up any ol' URL for the namespace. Each namespace has its own unique URL and you have to use the one supplied by the namespace's creator.

In other words, the two-part naming system says something like this: "Hey, Mr. XML processor! Over here! This attribute in my root element says that I want you to use a bunch of markup from another DTD in this document. For the purposes of simplicity, I'm going to call that something by a really convenient and easy-to-remember name (the namespace name, `xhtml`). Whenever you see this namespace name, go to this URL, `http://www.w3.org/1999/xhtml`, to find out more about it."

If the browser sees a namespace that it's not familiar with, it just displays the element using a default representation. You can find the namespaces recommendation at `www.w3.org/TR/1999/REC-xml-names-19990114/`.

Seeing a namespace at work

Seeing a namespace at work really brings the whole thing home to roost. Here we use a `clients.xml` document to demonstrate how you can use a namespace to use good ol' Web-page links in your custom XML documents. These aren't XLink links; we're not quite there yet. Here, we offer only an example of how to use namespaces. The following is a well-formed XML document that we could use to keep track of our clients:

```
<?xml version="1.0"?>
<?xml-stylesheet type="text/css" href="link1.css"?>
<Clients
  xmlns:xhtml="http://www.w3.org/1999/xhtml">
 <Client>
   <Name>John Smith</Name>
```

```
   <Address> 123 Elm, Sometown, Ohio</Address>
   <Phone>123-456-7891</Phone>
   <Fax>123-456-7891</Fax>
   <Email>
    <xhtml:a href="mailto:john@lanw.com">
          john@lanw.com</xhtml:a>
   </Email>
   <Website>
    <xhtml:a href="http://www.lanw.com">
          LANWrights</xhtml:a>
   </Website>
  </Client>
</Clients>
```

Type this XML document and link it with a suitable style sheet (see Chapters 13 through 16 for the lowdown on style sheets) that controls the formatting of the client information. A good style sheet might use the following markup:

```
Client,Name,Address,Phone,Fax,Email,Website{display:block;}
```

Now run the XML document in a namespace-enabled browser, such as Internet Explorer (IE) 5.5 or 6.0. In IE, you see that the content of the xhtml:a element looks just like the content of an XHTML a (linking) element. In other words, the content becomes a hyperlink (see Figure 17-1) — or at least hyperlink-like. The namespace you added to the XML document allows you to use the standard XHTML linking element (a) in your clients document. The browser already knows what to do with XHTML linking elements — create a hyperlink out of them — so you can take advantage of the browser's support for links but still use custom XML markup to define your content.

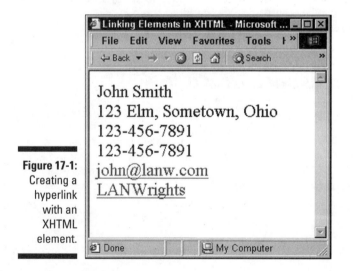

Figure 17-1:
Creating a hyperlink with an XHTML element.

When you run `clients.xml`, Internet Explorer does the following:

✔ Reads the root element, `<Clients xmlns:xhtml="http://www.w3.org/1999/xhtml">`, and sees that `clients.xml` uses the `xhtml` prefix to reference a namespace.

✔ Looks at the URL of the namespace, `http://www.w3.org/1999/xhtml`, and sees that this is the XHTML namespace (Internet Explorer is quite familiar with XHTML semantics).

✔ Looks at the abbreviation that we've chosen and notes that it should use XHTML semantics every time that it sees the prefix `xhtml:` before an element.

✔ Displays all `clients.xml` elements in accordance with the style sheet.

✔ Displays the `xhtml:a` element using XHTML semantics.

To see how easily you can integrate any markup from the XHTML namespace into your custom DTD, add an element such as `xhtml:h1` to this document and see what happens!

Using Namespaces to Link Elements in XLink

By now you're probably thinking, "Whoa there, cowboy. I thought this chapter was about linking in XML. What do namespaces have to do with XML? When am I gong to find out about the cool links you can create with XLink?" Never fear, the time is here.

XLink is — yep, you guessed it — an XML vocabulary, which means that it's written in XML syntax and you use it in your documents just like you use any other XML syntax. XLink defines a wide range of linking options, and you can use its elements and attributes in your documents with a wave of the namespace wand.

That's right. All you need to do to take advantage of XLink is to create a namespace reference to it in your document (as we've shown you how to do already) and then use the XLink elements and attributes to create links in your documents (which we'll show you now). It couldn't be easier.

A basic understanding of namespaces is essential to understanding the XLink specification, which resides at www.w3.org/TR/xlink. The standard HTML linking element, a, that's behind the scenes of every hyperlink you see on the Web today is powerful and has withstood the test of time. After all, this very simple tag connects pages all over the world. Even so, these connections are only the tip of the linking iceberg.

XLinks not only have all the utility of XHTML links, but they also promise to cause a revolution in linking practices at least as great as the original HTML a element did. To add an XLink to your XML document, you must do one of two things:

 ✔ Use the XLink namespace.

 ✔ Declare the XLink in a DTD; see the "Creating Link Elements" section later in this chapter.

To use an XLink namespace, you declare it in your document as we describe in the preceding section, "Using Namespaces." The URL for the XLink namespace is

```
http://www.w3.org/1999/xlink/namespace/
```

The following is clients.xml rewritten to use the simple linking element from the XLink namespace:

```
<?xml version="1.0"?>
<?xml-stylesheet type="text/css" href="link1.css"?>
<Clients xmlns:xlink="http://www.w3.org/1999/xlink/namespace/">
<Client>
    <Name>John Smith</Name>
    <Address> 123 Elm, Sometown, Ohio</Address>
    <Phone>123-456-7891</Phone>
    <Fax>123-456-7891</Fax>
    <Email>
     <xlink:simple href="mailto:john@lanw.com">john@lanw.com</xlink:simple>
    </Email>
    <Website>
     <xlink:simple href="http://www.lanw.com">LANWrights</xlink:simple>
    </Website>
  </Client>
</Clients>
```

To get the most intelligible results when viewing this document, you must use an XML-enabled browser such as IE 5.5 or higher with Microsoft XML (MSXML) installed, or the Amaya browser from the W3C (we cover this in Chapter 20).

A conforming XML browser must be able to understand the semantics of XLink for correct results to occur. Most general-purpose browsers will definitely support the linking semantics of XHTML (because they are really HTML links in well-formed XML documents) and a few may even support XLink. We hope that support for XLink semantics will be built right into all next-generation browsers.

Types of Linking Elements

The XLink specification describes four linking elements and a host of attributes. Here are the linking elements:

- ✔ `simple` is a simple linking element that acts much like the XHTML `a` element. It shares the `href` attribute with the XHTML element but also has additional attributes that you can work with.

- ✔ `extended` is a new brand of link that allows all kinds of wonderful linking possibilities. We look at these kinds of links in the section, "Extending Basic Linking Behaviors," later in this chapter.

- ✔ `locator` is always used as a child element in an extended link and is an empty element. We look at the `locator` element in some detail in the section, "Extending Basic Linking Behaviors," later in this chapter.

- ✔ `arc` is an empty element that's also used with extended links. We cover this element in the upcoming "Creating Link Groups" section in this chapter.

Simple XLink elements

The XLink `simple` element has almost the same type of functionality as an `a` element in XHTML except that it supports several more attributes. The attributes for an `simple` element are

- ✔ `href`, like in the `a` element of HTML, gives the location of the resource to which the simple element is linking. This is the only required attribute of the `simple` element. All other attributes are optional.

- ✔ `role` is a string that you can use to describe the element's role.

- ✔ `title` is the optional title for the `simple` link.

- ✔ `show` describes the behavior of the link when it fetches the resource at the other end. We discuss this element further in the "What can we show you?" section later in this chapter.

- ✔ `actuate` takes one of two values: `onRequest` or `auto`. If the value is `onRequest`, some active event, such as a mouse click, must occur for the link to be activated. If the value is `auto`, the link loads automatically. The `a` element in XHTML is an example of a link activated `onRequest`, and the `img` element in XHTML is an example of a link that usually activates automatically. The default behavior is `onRequest`.

What can we show you?

The show attribute requires a little explanation. It's an enumerated attribute that can take one of three values: new, embed, or replace. The default value is replace.

If the show attribute is left with the default value of replace when a link is activated, the resource that contains the link is replaced with a new resource. This is what happens for most instances of an XHTML link.

If given the value of new, the show attribute opens the requested resource in a new window. (To accomplish this in XHTML, you must use a script or the target attribute, where available.)

When given the value of embed, the show attribute embeds the requested resource in the existing document. Although you can do this with image resources in XHTML using a script, you can do this with any resource in XLink.

Describing local and remote links

A *link* is usually a fresh resource — a completely new document. Of course, you can link to a place inside the same document that contains a simple link. To do this, the href attribute must be an XPointer of some kind. (We discuss XPointers in Chapter 19.)

Typically, you use local links in a table of contents at the head of a document. You can use a full URI (User Resource Identifier, a reference mechanism that works much like a URL) as the value of an href attribute. If you do this, the link is no longer local; it's considered remote.

A *remote resource* is a document, an image, a sound file, or any other kind of resource located somewhere on the Internet. Remote resources are often identified by Universal Resource Identifiers (URIs). URIs identify a filetype, while Universal Resource Locators (URLs) identify the remote resource's filetype and its exact location on the Internet. (URLs are a kind of URI, by the way.)

Extending Basic Linking Behaviors

One of the most exciting things about XLink is the extended link, which you use to associate a series of links together. Whereas a simple link just takes the user of your document from one resource to another, an extended link gives users a bunch of selections from which they can choose.

The `extended` link requires helper elements to achieve full functionality. These elements are the `locator` element and the `arc` element.

Using the extended element

The `extended` element uses `locator` child elements to list the various links that it may access and uses attributes to describe the group behavior of such child elements. Here are the attributes for the extended element:

- ✔ `role` is a string that you can use to describe the element's role.

- ✔ `title` is the optional title of the extended link.

- ✔ `showdefault` is similar to the `show` attribute of the `simple` element but applies to the default behavior for all locator elements.

- ✔ `actuatedefault` is similar to the default behavior of the `actuate` attribute of the `simple` element and describes the default behavior for all child elements.

Using the locator element

The `locator` element defines the locations of all resources for an extended link. It takes an obligatory `href` attribute and optional `role` and `title` attributes. Here's a snippet from an XML document that uses both the `extended` and `locator` elements:

```
<Middle-ages xmlns:xlink="http://www.w3.org/1999/xlink/namespace/">
<!--The previous URL matches the draft specification -->
<!--Check the current spec for the current URL -->
<!--This is warfare.xml-->
[lots of text and markup here]

These <xlink:extended
      role="weapon list"
      title="Description of Weapons"
      showdefault="new"
      show actuate="onRequest">weapons
        <xlink:locator title="Longbow" href="longbow.htm"/>
        <xlink:locator title="Crossbow" href="crossbow.htm"/>
        <xlink:locator title="Stirrup" href="stirrup.xml"/>
    </xlink:extended>
revolutionized medieval warfare, making it more lethal and bloody
[lots more text and markup here]
</Middle-ages>
```

You must, as we did, declare the XLink namespace in the root element (`Middle-ages`). Best practice says you should declare all the namespaces for a document in the root element so that they are easy to find.

In this example, we added an extended link that highlights the word weapons. Theoretically, when someone with a newer browser (such as Internet Explorer 6) moves the mouse over the <u>Weapons</u> link, a tip box appears, showing the title of the extended link: <u>Description of Weapons</u>. When the user clicks the link, he or she is presented with a drop-down box with the titles of the optional pages as choices. Clicking any one of these selections displays a new window because showdefault is set to new.

Our discussion of how links might appear in a browser or other display tool is purely theoretical. Every tool will handle the links differently.

Okay, we've got to be honest: We don't know for sure if a tip box will show for the user in the previous example because the XLink specification gives no detailed description of how a browser is supposed to behave; it just says that a browser must recognize the markup and act on it in an appropriate way. Instead of a quaint tip box, your browser might make a drop-down box appear when you run your mouse across the link; another browser might flash something in a new window. Or perhaps links could be presented inline, just like standard Web page links are today. Read through the next section for more on inline links.

When Links Get Out of Line

Both the simple element and the extended element examples that we show in previous sections are examples of inline links. An *inline link* is a link in one of the participating resources. Or in non-nerdy language, with an inline link, all the markup that describes the link must be on the page where you click the link.

By using an XLink, however, you have the opportunity to take links out of line. In other words, you can place them in a different document. Here's how the example from the preceding section might look if you use an out-of-line link:

```
<Middle-ages
    xmlns:xlink="http://www.w3.org/1999/xlink/namespace">
<!--This is warfare.xml-->
[lots of text and markup here]
These <xlink:extended
        role="xlink:external-linkset"
        title="Description of Weapons"
          <xlink:locator href= "weaponlinkset.xml"/> weapons
</xlink:extended>
revolutionized medieval warfare, making it more lethal and bloody
[lots more text and markup here]
</Middle-ages>
```

Through this simple change, potentially hundreds of locator elements and the descriptions of their behaviors are moved into an external document called weaponlinkset.xml.

Relocating these `locator` elements not only cleans up the document that contains the link, but also allows different `show` and `actuate` behaviors for different resources. Perhaps even more importantly, a simple relocation like this allows a Webmaster to control all links for a site from a single location. Instead of editing thousands of documents when a link changes (yes, we know that automated software can do this, but it's still a pain), a Webmaster can simply edit a single link document. When links are out of line, though, some thought must go into the external document to create the necessary link groups.

When we refer to an out-of-line link, the `role` attribute of an `extended` element must take a special value. As shown in the preceding example, that value is

```
role="xlink:external-linkset"
```

When you specify this second value, it means that the browser should also follow up on any links referred to by the documents in a link document. Yipes — as you can imagine, this can get out of hand quickly because it could lead to every single link on the Web! For this reason, we recommend that you limit the links to those specifically declared in an `external-linkset`, which is what the first value does.

Creating Link Groups

When links are inline, you can easily tell which is the originating document and which is the destination document. When links are out of line, this isn't always so clear, so you use the empty `arc` element to spell it out.

Here's what the contents of `weaponlinkset.xml` might look like. The extended link description has two sets of child elements: the `locator` elements, which have all been given a unique `role` attribute value, and the `arc` elements, which describe the behavior of the links. Note also that the originating `warfare.xml` document is placed in its own `locator` element:

```
<WeaponLinks
      xmlns:xlink="http://www.w3.org/1999/xlink/namespace">
<!--This is weaponlinkset.xml-->
<xlink:extended>
<!--begin locator elements-->
        <xlink:locator
            title="Middle Age Warfare"
            role="sourcedoc"
            href="warfare.xml"/>
        <xlink:locator
            title="Longbow"
            role="longbow"
            href="longbow.htm"/>
        <xlink:locator
```

```
                  title="Longbow Picture"
                  role="longbowpic"
                  href="longbow.jpg"/>
              <xlink:locator
                  title="Crossbow"
                  role="crossbow"
                  href="crossbow.htm"/>
              <xlink:locator
                  title="Stirrup"
                  role="stirrup"
                  href="stirrup.xml"/>
<!--begin arc elements-->
          <xlink:arc
                  from="sourcedoc"
                  to="longbowpic"
                  show="embed"
                  actuate="auto"/>
          <xlink:arc
                  from="sourcedoc"
                  to="longbow"
                  show="new"
                  actuate="onRequest"/>
          <xlink:arc
                  from="sourcedoc"
                  to="crossbow"
                  show="new"
                  actuate="onRequest"/>
          <xlink:arc
                  from="sourcedoc"
                  to="stirrup"
                  show="replace"
                  actuate="onRequest"/>
          <xlink:arc
                  from="stirrup"
                  to="sourcedoc"
                  show="replace"
                  actuate="onRequest"/>
</xlink:extended>
</WeaponLinks>
```

The role of the locator elements in the preceding example is pretty straightforward: They describe the locations of the resources. But the arc elements
need a little more discussion.

An xlink:arc element describes what behavior a link in an out-of-line document should adopt. It defines which two resources to connect, the direction
of the link, what to do when the link is activated, and when to activate that
link. Here's a list of arc element attributes:

✔ The to and from attributes define the two resources to be connected.
Note that the preceding example references the role attribute of the
locator elements to reference the two resources to be linked.

✔ The to and from attributes provide information about the direction of
the link.

✔ The show attribute defines whether to embed the new resource in the old resource, replace the old resource with the new resource, or display the new resource in its own window.

✔ The actuate attribute defines whether the link should be activated as soon as it's recognized or wait for some kind of request.

Here's some additional information about the arc elements from the preceding example:

✔ The first arc element embeds a picture of a longbow (longbow.jpg) in the source document when it's loaded:

```
<xlink:arc
        from="sourcedoc"
        to="longbowpic"
        show="embed"
        actuate="auto"/>
```

✔ The next three arc elements describe what the browser does when a user clicks the weapons hyperlink in warfare.xml. The browser sees that the direction of the link is from sourcedoc to the other documents and creates a selection mechanism using the title attribute for the locator elements. When the browser fetches stirrup.xml, it replaces the current window and opens the two HTML documents in their own windows:

```
<xlink:arc
    from="sourcedoc"
    to="longbow"
    show="new"
    actuate="onRequest"/>
<xlink:arc
    from="sourcedoc"
    to="crossbow"
    show="new"
    actuate="onRequest"/>
<xlink:arc
    from="sourcedoc"
    to="stirrup"
    show="replace"
    actuate="onRequest"/>
<xlink:arc
    from="stirrup"
    to="sourcedoc"
    show="replace"
    actuate="onRequest"/>
```

✔ The last arc element is for a link that exists in stirrup.xml, which also references weaponlinkset.xml. It tells the browser to link to warfare.xml and to show the page by replacing the contents of stirrup.xml:

```
<xlink:arc
    from="stirrup"
    to="sourcedoc"
    show="replace"
    actuate="onRequest"/>
```

Creating Link Elements

In previous examples, we use the generic XLink elements with a namespace. Suppose that instead you want to designate a permanent linking element. Using clients.xml again, we make the Email and Website elements into linking elements and add an empty element, Picture, to embed a picture of the client in our document:

```
<?xml version="1.0"?>
<?xml-stylesheet type="text/css" href="link1.css"?>
<!DOCTYPE Clients SYSTEM "Clients.dtd">
<Clients
  xmlns:xhtml="http://www.w3.org/1999/xhtml">
 <Client>
   <Name>John Smith</Name>
   <Address> 123 Elm, Sometown, Ohio</Address>
   <Phone>123-456-7891</Phone>
   <Fax>123-456-7891</Fax>
   <Email
       xlink:href="mailto:john@lanw.com">
               john@lanw.com
   </Email>
   <Website
    xlink:href="http://www.lanw.com/jsmith.htm"
    xlink:role="Clients web site"
    xlink:title="Clients web site"
    xlink:show="new"
    xlink:actuate="onrequest"
    >
               LANW
   </Website>
   <Picture
    xlink:href="jsmith.jpg"
    xlink:role="Clients picture"
    xlink:title="John Smith"
    xlink:show="embed"
    xlink:actuate="auto"
    />
 </Client>
</Clients>
```

Here's how we declare these elements in the DTD:

```
<!ELEMENT  Email (#PCDATA) >
<!ATTLIST Email
    xmlns:xlink  CDATA  #FIXED " has http://www.w3.org/1999/xlink/namespace "
    xlink:href   CDATA   #REQUIRED
    xlink:type   (simple|extended|locator|arc)
    #FIXED "simple"
>
<!ELEMENT  Webpage (#PCDATA) >
<!ATTLIST Webpage
    xmlns:xlink  CDATA  #FIXED " http://www.w3.org/1999/xlink/namespace /"
    xlink:href   CDATA   #REQUIRED
    xlink:type   (simple|extended|locator|arc)
    #FIXED "simple"
    xlink:role   CDATA   #IMPLIED
    xlink:title  CDATA   #IMPLIED
```

```
      xlink:show    (new|embed|replace) "new"
      xlink:title   (onRequest|auto) "onRequest"
`>
<!ELEMENT  Picture #EMPTY >
<!ATTLIST  Picture
      xmlns:xlink  CDATA  #FIXED " has http://www.w3.org/1999/xlink/namespace "
      xlink:href   CDATA   #REQUIRED
      xlink:type   (simple|extended|locator|arc)
      #FIXED "simple"
      xlink:role   CDATA   #IMPLIED
      xlink:title  CDATA   #IMPLIED
      xlink:show   (new|embed|replace)   "embed"
      xlink:title  (onRequest|auto)      "auto"
  >
```

What's going on here? Here's what you need to know:

✔ In each case, you must declare `xmlns:xlink` as a `#FIXED` attribute with the XLink namespace. This means that the parser always considers it to be present even though it's not typed.

✔ You must explicitly include any `colonized` attributes of the `xlink:simple` element that you want to use in your markup. The `xlink:href` attribute is compulsory. Add whatever others you want.

✔ Nothing is stopping you from adding your own attributes, but they shouldn't employ the `xlink:` prefix because that's the standard prefix you use when you reference the XLink namespace in your documents.

✔ In the `Email` element, you can expect a conforming browser to open your e-mail client with the correct address already inserted. This behavior varies from client to client because the semantics are not spelled out in XLink. In fact, it would probably be better to use an XHTML `a` element here because it's supported in just about every browser known to man.

✔ In the `Webpage` element, you decide to have any Web page that you access opened in a new window.

✔ In the `Picture` element, you decide that you would like the picture to be embedded in the page automatically (just like the `img` element in XHTML). You could use the XHTML `img` element for this.

XHTML versus XLink

Many simple linking tasks can be carried out with XHTML elements instead of XLink elements. XHTML 1.0 mimics the linking behavior of HTML, whereas it's expected that XHTML 2.0 will adopt the linking behavior of XLink.

Most XML browsers will probably support XHTML semantics before they support XLink semantics (because XHTML is a more mature specification), so you may want to adopt XHTML namespaces for your simple linking tasks.

Chapter 18

The XML Path Language

*I*n eXtensible Markup Language (XML) documents, you need something to tell the software where to go in the document. XPath does just that, providing a concise language describing the location of specific elements, attributes, and their values in an XML document.

In this chapter, you find out how XPath creates paths to help computer systems find every little piece of markup or content in your XML document. You also discover where those paths lead, what markup to use to describe them, and how to correctly document them.

Where Do XPaths Lead?

The word *path* has two meanings: It can mean the physical path that you walk along (that sunny lane that leads to your favorite coffee house) or it can mean the direction you take. When you leave your house and walk to the local coffee house, you walk on a path — probably a sidewalk. When you end up at the coffee house, you can trace your path (up a hill, turning right at the old oak tree at Helen's house, and making a sharp left at the corner of Main and Central).

Suppose that your friend George comes to stay with you, and he wants to know how to get to a bar, not the coffee house. You might tell him something like this: "Take a left out the front door, go down to Main Street, and then make a right. The bar is the third building on the right side, and it has a sign that says McGinty's."

An XML document also has a set of paths that you can navigate using software, tracing a path through the document from one point to another.

Where XML paths are concerned, you need a starting point and an ending point. You also need a route and a set of directions. There are stages to the journey. Each stage has not only a starting point and an ending point, but also a direction of travel. The final destination is also described in some detail; the complete description could be written as follows:

```
front door-right-Main St./(Main St.)-left-McGinty's[3rd on right]
```

Here are the pieces you need to know to translate this example into XML:

- ✔ **(Stage 1):** This is equivalent to the front door, George's starting point.
- ✔ **(Stage 2):** This is the actual path that George follows.
- ✔ **(Stage 3):** This is the final product, George's ending point, where he's rewarded with a nice, frothy, cold beer.

When you navigate through an XML document, you move along the paths of the XML document and trace a path that can be described. What you need is a succinct language that describes the paths built into a document as well as how to follow a route through that document.

Here's how you might describe a path through an eXtensible HyperText Markup Language (XHTML) document:

```
"Starting at the top of the document, go to the root element <html>,
then go to the <body> element, and then find the third <p> element."
```

This is quite simple and understandable to a human reader, but what you really want is a common simple language that you can use to describe this path to software. XPath is such a language.

The XPath specification, which you can find at www.w3.org/TR/xpath, is all about naming the XML paths that run through a document and providing a concise language to describe directions for how to get from one place to another in an XML document. The XPath specification is a stable recommendation.

Why do you need directions?

In XML, you need to know how to get from point A to point B only if there's some purpose to your journey. XML has no equivalent to the Sunday afternoon drive to see the fall colors. XML gurus navigating XML documents are like stern Puritans who travel only when they have a purpose. In other words, if you don't need to worry about paths, hooray. Don't bother. But if you do need to know your document's path, you need to use a specific XML-based language.

In XML, you need a language to describe how to move about a document for two primary reasons:

✔ **To find your way to and describe a section of a document that needs to be transformed or formatted for display.** This task involves XSL Transformations (XSLT) or XSL Formatting Objects (XSL-FO). See Chapter 15 for more information.

✔ **To be able to point to a certain part of the document.** This task involves the use of XPointers. See Chapter 19 for more information on XPointers.

For example, if you want transform every paragraph element that contains the word W3C into an indented block with a purple background for display, you have be able to find those specific paragraphs, which you can do with XPath. Or if you want to create a link from the W3C to every paragraph element that contains the word W3C, you have to be able to locate those paragraphs so that you can link to them.

XPath may be used for other purposes as well, but these two tasks provided the motivation for writing the XPath specification.

The paths and way stations of XML

To understand how XPath describes paths and directions, we use the `clients.xml` document that we use in Chapter 17.

This is an example of an XML document that we could use to keep track of clients:

```
<?xml version="1.0"?>
<!-- Clients.xml-->
<Clients>
<!--This is the root element of Clients.xml-->
 <Client id="c1">
  <Name>Jon Smith</Name>
  <Phone type="home">440-123-3333</Phone>
  <Fax>440-123-3334</Fax>
  <Email>jon@acme.com</Email>
 </Client>
 <Client id="c2">
  <Name>Bill Jones</Name>
  <Phone type="cellphone">330-124-5432</Phone>
  <Fax>440-123-5433</Fax>
  <Email>bjones@someinc.com</Email>
 </Client>
 <Client id="c3">
  <Name>Matt Brown</Name>
  <Phone type="work">220-125-1234</Phone>
  <Phone type="cellphone">233-344-4455</Phone>
  <Phone type="home">234-567-8910</Phone>
  <Fax>220-125-1235</Fax>
  <Email>matthew@hotstuff.com</Email>
 </Client>
</Clients>
```

This document can be laid out like a tree, as shown in Figure 18-1.

In Figure 18-1, all elements and comments in the `clients.xml` file appear as boxes. In XPath terminology, these are called nodes. *Nodes* in XPath are related to each other by using the language of the family tree: child, parent, sibling, descendant, ancestor, and so on. (See Chapter 16 for more information.)

The name *node* is borrowed from biology. When a tree or a plant branches, that's a node. Sometimes this comparison is carried even further so that a node with no children is called a *leaf*. To clear up a potentially confusing point, various kinds of nodes in XML have different names, such as text node, element node, comment node, document node, and root element node. For details on these terms, see the "XPath Directions and Destinations" section later in this chapter.

For examples of some text and attribute nodes, see Figure 18-2. The text nodes contain the text content (such as the actual name, phone numbers, fax numbers, and e-mail addresses) for each of the element nodes (`Client`), and the attribute nodes represent the attributes of these elements, namely the `id` attributes of client elements and the `type` attributes of `Phone` elements.

Here are some examples of the XPath relationships among the various nodes in `clients.xml`:

- A single node called the *document node* contains the whole document.

- The document node contains three children: the version declaration, a comment node, and the root element node (`Clients`). These three very different nodes are all siblings.

- The Clients node is the root element of the document. It's sometimes called the *document element*.

- The Clients node has four child nodes: a comment node and three Client nodes.

- The parent of the #comment node is the Clients node. The #comment node has no children (the text of a comment is considered part of the node) but has three siblings in the form of Client nodes.

- Each Client node has children of its own. For example, the third Client node has six children: a name node, three phone nodes, a fax node, and an e-mail node. All these nodes are siblings of one another.

- Each of these nodes has a text node, which is not shown in Figure 18-1, as a child.

- The parent of every phone node is a Client node.

- The grandparent of every phone node is the Clients node.

- All nodes, including all text nodes and attribute nodes, are descendants of the Clients node.

✔ Every node in the document, including the root element node and all attribute and text nodes, has the document node as its ancestor.

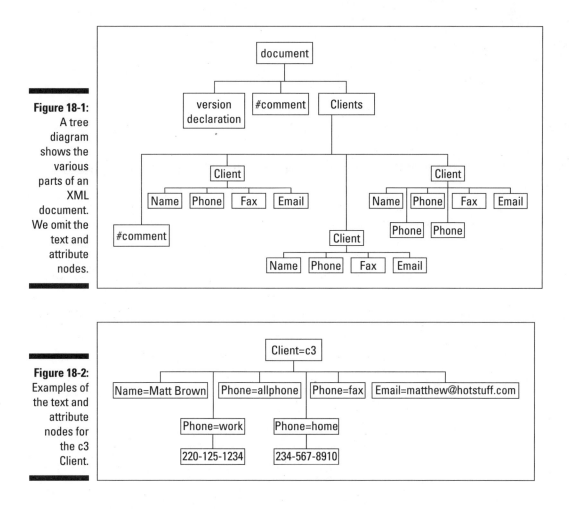

Figure 18-1:
A tree diagram shows the various parts of an XML document. We omit the text and attribute nodes.

Figure 18-2:
Examples of the text and attribute nodes for the c3 Client.

The XPath specification considers the parent of an attribute to be the element that contains it. But the W3C Document Object Model (DOM) considers an attribute to be a *property* of the element that contains it.

Bottom line: In the XPath specification

✔ The attribute nodes (not shown in Figure 18-1) have elements as their parents.

✔ Attribute nodes are not child nodes of their parents.

Got that?

Believe it or not, although the attribute of an element is considered to have the element that contains it as its parent, it's not considered to be the child of its parent. (Shades of Oedipus, anyone?) The reason for this contorted reasoning is all nerdy stuff that has to do with namespaces, which we don't even touch in this book. If you want a beginner's guide to namespaces, take a peek at Chapter 17. To read even more about the topic of namespaces and how they relate to all manner of XML goodness, we suggest picking up a copy of *XML Bible,* 2nd edition, by Elliotte Rusty Harold (Hungry Minds, Inc.).

In addition to the nodes in our document, the XPath specification recognizes namespace nodes and processing instruction nodes — neither of which you need to consider further.

Before moving on and looking at how XPath gives out directions, here's a summary of the various node types recognized by XPath:

- **Document node:** The *document node* contains the whole document, including all the version declarations and prolog, as well as the root node. (Check out Chapter 6 for the details about these key document structures.)

- **Root nodes:** The *root node* is the node that contains the whole written content of the document proper that comes after the prolog.

- **Element nodes:** The name of an *element node* is the same as its tag name.

- **Text nodes:** *Text nodes* are the text content of the elements.

- **Attribute nodes:** The name of an *attribute node* is the same as its attribute name.

- **Namespace nodes:** *Namespace nodes* are beyond the scope of this book. You just need to know that they exist.

- **Processing instruction nodes:** Ditto, *processing instruction nodes* are also beyond the scope of the book. Just know that they exist.

- **Comment nodes:** The *comment nodes* include the comments. This is not considered a separate text node.

XPath Directions and Destinations

In this section, you look at the language that XPath uses to describe a route through a document. We need to clarify that an XPath is a terse set of directions presented as a string, which is read by suitable software and is said to return a *destination node* or a set of nodes.

A *string* is a nerdy term for a line of text. Nerds would much rather talk about a *string of characters* than use a regular English expression such as *a phrase* or *a piece of text.* Similarly, when nerds talk about something being *returned,* they're talking about the *answer* that a piece of software gives if you ask it a question.

Different software systems can use the set of directions in XPath in various ways. For example, a transformation system takes what it finds at the end of the path and applies transformation rules to apply new markup to it. The XPointer specification uses this set of directions in its fragment identifier, and the XSL specification uses it as an attribute.

XPath says nothing about what to do with a destination after it's been reached. Again, this is left up to the individual system that uses XPath for its own purposes.

Every trip has three parts, and here is what XPath has to say about each part:

- ✔ **The starting point** is usually from the root node of the document. Sometimes, however, it may be another node in a document. Where the journey starts is called the *context node.*

- ✔ **The journey itself** consists of both a direction and a number of steps. XPath describes each of these steps using its syntax. Each step is separated by a forward slash (/). Sometimes a journey consists of one step; at other times, a journey may involve many steps. In the following section, we look at several examples of these steps. Note that XPath calls the most important of its set of directions a LocationPath.

- ✔ **The destination** can be either a single node or a collection of nodes. This concept shouldn't be too difficult. For example, in a real journey, you could say that your destination is 27 Palace Court, London, W1; or Europe; or England; or London, UK. All these statements are correct.

XPath says nothing about what to do when you reach your destination: It just describes the destination and how to get there.

LocationPaths: Describing the Journey

XPath uses two types of syntax: an abbreviated form and an unabbreviated form. In this section, we show you both forms. We start with the unabbreviated syntax because it's a little more descriptive and easier to follow.

A LocationPath searches for a node depending on the information that you give it. The general syntax for a LocationPath is as follows:

```
axisname :: nodetest[expression1] [expression2] ...
```

Each part of this syntax is as follows:

- axisname is the type of selection that you want to perform. It also tells you the direction in the document that you need to travel. If you select child, descendant, or following-sibling as an axis, you travel forward in the document. If you select parent, ancestor, or previous-sibling, you travel backward in the document. If you select self, you stand still.

- nodetest tests for the type of node that you want to select. This is usually the name of a node.

- expression appears in square brackets and further refines your selection process for a node or set of nodes. You can use more than one expression (which may sometimes be called a *predicate* in the XPath specification).

Before getting into some of the details of XPath, here are a few simple examples of LocationPaths using the clients.xml document. In the examples in the following sections, the starting point (the context node) is the root element node (Clients) of clients.xml, unless otherwise stated.

Some simple location paths

Here are some simple examples of selection paths. First, we show you the code, followed by a brief description. In this example

```
child::Clients
```

the axis is child, and the node test is Clients. This selects all the child nodes of the context node named Clients:

```
child::*
```

The axis is child and the node test is *, which stands for a wildcard selection. This selects all the child nodes of the type element from the context node. Because an XML document can have only one root element, this example also selects all the nodes called Clients:

```
child::node()
```

The axis is child and the node test is node(), which selects all the child nodes of the document root, including the XML version declaration, the comment node, and the element node Clients.

Adding expressions

Here are some simple examples of expressions, which further refine the selection process. As before, first we show you the code, and then we give a brief description. Here's the first example:

```
child::Clients[position()=1]
```

The axis is `child`, and the node test is `Clients`. We add an expression, `[position()=1]`, which selects the first child node named `Clients` of the context node.

Note the single `Clients` node: It's the root element. Even though this seems obvious, be sure that you still name the position of the specific node that you want because software isn't smart enough to tell the difference between a list containing just one item and a single item. As far as software is concerned, `child::Clients` returns a list with a single item, and `child::Clients[position()=1]` returns a single node.

In this case, you could also use the `last()` function to return the last node in the list:

```
child::Clients[position()=last()]
```

Because there's only one node, this last node is identical to the first node in the list.

Taking steps

Having taken one step on the path, take another one and step into the document properly. XPath uses a forward slash (/) to tell you when to take another step. The new context node is the node selected in the preceding step:

```
child::Clients[position()=1]/child::Client
```

After that step, you make a new LocationPath. The previous syntax selects all the `Client` element children of the root element.

More on adding expressions

The use of the `position()` function is pretty obvious:

```
child::Client[position()=last()]
```

The axis is `child`, and the node test is `Client`. We add an expression, `[position()=last()]`, which selects the last child node of `Clients` named `Client`.

Looking at attributes

You can use the value of attributes to narrow your selection of a destination node. For example, the axis is `child` and the node test is `Client`, as shown here:

```
child::Client[attribute::id="c3"]
```

The expression is itself another LocationPath with an axis of `attribute` and a node test of `id="c3"`. The expression selects all the child elements of `Clients`, which are not only named *Client* but also have an `id` attribute with a value equal to `c3`. In other words, the last `Client` element is selected.

May we see your ID?

Because an `ID` attribute is unique in an XML document, you can use a special function, the `id()` function, to select a node in the document. You don't need to describe any steps or trace any paths. If you just write the following path, the software will find the correct node:

```
id()="c3"
```

For this to work, the document must have a Document Type Definition (DTD) so that the software can make sure the attribute that you called `id` is indeed of type `ID`. See Chapter 19 for more details on IDs.

Going backwards

You can also step backwards. If you start from the document root, you have nowhere to go. It's like the old joke of the man taking a picture of his wife on the edge of the Grand Canyon! ("Just take one more step back, dear.")

For these next examples, we assume that the context node is the last `Email` element of the third `Client`, that is, the `Email` element with the content `matthew@hotstuff.com`. Here's the first example:

```
preceding-sibling::Fax
```

Using this code returns all the preceding sibling elements called `Fax` — in other words, just one element. The next example returns all the preceding `sibling` elements called `Phone`:

```
preceding-sibling::Phone
```

When you apply this to the `clients.xml` file, it describes the three phone elements.

Finally, the following path returns the parent element, provided that it's named `Client`:

```
parent::Client
```

When applied to the `clients.xml` file, this path indeed returns its parent.

Reversing direction

When you start going backwards, you also reverse the direction of counting for the `position()` function. So, if you assume the same context node as in the preceding section, this example returns the phone node of `type="home"`:

```
preceding-sibling::*[position()=1]
```

This example returns the `name` node:

```
preceding-sibling::*[position()=last()]
```

Null results

Sometimes you ask for something and nothing is there! For example, this returns the preceding parent element provided that it's called `MoneyBags`:

```
parent::MoneyBags
```

Alas, there's no parent called `MoneyBags`, so XPath returns a null value.

Null is one of those nerdy terms that crops up from time to time, and it refers to a real value with nothing in it. Not only is nothing there; nothing has _ever_ been there. Null is different from empty, nothing, or zero. It's the black hole of XML, only it doesn't suck you into it and it's not an astronomical element. Okay, so it's just weird, hard to explain, and plain old goofy, but we'll do our best to give you an example of the difference between a null value and nothing.

Consider a text box in a form. If you ask (through code) for the contents of that text box before anything has been filled in, you receive a null value. If you fill out the form with your name, you receive a value that's the same as your name. If you erase your name so that the box is empty, you don't receive a null value: You receive an empty string value.

Getting to the root of things

The root of a document is different from the root element because it's one step behind the root element. You can always go back to the root of a document by using the forward slash (/). If the context node is still the e-mail node, the following selects the root element of the document `Clients`:

```
/child::*
```

The / takes you back to the root of the document (think of it as the top of the document, before the root element), `child` is an axis that selects the children, and * makes sure that you only select the element children. Because of the rules of XML, there can only be one root element, which means that this construct always selects the root element of the document.

The Axes of XPath

Here are the various axes that XPath provides and a brief description of each:

- ✔ `child` selects the children of the context node.
- ✔ `descendant` selects from any of the descendants of the context node.
- ✔ `parent` selects the parent node.
- ✔ `ancestor` selects from all the ancestor nodes.
- ✔ `following-sibling` selects from all the following siblings.
- ✔ `preceding-sibling` selects from all the preceding siblings.
- ✔ `following` is any following node other than attribute or namespace nodes.
- ✔ `preceding` is any preceding node other than attribute or namespace nodes.
- ✔ `attribute` contains the attributes of the context node.
- ✔ `namespace` is beyond the scope of this book; you just need to know that it exists.
- ✔ `self` contains just the context node itself.
- ✔ `descendant-or-self` contains the context node or any of its descendants.
- ✔ `ancestor-or-self` contains the context node or any of its ancestors.

The Short Version

XPath is designed to be used with XPointers when it will be part of a fragment identifier, or with XSL where it will be part of an attribute. For this reason, it makes sense to provide less verbose syntax. This is called *abbreviated syntax* for XPath.

The most important abbreviation is `child::`. This abbreviates to . . . wait for it . . . nothing!

Client axis abbreviations

Here are some of the previous examples from this chapter set out with their abbreviated equivalents:

- `child::Client` abbreviates to `Client`.
- `child::*` abbreviates to `*`.
- `child::node()` abbreviates to `node()`.
- `child::text()` abbreviates to `text()` and selects all text nodes of the context node.

Attribute axis abbreviation

Other important abbreviations are of the `attribute` axis and some of the predicates. The `attribute::` axis abbreviates to the @ symbol. So the example

```
child::Client[attribute::id="c3"]
```

abbreviates to

```
Client[@id="c3"]
```

Predicate and expression abbreviations

There are several useful abbreviations for the expressions. The `position` expression abbreviates to nothing; therefore

```
child::Client[position()=1]
```

abbreviates to

```
Client[1]
```

This simply selects the first Client element of the context node. The next expression selects the last child of the context node:

```
child::Client[position()=last()]
```

It must retain the empty parentheses; otherwise, it will look for other child elements. Therefore, it abbreviates to

```
Client[last()]
```

Here are some other abbreviations:

- ✔ Client[>1] selects all the client nodes other than the first client node.
- ✔ Client[< last()] selects all the client nodes other than the last client node.
- ✔ Client[last()-1] selects the client node immediately before the last client node.
- ✔ child::Client[position()=1]/child::phone abbreviates to Client[1]/phone.

Some more abbreviations

Here are a few more abbreviations. The context node abbreviates to a dot (.). The descendant axis abbreviates to a forward slash, so the following:

```
descendants::Phone
```

which selects all the Phone elements in the document, abbreviates to

```
/Phone
```

Several more XPath abbreviations and functions are possible, but the previous examples are the ones that you'll use in all but the most esoteric cases. To see the other examples, consult the specification at www.w3c.org/TR/xpath.

Using XPath with XPointer and XSL

By themselves, XPath expressions are not much good. They're just part of a language that describes how to select a set of nodes or a single node from a document. To be of use, you must combine them with some other application:

- ✔ In XPointers, the expressions of XPath are used to point software to a particular spot in the document. See Chapter 19 for more information.

- ✔ In XSL, XPath expressions are used to select a node or a whole series of nodes so that they can either be transformed from one XML element set to another element set or have styles applied to them.

- ✔ Other potential uses for XPath expressions include a simple XML query language for retrieving hunks of data from an XML document.

Where to Now?

One fun application of XPath occurs in a language called Schematron (an alternative to XML Schema, in fact), which uses XPath (and some XSL) to describe document structures. (To find out more about Schematron, visit `www.ascc.net/xml/resource/schematron/schematron.html`.) To you, all this XPath stuff might not seem like fun, but in the drab lives that document nerds live, it looks like Mardi Gras!

Chapter 19

The XML Pointer Language

In This Chapter

▶ Examining the purpose of XPointers

▶ Figuring out what XPointers do

▶ Discussing how XPointers work

*I*n this chapter, we cover XML Pointers (XPointers), which provide mechanisms to create links into specific document locations. We also show you how to use XPointers to pinpoint locations within a document.

To get an idea of just how useful XPointers can be, put on your imagining hat and picture this: a browser based on the new XML-based XPointers that can give you the option of choosing only a part of a document (say, only news items with a date of yesterday or later) for download and display. To do this, the browser needs a mechanism to identify the start point and the end point for the display. XPointer syntax makes this possible because it enables you to select a range in the document. In other words, with XPointer syntax you can isolate a complete section of a document.

You read more about selecting specific chunks of text in the upcoming section, "How much can I get you?" For now it's important to know that XPointer lets you get at pieces and parts of your document so that you can do cool things with them.

Anchors (And Fragments) Away

A *pointer* takes you to a specific spot inside a document. If you've surfed the Web, you've used pointers, even though you might not have realized it at the time. When you click a hyperlink, you're taken to a location in a Web document, or maybe even given the option to download a remote file, such as a sound clip or PDF document. The pointer part of the element (the `href` attribute for your HTML geeks out there) specifies exactly where the link takes you (the page or the resource). An XHTML pointer can lead you to the head of a new page, to the middle of a page, or to a specific heading in a page — that's how accurate they are.

The concept of pointers in XML is heavily based on hypertext pointers (the kind you use on the Web). Think of Web pointers as the granddaddy of XML pointers. We start with a discussion of Web pointers because they will give you great insight into how pointers work in XML. In the end, XML pointers are just Web pointers on steroids.

Pointers are also at work when you click an item in a table of contents on a Web page and are automatically taken down the page to a specific part of the page. Figures 19-1 and 19-2 illustrate this very cool pointer functionality. Figure 19-1 shows the top of a page on the LANWrights, Inc. site devoted to listing of magazine articles we've written. Notice that you don't see any articles, just a list of hyperlinked magazine names.

If you click any magazine name, you don't jump to another Web page, but rather to a spot further down on the page. The pointer doesn't take you off the page, but to a specific chunk — more technically called a *fragment* — of the page, as shown in Figure 19-2.

You can see this pointer functionality for yourself online at `www.lanw.com/mags.htm`. If you really want to know what HTML makes this page tick, view the source for the page.

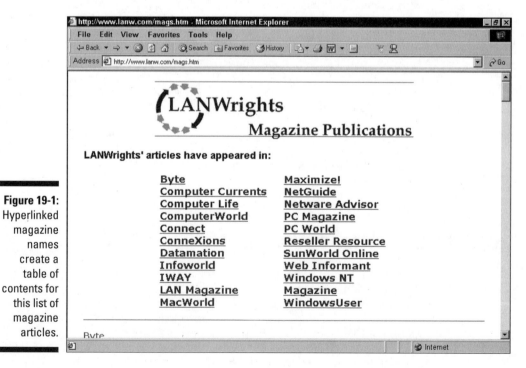

Figure 19-1:
Hyperlinked magazine names create a table of contents for this list of magazine articles.

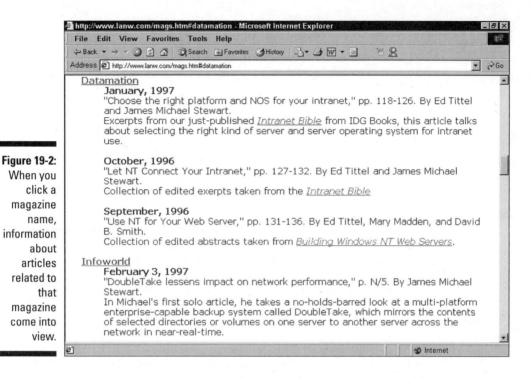

Figure 19-2:
When you
click a
magazine
name,
information
about
articles
related to
that
magazine
come into
view.

Three markup components are at work here: elements, document fragments, and fragment identifiers. The elements (the headings that hold the magazine names) have links with pointers attached to them. When you click the link, the pointer is activated. A *document fragment* is a piece of the document you call out so that you can link to it. In this case, the magazine document is composed of many fragments, each one holding a list of articles we've written for each magazine.

Finally, the *fragment identifier* is the thing that connects the two. The fragment itself (each list of magazine articles) has an identifier (invisible to the naked eye) that we've placed beside it in the XHTML that drives the page. For example, the identifier for the listing of articles for Byte magazine is byte (this is a no-brainer). We reference the identifier in the link element around the magazine's name, and poof, like magic, when you click the magazine's name, the link looks for the fragment identifier and brings the fragment into view. Cool huh?

Why Do You Need XPointers?

So far you've seen how pointers work on the Web (and consequently in XHTML), and in general, they work fairly well. However, Web pointers as they exist today have one major drawback: To point into a fragment on a page, not only do you have to create a document with a link to the fragment, but you have to be able to tag a fragment identifier onto the fragment itself. No fragment identifier, no link to fragment. In other words, if you don't own the document and all its fragments that you want to point to, you're out of luck.

Another drawback of existing Web pointers is that they require you to download the whole document to your computer to work. Going back to our earlier magazine example, the browser downloads the whole list of magazine articles and then brings the articles for a particular magazine to view when you click the magazine's name. Even if you're not interested in the other sections of that document, you must still download and display them. For a page that only lists 50 or 60 articles, this isn't a big deal. Imagine one with 10,000 instead. You can run out for coffee and a bagel while you wait for it to load. There's a better way.

This is where the pointers on steroids we mentioned earlier come in. The gurus of XML wanted you to have a way to point to fragments inside documents that you don't own (wasn't that nice of them). They also wanted you to be able to work with only those fragments (for display or any other reason) instead of having to work with a whole document just to get the fragment. To make this happen, you need a method for identifying fragments inside a document even when you don't have editing privileges for that document and can't mark them as fragments yourself. You also need a way to specify where the fragment you want starts and ends.

Enter the XPointer Specification. XPointer provides several mechanisms to create links to specific locations (a word often used interchangeably with fragments in XPointer discussion) within any given document. Think back to the magazine article example from a bit earlier in the chapter. Imagine that Byte magazine (one listed on the site) wanted to point only to the listing of magazine articles from its Web site. XPointer would allow them to point inside the LANWrights, Inc. Magazines page even though Byte doesn't have access to the page to add in its own fragment identifiers.

Of course, it takes a browser that supports XPointer for this approach to actually work. The XPointer specification tells you how to create and use pointers, but it's up to your software to implement them. (Note that very few browsers support XPointer. Most are experimental and not in the mainstream. Check out www.xmlsoftware.com to see whether more have been released since the writing of this book.) To paraphrase how Winston Churchill might have addressed browser makers, "We can give you the tools, but you will have to finish the job yourself."

The XPointer language is a Candidate Recommendation, so it may change slightly before becoming a full-blown recommendation. As always, check out the official source for the information at `www.w3.org/TR/xptr`.

Understanding XPointer Syntax

XPointer provides three methods to point into a document:

- ✔ A shorthand method that employs fragment identifiers (IDs) for specifically naming and referencing a chunk of content.

- ✔ A shorthand method that uses a simple syntax to step you through a document.

- ✔ Full-blown XPath syntax. In this method, XPath is combined with XPointer to use complex path notation to find a spot in a document and then create a pointer out of it. XPointer also provides a mechanism to select a section or a range within a document.

See Chapter 18 for more information on XPath. In that chapter, we use an example `clients.xml` document to show how you can create complex paths that lead a processing system to very specific pieces of a document.

Show me your ID

Speaking of the `clients.xml` document, we're using another `clients.xml` document (Listing 19-1) in this chapter. This document incorporates the same clients DTD from Chapter 18 to give you a look into how XPointer works. In the real world, this document would hold a list of clients' contact information, and you could use XPointer to point into it and work with information about a particular client.

This `clients.xml` document uses predefined fragment identifiers (one of XPointers methods of pointing to a chunk of document) to assign a unique identifier to each set of client information. Look for the `id` attribute in each `Client` element to see these identifiers at work.

Listing 19-1: The clients.xml Document

```
<?xml version="1.0"?>
<!DOCTYPE clients SYSTEM "clients.dtd">
<Clients>
<!-- This is Clients.xml -->
 <Client id="c1">
  <Name>Jon Smith</Name>
  <Phone type="home">440-123-3333</Phone>
  <Fax>440-123-3334</Fax>
  <Email>jon@acme.com</Email>
```

(continued)

Listing 19-1 *(continued)*

```
<Phone type="home">440-123-3333</Phone>
<Fax>440-123-3334</Fax>
<Email>jon@acme.com</Email>
</Client>
<Client id="c2">
<Name>Bill Jones</Name>
<Phone type="cellphone">330-124-5432</Phone>
<Fax>440-123-5433</Fax>
<Email>bjones@someinc.com</Email>
</Client>
<Client id="c3">
<Name>Matt Brown</Name>
<Phone type="work">220-125-1234</Phone>
<Phone type="cellphone">233-344-4455</Phone>
<Phone type="home">234-567-8910</Phone>
<Fax>220-125-1235</Fax>
<Email>matthew@hotstuff.com</Email>
</Client>
</Clients>
```

Three clients are listed in this document, and each has a unique ID — c1, c2, and c3 respectively. Here's how to use XPointer to create an ID shortcut in your XML documents:

1. **In your XML document, assign ID attributes to each fragment you want to identify.**

   In the clients.xml document, we assign an ID to each Client element because the Client element holds all other information about the client. The elements you assign IDs to will be based on how small you want your fragments to be and how your documents are structured. We chose clients because we wanted all client information to be included in our fragments. If we were only interested in client names, we would have assigned IDs to Name elements instead.

2. **Create links that include a reference fragment identifier. (In our example, the fragment identifiers are c1, c2, and c3, which refer to the ID attribute values.)**

   The fragment identifier is always the same as the value of the id attribute. When you create a pointer to the fragment, you use the name of the document followed by the pound sign (#), followed by the fragment identifier (the value of the id attribute). The pointer to the third client (Matt Brown) in our clients.xml file looks like this:

   ```
   clients.xml#c3
   ```

   If the pointer-enabled browser can't find a c3 ID, the browser points to the top of the remote resource.

Please step me through this!

If you don't want to create predefined fragment identifiers in documents (as we showed you in the previous section) or if you don't have access to the documents in the first place to add the identifiers, don't despair. You can include XPointer in your XML documents to point to fragments in any XML document, even when those fragments don't have predefined IDs. The syntax for these kinds of pointers uses a set of integers separated by forward slashes (/) to help you identify the fragment.

A slash represents a level of nesting in the document you are pointing to; the number of slashes represents the nesting level's closeness to the root element. The root element is always represented in the markup by the number 1. Each integer represents the position of an element within that nesting level. (The lower the number, the closer the element appears sequentially to its parent element.)

The first forward slash represents the root of the document. Because there can be only one root element, it's always followed by 1. Check out the `clients.xml` document back in Listing 19-1 to see what we mean. The following points you to the `clients.xml` root element, which just happens to be called `Clients`:

```
Clients.xml#/1
```

An added slash points the browser to the second child element of the `Clients` element: namely, the second `Client` element that contains Bill Jones' contact information:

```
Clients.xml#/1/2
```

Finally, the following points you to the fourth child of the second child of the `Clients` element — namely, the `Email` element of the second `Client` element:

```
Clients.xml#/1/2/4
```

This part of the XPointer syntax is hierarchical just like XML document structure is. Coincidental? We think not. This is a good thing because it means XPointers point exactly where you want them to. If you say fourth child of the second element, that's what you're going to get, not the 3rd child of the fifth element.

Here's a harder one:

```
Clients.xml#/1/3/1
```

It's the first child of the third child of the `Clients` element, namely the `Name` element of the Matt Brown record.

Show me the path

The third method for XPointers is very powerful. You can use XPath to describe a document location with XPointers. To use this method, you use the xptr() function in the fragment identifier. (See the "Show me your ID" section to find out more about fragment identifiers.) XPath is used by both eXtensible Stylesheet Language Transformations (XSLT) and XPointer. We discuss XPath in Chapter 18.

The general syntax for a fragment identifier used with XPath, xptr, must be all lowercase characters and tells the browser that we're about to use an XPath as a locating device:

```
#xptr( XPath expression )
```

Now all we have to do is insert an XPath expression. This expression points to the second Client element in our document:

```
Clients.xml#xptr( child::Clients[1]/child::Client[position()=2]) )
```

Here's an abbreviated version:

```
Clients.xml#xptr(Clients[1]/ Client[2]) )
```

Here's an even more abbreviated version:

```
Clients.xml#xptr(// Client[2]) )
```

In XPath, the *root node* of a document is a node that contains the whole document, including the version declaration and the document element. This means that when you use XPointer with XPath (as opposed to the simple XPath syntax you saw in the last section), the pointer starts at the document level, not the root element.

What If I Don't Have My ID?

In the United States, if you have a baby face and want to buy beer, chances are that you'll be asked to show an ID to prove that you're of legal drinking age. You know the drill: "No ID, no beer!" (Some of us are long past the age where anyone asks for our ID, though. Sigh.)

A similar thing happens with XPointers. When an XPointer-enabled browser comes across a fragment identifier that claims to point at an ID, it demands to see some proof that the attribute is indeed of the type ID. The only way that it can do this is to look at the document type (DOCTYPE) declaration. If a

Document Type Definition (DTD) isn't present or can't be found, a similar rule applies: "No ID, no can point!" See Chapters 6, 7, and 10 for more information on DTDs.

But the lords of XML are not as hard-hearted as our enlightened legislators. You have an alternative if a browser fails to find a document's ID. You can string two pointers together so that, if the first pointer fails, the browser can next try a second pointing method! (Sort of like going to another store in the hopes that the clerk thinks that you actually look old enough to pound a few.)

Here's how this works. The following is the fragment identifier that can find an ID:

```
#xptr( id()="c3")
```

This alternative works just fine if your browser can find the DTD for `clients.xml`. But what if it can't? In that case, your browser returns an error and shows you the whole document starting from the top. The DTD may very well be there, but for some reason the browser just can't access it — an all-too-common occurrence.

On the other hand, if you use the following markup instead, your browser goes on to evaluate the second XPointer expression if the first fails:

```
#xptr( id()="c3")xptr(//*[@id="c3"/parent::node()])
```

Because the second expression doesn't rely on the fact that the `id` attribute is of type `ID`, the pointer successfully locates the remote resource being pointed to.

You just provided yourself with a savvy insurance policy. You can run together as many `xptr()` expressions as you want; they're evaluated from left to right. The second is evaluated only if the first returns an error; the third is evaluated only if both the first and second return an error; and so on. Just another case of persistence paying off.

How Much Can 1 Get You?

One of the cool things about XPointers is that they can identify a start point and also a whole section of a document. XPointers enable you to display just a portion of a remote document because you can use them to can specify a range by using the `to` keyword with an XPath expression on either side. For example

```
xptr(id("c2") to id("c3"))
```

selects the following part of the `clients.xml` document:

```
<Client id="c2">
  <Name>Bill Jones</Name>
  <Phone type="cellphone">330-124-5432</Phone>
  <Fax>440-123-5433</Fax>
  <Email>bjones@someinc.com</Email>
</Client>
```

Ranges can get quite complicated, but the most important thing to remember is that the start of the range must occur before the end of the range, and the range must occur in the same document.

Part VI
XML in the Real World

The 5th Wave
By Rich Tennant

©RICHTENNANT

" What I'm looking for are dynamic XML applications
and content, not HTML innuendoes and intent. "

In this part . . .

The real power of XML comes from its capability to capture, organize, and represent data of many different kinds and to make it available for all kinds of cool uses. Part VI helps give some substance to this claim, as you explore tools, services, and genuine workplace applications for XML data, documents, and technologies.

Chapter 20 covers a collection of useful and interesting XML software tools, from XML editors, to XML document managers, to XML-enabled Web browsers and more — many of which you'll find ready for your personal exploration on the companion CD for this book. Chapter 21 explores the world of so-called "Web services," which rely on a potent combination of XML applications to advertise, describe, and broker connections between service providers (companies or organizations with data or online services to offer the public) and service consumers (users who are willing to meet the terms and conditions necessary to gain access to service offerings). Chapter 22 concludes this part of the book with a quick overview of how several well-known companies that are using XML documents and tools for a variety of interesting business purposes. Because these companies have invested millions of dollars in these systems and the XML data and documents they manage, it doesn't get any more real than that! It also covers a plethora of other interesting uses for XML markup, in case you're looking for more reasons why businesses are going so gaga over XML.

Chapter 20

Cool XML Tools and Technologies

. . . .

In This Chapter

▶ Discovering the tricks of the trade

▶ Creating XML documents with your favorite tools

▶ Validating like a breeze with a parser

▶ Viewing XML documents gets easier

▶ Converting XML documents

. . . .

*N*obody tackles a lot of eXtensible Markup Language (XML) authoring without the help of some authoring tool, and no one should try to manage a collection of XML documents without using some software tools along the way. To help you, we offer here a list of some of our favorite tools for authoring, checking, viewing, and converting XML documents. If your resources or your time are limited — and whose aren't these days? — these are the essential tools that you absolutely must check out.

At the beginning of each section, you find a quick reference table (Table 20-1 through Table 20-5) that lists all the tools discussed in the section, along with the most pertinent of details: how much it costs and where to find out more. Also, don't forget to check out Appendix A, where you can discover which of these tools we've included on the CD-ROM that accompanies this book.

Creating Documents with Authoring Tools

Table 20-1	XML Authoring Tools		
Product Name	*URL*	*Single User Price*	*Free Demo Copy?*
Epic Editor	www.arbortext.com	$695	N/A
Turbo XML v2.2	www.tibco.com	$269.95	Yes

(continued)

Product Name	URL	Single User Price	Free Demo Copy?
XMetaL 2.1	www.softquad.com	Less than $500	Yes
XML Pro v2.0	www.vervet.com	Less than $199	Yes
XML Spy 4.3 Suite	www.xmlspy.com	$399	Yes

Table 20-1 *(continued)*

The first step in working with XML is to create a document, and you may have already gotten around to using your trusty old text editor to create your first XML documents. Don't feel like you have to go it alone, though, because we've found a few XML-specific editors that might change your habits.

To help you get your documents under construction, the following sections list of some of the best XML authoring tools available that we know of. Keep in mind that as long as XML continues to create a buzz, more tools will emerge on the scene. To keep up to date on the latest technology, be sure to read Chapter 24 for more on XML resources.

Epic Editor

Arbortext has built Standard Generalized Markup Language (SGML) editors for years and has helped pave the way for XML tools. Epic Editor comes from that SGML background and has been adapted for XML.

Epic Editor, which has earned worldwide recognition for its power, performance, and capabilities, enables you to author and edit a medium to large volume of XML-based business documentation that needs to be disseminated in multiple forms (across the Web, on a CD-ROM, in print, and through wireless devices, for example). Use Epic Editor when you need to handle large document collections or documents with multiple authors.

This product is definitely designed for advanced XML creation. Although Epic Editor is expensive, it's complete and worth every pretty penny if you're building complex documents with XML or SGML. Visit the Arbortext site at www.arbortext.com to learn more about this groovy tool.

Turbo XML v2.2

Turbo XML v2.2, from TIBCO Software, Inc., is a graphical design tool that accelerates the creation and enhances the management of schemas. It includes a toolset to help convert existing application and document structures to schemas, defining the basis for well-formed and valid XML documents. In addition, it has import and output support for XML Schema, External Data Representation (XDR), BizTalk, Schema for Object-Oriented XML (SOX), and Document Type Definitions (DTDs).

This fabulous upgrade includes new documentation, syntax checking, and import/export features. Well worth the money (only $269.95), Turbo XML is not designed for the beginner; a working knowledge of XML and an understanding of schema design basics are assumed. Turbo XML fully supports and extends the XML Schema specification. Read more about Turbo XML at www.tibco.com.

XMetaL 3

SoftQuad Software — best known as the maker of the popular HTML editor HoTMetaL PRO — developed XMetaL. It's not badly priced ($399 in the U.S.). Like many XML editors, XMetaL offers users a familiar word processing environment that's easy to use. XMetaL anticipates the next generation of browsers by offering Cascading Style Sheets (CSS) editing capabilities. XMetaL also supports both DTDs and XML Schema. It conforms to numerous standards including SGML, XML, CALS tables, Document Object Model (DOM), CSS, and HTML. Find out more at www.softquad.com.

XML Pro v2.0

A more basic product — and a less expensive alternative to XMetaL — is XML Pro, developed at Vervet Logic. XML Pro sure can edit but doesn't claim to do much more.

You can create and edit XML documents while using a clean and easy interface. The newest release claims to be fully W3C XML 1.0 compliant and features the IBM XML4J parser. Currently, there's no support for document conversion, DTD creation, or style sheet design. You can read more at www.vervet.com.

Because many of the editors listed come at a hefty price, we recommend that you test drive demo versions when they're available. Demos should be accessible on the product pages.

XML Spy 4.3

XML Spy 4.3 Suite is one of the sweetest XML multi-tools around. Okay, maybe it can't slice, dice, chop, and pare, but it does handle XML and knows how to deal with XSLT and XML Schemas. But wait, there's more: It also supports graphical design, schema- or DTD-based validation, database connectivity, and so much more. At $399, its price is comparable to other tools, but it does an awful lot for the money. To discover more about this cool tool, visit www.xmlspy.com (a 30-day evaluation copy is also available for downloading).

Checking Documents with Parser Tools

Table 20-2		Parsers	
Product Name	**Validating?**	**URL**	**Single User Price**
Ælfred	No	www.opentext.com/microstar	Free
expat v1.2	No	www.jclark.com/xml/expat.html	Free
Lark	No	www.textuality.com/Lark/	Free
SP v1.3	Yes	www.jclark.com/sp	Free
XML4J Parser 3.2.1	Yes	www.alphaworks.ibm.com/tech/xml4j	Free

Your XML document is a carefully crafted work of art and adheres to strict XML 1.0 compliance. You believe that you've followed the rules, and now you're ready to check your work. Luckily, you don't have to check each element by hand — parsers do that for you!

Use a parser to ensure that your XML documents are well formed and, if linked to a DTD, valid as well. (See Chapter 4 for more information on valid and well-formed XML documents.)

Parsing is a basic but important step in XML publishing. Errors can be the death knell to any XML document. Forget those old HTML days when browsers picked up your slack. An XML document must be well formed, and it must also be valid if it uses a DTD. Parsers help enforce these requirements.

Some parsers check only that a document is well formed; others also check for validity. Make sure you examine the parser's capabilities when you're selecting one that's right for your needs. Look back at Chapter 13 for a discussion of how to choose the right parser to meet your needs.

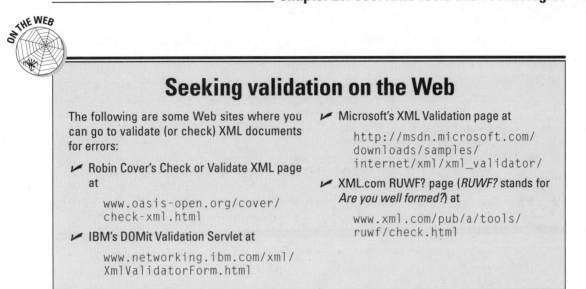

ON THE WEB

Seeking validation on the Web

The following are some Web sites where you can go to validate (or check) XML documents for errors:

✔ Robin Cover's Check or Validate XML page at

    www.oasis-open.org/cover/
    check-xml.html

✔ IBM's DOMit Validation Servlet at

    www.networking.ibm.com/xml/
    XmlValidatorForm.html

✔ Microsoft's XML Validation page at

    http://msdn.microsoft.com/
    downloads/samples/
    internet/xml/xml_validator/

✔ XML.com RUWF? page (*RUWF?* stands for *Are you well formed?*) at

    www.xml.com/pub/a/tools/
    ruwf/check.html

Ælfred

The folks at Microstar offer their Java-based parser to the public for free. (Can't squawk about the price.) Ælfred is a non-validating parser, which means that it checks documents only for well-formedness. According to its designers, Ælfred concentrates on optimizing speed and size rather than error reporting, so it's most useful for deployment over the Internet. Read more at www.opentext.com/microstar.

expat v1.2

James Clark is a legend in the SGML community because of his amazing collection of tools that support all kinds of cool functionality — most of it in the form of freeware that works like the dickens. This James Clark contribution, expat v1.2, is a non-validating XML parser written in C. Check out this free and quite useful parser at www.jclark.com/xml/expat.html.

Lark

Tim Bray offers the Java-based XML processor Lark, which he built as a way to sanity-check the XML design requirement so that ". . . it shall be easy to write programs that process XML documents." Tim Bray has been a member of the W3C's XML Working Group since long before it operated under that name. (It all started as a special interest group within the SGML cadre at the

W3C.) His work on XML is widely recognized and deservedly renowned. Among other things, Tim was the coeditor of the XML specification.

Lark, a non-validating parser, could be useful for other programmers who seek to follow in his footsteps, but it's also a pretty great tool in its own right. The parser is solidly built and has been tweaked over time to meet most programmers' needs. The fruits of Tim's labor are available for download at www.textuality.com/Lark.

 Much of the software listed in this chapter is free for the downloading. The only payment that you will be asked to give is feedback. XML tools are still pretty green; this means you must watch out for bugs. Make sure that you report any bugs that you find to the responsible parties. They'll thank you for it!

SP v1.3

Here's another great contribution from legendary James Clark. His state-of-the-art SP parser, SP v1.3, can be configured to parse and validate XML as well as SGML. What a dandy tool. If you want a validating version of Lark, this is it.

XML4J Parser 3.2.1

IBM offers a validating XML parser, XML4J, that's written in Java and available to users for free. This parser is the subject of a lot of buzz and seems to lead the pack in online reviews, probably because the crack team at IBM put it together. Tools like this help to explain IBM's stellar reputation in the tool development department. Big Blue is creating many XML tools, technologies, and resources as it expands its technology arsenal. Find more information about XML4J and other tools at www.alphaworks.ibm.com/tech/xml4j.

Viewing with XML Browsers

Table 20-3	XML-Enabled Web Browsers	
Product Name	**URL**	**Single User Price**
Amaya	www.w3.org/Amaya/	Free
Internet Explorer 6	www.microsoft.com/windows/ ie/default.asp	Free

Product Name	URL	Single User Price
Mozilla	www.mozilla.org	Free
Opera	www.opera.com	Free

According to most Web designers, XML can revolutionize the way that people look at and transfer information across the Web. However, before XML can start that revolution, browsers must provide their support. Netscape Navigator doesn't currently support XML fully. A few other browsers, such as Amaya and Opera, however, do provide such support. We find the browsers that we cover in this section to be noteworthy.

Amaya

Amaya is the W3C browser and authoring tool that you can use to demonstrate and test many new developments in Web protocols and data formats. Amaya is versatile and extensible, which makes it easy to add new features. Along with support for XML, Amaya supports HTML, eXtensible HyperText Markup Language (XHTML), MathML, and CSS 2. It also has limited Scalable Vector Graphics (SVG) support. (See Chapter 2 for more information on XHTML.) If it's good enough for the W3C, it should be good enough for you! Read more at www.w3.org/Amaya and then download the software for free.

Internet Explorer 6

The Microsoft king of browsers can't be left in the cold. Internet Explorer (IE) also offers XML support: Microsoft XML (MSXML) version 3.0 specifically. IE 6 also fully supports Dynamic HTML (DHTML), CSS 1, and DOM 1. It also provides some support for Synchronized Multimedia Integration Language (SMIL). You can't beat the price — free! — and if you're using one of the current flavors of Windows, you probably already have it. Download the latest version of IE from www.microsoft.com/windows/ie/default.asp.

Mozilla

Like many free XML tools, Mozilla is built around publicly available source code. Mozilla is fully compliant with standards for HTML 4.0, XML, CSS, and DOM. It includes expat (see the "expat v1.3" section earlier in this chapter) for XML parsing, supports CSS display for XML, and provides partial support for namespaces and simple XLinks (Chapter 17).

The folks at Mozilla.org are dedicated to debugging and updating this software, and you should be, too. Mozilla.org provides users with an open forum to report bugs. To download this free software or keep up with changes, visit www.mozilla.org.

Opera

The brainchild of the markup gurus at Opera Software ASA in Norway, Opera is easily the most international and platform friendly browser around. In addition to support for common operating systems such as Windows, Macintosh OS, and Linux/Solaris, Opera also runs on BeOS, OS/2, QNX (a real-time version of Unix), and Symbian (a hand-held device OS popular in Europe). This browser really gets around and is much smaller, faster, and easier to customize than some other browsers that we know. Opera also claims to provide " . . . full support for the XML 1.0 recommendation" and does a good enough job of delivering on that claim to be a part of our standard XML test environment.

You can get Opera for free (in which case, you must submit to the banner ads that support this mode of operation) or you can buy it for a modest $30 or so per copy. Discover more about this fine tool at www.opera.com.

Using XML Parsers and Engines

Table 20-4	XML Parsers and Engines	
Product Name	**URL**	**Single User Price**
XML C Library for Gnome	xmlsoft.org	Free
Java XML Pack	java.sun.com/xml/download.html	Free
Xerces	xml.apache.org	Free

XML parsers and engines provide tools that can ingest and interpret the contents of XML documents (with or without governing DTDs or schemas against which to validate). Basically, such tools sit at the core of most of the other tools that we cover up to this point in this chapter.

XML C Library for Gnome

Daniel Veillard's XML C Library for Gnome (libxml) is a case in point. This collection of C language routines implements a validating XML parser that can work with various XML document models (including the DOM, and the so-called Simple API for XML, or SAX). It also implements support for XPath and XPointers, as well as lots of other goodies. (For more on XPath and XPointers, see Chapters 18 and 19, respectively.) Check it out at xmlsoft.org.

Java XML Pack

Sun Microsystems, Inc. offers a cornucopia of Java-based XML tools, APIs, and more. Visit its Java Technology and XML page at java.sun.com/xml/download.html to find the Java XML Pack. This site includes some of the most popular Java XML tools, including:

- **JAXM:** The Java API for XML Messaging
- **JAXP:** The Java API for XML Processing
- **JAXR:** The Java API for XML Registries
- **JAX-RPC:** The Java API for XML-based Remote Procedure Call

Of these elements, JAXP offers a reasonably complete XML processing engine, but the other tools will be of interest to those building distributed applications using Java and XML as well. Visit java.sun.com/xml/download.html for more information.

Xerces

The Open Source Apache project is famous for producing the world's most popular Web server software, but that's just the barest suggestion of its large and interesting collection of Web- and document-related software tools and technologies. Among the many Apache offerings, the Xerces-C++ Parser 2.0 is of great interest if you're looking for a powerful yet compact XML parser to build around. The Apache library of routines can handle a wide range of XML tasks from parsing to generating, validating, and manipulating XML documents. The library is definitely worth your time. Discover more at xml.apache.org/xerces-c/index.html. You can also find the most current version of a Java Xerces available at xml.apache.org/xerces2-j/index.html.

Employing Conversion Tools

Table 20-5	XML Conversion Tools		
Product Name	*URL*	*Single User Price*	*Free Demo Copy?*
HTML Tidy	`tidy.sourceforge.net`	Free	N/A
XMLPDF library	`www.xmlpdf.com/ overview.html`	$199	No
Xml2lit library	`www.ebookstools.net/ xml2lit/xml2lit_e.htm`	Free	N/A
XPS	`softml.net/xps`	Free	N/A

When it comes to making XML content as accessible as possible, consider using a tool to convert it from its native document format into something else. Many of these tools use XSLT (or implement similar capabilities) to do their thing. As you look at some of the conversion tools that we cover here, you should get a good idea that *something else* covers a lot of territory!

HTML Tidy

W3C stalwart Dave Raggett has created a wonderful tool called HTML Tidy that can validate against a whole slew of HTML, XHTML, and other DTDs. This conversion tool can even convert HTML into XHTML or other forms of XML as well. In fact, Dave's tool sits at the heart of numerous extremely good HTML tools including HTML-Kit (available free from `www.chami.com`) that puts a friendly face on Tidy and adds lots of additional functionality. For more information on Tidy, please visit `tidy.sourceforge.net`.

XMLPDF library

The XMLPDF library provides a set of routines that can convert XML documents into the popular Adobe portable document format (PDF) for viewing or printing. This code works on a Web server to read XML input and to send PDF output to users so that the burden of conversion is handled on the server side. Output documents can draw on multiple sources of input, and content may also be dynamically generated at run-time. This is a pretty neat toolbox for making sophisticated XML content available to garden-variety users using widely adopted PDF viewers such as Adobe Acrobat. For more information, please visit `www.xmlpdf.com/overview.html`.

Xml2lit library

Mark Lipsman's Xml2lit library provides tools to transform XML into various e-book formats. Supported formats include those required for the Microsoft Reader (LIT format), Mobipocket Publisher (XDOC), plus TXT and HTML formats, which can be further transformed into PalmDoc formats for Palm-powered devices, such as the 3COM Palm or the Handspring Visor. For more information visit `www.ebookstools.net/xml2lit/xml2lit_e.htm`. For the whole package, download `xml2lit.zip` from `www.ebookstools.net/xml2lit`.

Extensible Programming Script (XPS)

SoftML Pte Ltd has created the powerful transformation tool *XPS* that can translate XML into other formats, or other formats into XML, all based on an XML data manipulation language. XPS supports easy transforms to or from Structured Query Language (SQL)- or Open Database Connectivity (ODBC)-compliant databases as well as more text-intensive document types. For more information, please visit `softml.net/xps`.

The Ultimate XML Grab Bag and Goodie Box

All the other products that we list in this chapter have a focus on a particular piece of an XML solution — editing, validating, and so on. However, some companies do it all. Here are a few of our favorites.

Microsoft does XML, too!

In its search to extend the reach and capability of its Internet software, particularly the Internet Explorer browser, Microsoft is an unexpected and ardent XML supporter, particularly for the Channel Definition Format (CDF) and the Resource Definition Framework (RDF) — among other XML applications. As it begins to add additional XML support to the next release of Internet Explorer, Microsoft offers numerous other XML tools as well. To read more about the Microsoft view of XML, visit `msdn.microsoft.com/xml`.

webMethods automates XML excellence

webMethods, Inc. has constructed the core of its Web services toolkit (the webMethods integration platform) around XML and Java technology. This toolkit is marketed heavily for use in electronic commerce and related applications, and for automating access to a variety of Web-based data and services, both in HTML and XML. The webMethods integration platform has been well received in the marketplace and is worth investigating for those who seek to improve data access, data handling, and data security on their Web sites.

To obtain an evaluation copy of the webMethods integration platform, or for more information about the company and its products, visit www. webmethods.com.

 We can't cover all the wonderful XML tools available. To find a complete guide on XML software, check out www.xmlsoftware.com.

We hope you enjoy some of our favorite XML tools as much as we do. And don't overlook these two great tools: Consult the "About the CD" appendix to help you explore the accompanying CD's contents; flip through this book's glossary for great help in decoding the sometimes-mysterious terminology you're likely to encounter when canvassing the wild and wooly intellectual landscape of XML.

Chapter 21

XML and Web Services

*T*he Internet and the Web are in the process of remaking the world of computing as we know it today, promising to reshape it in fundamental ways for the world of tomorrow. And of course, XML also has a key role to play in this reshaping because XML documents — at least, those governed by Document Type Definitions (DTDs), XML Schemas, or other alternative forms of documentation — are sufficiently self-describing to carry their descriptions along with their content and make themselves understood to any XML-capable software program.

The world breaks up into two broad classes of computer users: Those who have specific information gathering or processing needs to fulfill (we dub them *service consumers*), and those who have specific information resources or processing capabilities to offer (*service providers*). Basic supply and demand.

A service provider can also be a service consumer because, in addition to providing its own unique data, the provider may provide content that it digested from another resource. For example, say an accounting firm offers access to IRS tax code information. The service provider then passes on the content to end users, along with useful tips on reading and interpreting the code. This is what Web services are fundamentally about — the use, reuse, augmentation, and dissemination of information — and financial gain, of course.

This chapter gives you a birds-eye view of how XML plays a role in the exchange and storage of data for consumers and providers.

What's Up with Web Services?

In a virtual world where Web services help define a basic model for computing, the Internet and the Web explode into action. In this world, services consumers — that may be individuals, corporations, organizations, associations, or institutions — seek to find the best resources and the best deals for their information and processing needs. In this same world, services providers seek to advertise and promote their services so that service consumers can take a look at the wealth of cool resources and pass these services on to consumers.

In the process of passing on the information and services that customers want, service providers

- Establish and confirm the consumer's identity.
- Establish the consumer's credit and ability to pay.
- Set up an account and a user profile, which govern what services the consumer can access from a provider.

For example, most people run an e-mail client on their desktop, downloading and managing e-mail messages locally. When you're ready to read your e-mail, you click the Receive button (or something similar) to send a message to your e-mail server requesting a download of all your e-mail messages. The server complies and sends them to you. Your e-mail client handles all this for you (that's what clients are supposed to do, after all). When you're ready to send an e-mail message, you type it up in your e-mail client's editor and click the Send button. Your client shoots the message off to the outgoing mail server, and the mail is off and running. Figure 21-1 illustrates how an e-mail client on the desktop sends and receives messages with mail servers on the Internet.

The e-mail software and the entire store of e-mail messages reside on your desktop machine, but this information made its way to your desktop through the Internet. As the collection of e-mail piling up in your mailbox is evidence of, service providers have created elaborate systems designed to make it possible for you send and receive e-mail seamlessly from a server somewhere on the Internet.

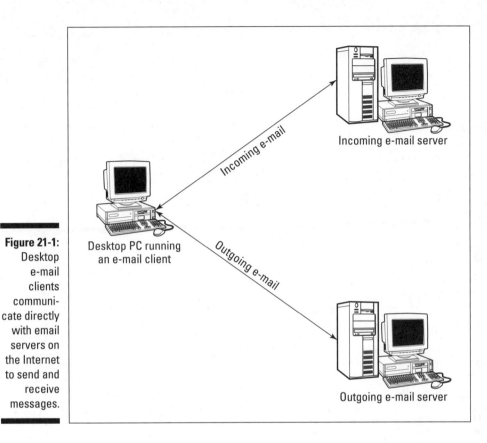

Figure 21-1:
Desktop
e-mail
clients
communi-
cate directly
with email
servers on
the Internet
to send and
receive
messages.

Incoming e-mail

Incoming e-mail server

Desktop PC running
an e-mail client

Outgoing e-mail

Outgoing e-mail server

A Web services model for e-mail (of which many implementations are already available, including Hotmail, Yahoo! Mail, and others) takes a different approach to e-mail access for the user. To use one of the Web-based e-mail services, you set up an e-mail account and use your Web browser to send and receive e-mail. The brains that drive the e-mail software are split between your desktop and the remote e-mail server that holds your messages and folders. Figure 21-2 shows how the e-mail Web service approach is different from the desktop client e-mail approach.

In this e-mail scenario, you manage the e-mail interface, decide what to do with incoming e-mail messages, and create outgoing e-mail messages just as you do with a desktop e-mail client. However, a server somewhere on the Web handles all the dirty work: requesting and sending messages, storing messages, filing messages, and such. With most of these Web-based e-mail services, you get the same functionality as you do with your favorite desktop client, and as a bonus, you can access your e-mail from any computer with a Web browser and Internet connection.

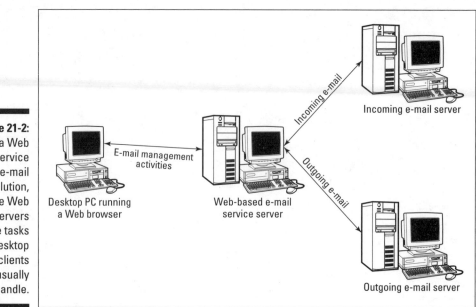

Figure 21-2:
In a Web
service
e-mail
solution,
remote Web
servers
handle tasks
that desktop
clients
usually
handle.

Incoming e-mail

Incoming e-mail server

E-mail management activities

Outgoing e-mail

Desktop PC running a Web browser

Web-based e-mail service server

Outgoing e-mail server

You have to access a Web page and provide an account name and password to supply proof of identity before you can access the data store (the collection of folders and saved messages in the case of e-mail) and the Web application service (the Web-based e-mail service you use to send and receive, read and write, and otherwise manage e-mail messages).

The concept of Web-based applications goes way beyond e-mail. Applications, such as word processing, spreadsheets, database management systems, and presentation systems, can become service based. The great benefit of Web services is they aren't tied to any single computer like traditional software applications are. Both the application functionality and the data are stored in a centralized server. This makes the functionality and content more accessible and encourages online collaboration.

But how? Patience, Grasshopper. If a service provider maintains a current, correct copy of the Web-based application and gives you access to all the necessary data (e-mail messages for e-mail services, documents for word processing, spreadsheets for spreadsheet services, and so on), just about any conceivable form of computing could fall into the Web services model. We think this explains why many software vendors are moving away from selling software outright and are instead beginning to license software on a renewable term.

Okay, what does this have to do with XML?

In fact, no compelling reason exists as to why other common monolithic applications — such as word processing, spreadsheets, database management systems, presentation systems, and so forth — have to remain monolithic in the future.

A Web Services Architecture

Because XML is well suited to describing all kinds of documents and data, and because such descriptions are easy to exchange across the Internet, XML is a natural foundation on which to construct an abstract model for Web services in general. In fact, XML experts have constructed a general model for how XML Web services should work; this model is known as the XML Web Services Architecture.

The Web Services Architecture is divided into four individual layers, each of which depends on access to one or more XML applications to support that layer's specific functions. In this section, we examine the entire model and provide only brief explanations of the layers involved. But in the following sections, we explore each layer in more detail and introduce some of many XML applications that various Web services implementations require at each layer.

In addition, the following list is presented top-down, so that the highest layer in this stack of names represents the most abstract functions, and the lowest layer in this stack represents the least abstract functions. As is the case with many layered models for communications (and that's a big part of what Web services is about), higher layers depend and build on the capabilities supplied at lower layers. In the following sections, we tackle the Web Services Architecture from the bottom up, starting with the Transport layer and working up to the Discovery layer. Here's the list:

- ✔ **Discovery:** This is the part of the Web services environment where service providers can supply descriptions of the information and services that they have to offer. This is also where would-be service consumers can make inquiries about what services are generally available or request details about specific available services. This layer generally addresses the question, "What's available out there?"

- ✔ **Description:** This is the part of Web services where available services and information are described in detail, along with the mechanisms necessary to describe how prospective service consumers and service providers can exchange messages with one another. This layer generally addresses the questions related to: "For Service X, what are the details involved in accessing this service, and what kinds of messages and data objects must be exchanged to take advantage of that service?"

   ✔ **Packaging/Extensions:** This is the part of Web services where issues related to managing, packaging, and securing exchanges of information between a service consumer and a service provider are handled. This layer generally addresses questions related to: "What kinds of requests and replies are reasonable for consumers and providers to exchange, and how will that message traffic be managed, controlled, secured, packaged, and represented?"

   ✔ **Transport:** This is the part of Web services where issues related to moving messages from a sender to a receiver are established. (Note that both consumers and provider can be senders and receivers; this will change among the latter roles as needed to maintain a working consumer/provider relationship.) This layer addresses questions related to: "What kinds of messages will be sent or received across the network, and what kinds of requests and replies do those messages represent?"

If you're familiar with the construction of network protocol stacks, you'll notice an intentional resemblance between the names and definitions we list here and the OSI Reference Model.

At each step along the way, we briefly mention important XML applications that are invoked in various implementations of this model.

Microsoft and IBM share a common view of the model at the level to which we've explained this so far. But as you might expect, these two companies do differ on the exact details involved, more at some layers than at others.

Transport: Moving XML messages

At the Transport level, the bottom of the stack, software clients (like Web browsers) and service delivery software on Web servers communicate with each other. In general, browsers and servers talk to each other at this level without requiring much user knowledge or interaction, if any.

Bottom line? The *Transport layer* acts like the highway that carries messages from senders to receivers; as long as the messages are suitable for the underlying road, things work just fine.

The Web services model is nearly unanimous in its adoption of the XML application known as Simple Object Access Protocol (SOAP) for exchange of self-describing, XML-based messages between senders and receivers (or consumers and providers, if you prefer). In fact, nearly every major XML player has endorsed SOAP as a basic mechanism whereby messages can be exchanged across the Internet. Some of the organizations that endorse SOAP include:

  ✔ Hewlett-Packard

  ✔ IBM

  ✔ Netscape Communications

  ✔ Microsoft

  ✔ OASIS (Organization for the Advancement of Structured Information
    Standards Consortium)

  ✔ Sun Microsystems

  ✔ W3C (World Wide Web Consortium)

Underlying protocols in SOAP not only include the same HyperText Transport
Protocol (HTTP) already used for everyday Web communications, but also
include other implementations of HTTP as well, including secure HTTP implementations and a newly minted *reliable HTTP* (also known as HTTPR).

For more information about the SOAP specification, please visit `www.`
`w3.org/2002/ws`. You can find the Primer, Messaging Framework, and
Adjuncts documents for SOAP listed about halfway down that page.

Packaging/Extensions: Managing information exchange

One layer up from the Transport layer in the Web Services Architecture is the
Packaging/Extensions layer. This layer is primarily concerned with establishing, managing, securing, and packaging information for exchange between
service consumers and producers.

The functions associated with this layer are aptly named. *Packaging* permits
text information, images, and other kinds of binary data to be neatly encapsu-
lated and sent to another other party over a network.

Extensions address enhancements to basic messaging services for the following reasons:

  ✔ To increase the level of security through encryption

  ✔ To strengthen the credentials that establish consumer and producer
    identities (such as digital signatures or certificates, which act the same
    way for virtual proofs of identity that inspections of driver's licenses or
    passports act for visual proofs of identity)

  ✔ To manage how messages are delivered from sender to receiver

Here's a brief annotated list of XML applications that you're likely to encounter when exploring the Packaging/Extensions layer of the Web Services Architecture:

- **WS-Referral (Web services Referral)** handles SOAP node configuration and message routing

  ```
  msdn.microsoft.com/library/default.asp?url=/library/
      en-us/dnglobspec/html/wsreferspecindex.asp
  ```

- **WS-Routing (Web services Routing)** routes SOAP using Transport Control Protocol (TCP), User Datagram Protocol (UDP), or HTTP

  ```
  msdn.microsoft.com/library/default.asp?url=/library/
      en-us/dnglobspec/html/wsroutspecindex.asp
  ```

- **WS-Security (Web services Security)** handles credential exchange, message integrity and confidentiality

  ```
  msdn.microsoft.com/library/default.asp?url=/library/
      en-us/dnglobspec/html/wssecurspecindex.asp
  ```

- **WS-License (Web services License)** provides descriptions for X.509 certificates, Kerberos tickets, and so on

  ```
  msdn.microsoft.com/library/default.asp?url=/library/
      en-us/dnglobspec/html/wslicspecindex.asp
  ```

- **SOAP-DSIG (SOAP Digital Signature)** permits use of XML Digital signatures in SOAP messages

  ```
  www.w3.org/TR/SOAP-dsig
  ```

- **SWA (SOAP Messages with Attachments)** packages SOAP messages into Multipurpose Internet Mail Extensions (MIME) messages

  ```
  www.w3.org/TR/SOAP-attachments
  ```

- **DIME (Direct Internet Message Encapsulation)** a binary format to package one or more payloads into single message

  ```
  search.ietf.org/internet-drafts/draft-nielsen-dime-01.txt
  ```

Description: Specifying services and related components

The Description layer is where things start to get more interesting from the overall perspective of what Web services are and can do (as compared with how they're packaged, delivered, and addressed). In fact, the Description layer encompasses a number of various XML applications designed to describe the following:

- How services are composed
- How they may be used

✔ How they can interact with other services

✔ How they must behave

✔ What they can offer potential consumers

These are all of some interest to consumers, and some aspects of the data available from these XML applications may actually be involved in selecting or using such services. Here's a summary of the Description layer services:

✔ **WSCM (Web Services Component Model)** defines mechanisms to package a Web service's display components

```
www.oasis-open.org/committees/wscm
```

✔ **WSXL (Web Services Experience Language)** is the component model for interactive Web applications

```
www-106.ibm.com/developerworks/webservices/library/ws-wsxl
```

✔ **WSUI (Web Services User Interface)** adds user interface and multistage interaction to SOAP-based message services

```
www.wsui.org/doc/20010629/WD-wsui-20010629.html
```

✔ **WSFL (Web Services Flow Language)** describes usage and interaction patterns for Web Services interactions

```
www-4.ibm.com/software/solutions/webservices/pdf/WSFL.pdf
```

✔ **WSEL (Web Services Endpoint Language)** describes cost and quality of service characteristics for service endpoints

```
www.w3.org/2001/04/wsws-proceedings/rod_smith/rod.pdf
```

✔ **WSDL (Web Services Description Language)** describes network services as a set of endpoints that operate on messages containing document- or procedure-oriented data

```
www.w3.org/TR/wsdl
```

✔ **XLANG (Web Services for Business Process Design)** describes message exchange behavior among participating Web services

```
www.gotdotnet.com/team/xml_wsspecs/xlang-c/default.htm
```

✔ **WSML (Web Services Meta Language)** maps operation of a service to specific methods in Microsoft's Common Object Model (COM)

```
msdn.microsoft.com/library/default.asp?url=/library/
    en-us/soap/htm/soap_overview_72r0.asp
```

The preceding lists a lot of potential or emerging XML applications, many of which are tailored for specific IBM or Microsoft views of Web services. Others in the list are designed to make it easier for multiple service providers to interact and exchange data on behalf of shared service consumers.

Of greatest interest at present is the Web Services Description Language (WSDL), which describes what kinds of information and services a specific service provider has to offer. Yep, that's right, a service that lists the services you can provide. Think about how many services a company like Yahoo! has to offer: e-mail, chat, bill pay, shopping, and more. WSDL could provide a catalog of Yahoo!'s many services and the particulars of them. The Web Services Endpoint Language (WSEL) is an IBM initiative that may take on wider interest as a replacement for WSDL if its ability to communicate about service quality and cost information is more widely adopted.

Discovery: Finding what's available

At the top of the Web Services Architecture is where you find XML applications geared to registering Web services for discovery by searching for services, inquiring about specific services, or inspecting what services some particular service provider may claim to offer. This is sort of like Google for Web services consumers. The customers can go out and search for which providers have what services (how many e-mail or shopping services there are for example). The three XML applications that you encounter in this context are:

- ✔ **UDDI (Universal Description, Discovery, and Integration)** enables businesses to discover one another, to define how they can interact, and to share service descriptions in a global registry

  uddi.org

- ✔ **USML (UDDI Search Markup Language)** aggregates queries to search various UDDI registries for specific criteria

  xml.coverpages.org/BE4WS-HowToWriteUSML-200112.html

- ✔ **WS-Inspection (Web Services Inspection Language)** assists in performing inspections of specific sites for Web services, along with rules for publishing information derived from inspection

  www-106.ibm.com/developerworks/webservices/library/ws-wsilspec.html

Providers readily understand that providing information to assist the discovery process is essential. The more information a provider system can tell a consumer system about a service, the greater the chances are that a user can use the consumer system to take advantage of the provider system. If an online bill paying service (the consumer system) can't communicate with a biller (the provider system) to electronically exchange bills and payment, then the user won't be able to receive bills online or pay them online.

Providers also recognize that documenting how they can interact with other services is similarly important. Consumers use the discovery process to identify potential providers and to begin the inquiry process that may or may not lead them to establish an ongoing relationship with one or more providers.

In a sense, discovery is the public face that drives the Web Services environment. The remaining layers of the Web Services Architecture are what make it possible to request and obtain services; to handle matters of payment, identity, and security; and to make sure that consumers and providers can communicate seamlessly and successfully with one another.

For example, a user asks his or her online bill paying service to request and pay bills from billers. This request launches the discovery that sends the service out to find out if it can get the bill, and if it can pay the bill online. The results of the discovery drive what the user sees in the online system. If Web service communication is possible, the bill paying system displays the bill, prompts the user to pay the bill, and manages the electronic funds transfer (EFT) of the paid amount from the user's bank account to the biller's bank account (yet another example of Web services). If the Web service communication isn't possible, then the online bill paying service has to use another tool to display bills and make payments (such as scanning in printed bills and mailing printed checks for payment).

Where Will Web Services Lead?

Certainly, those who build Web-based applications — or should we say those who offer Web services? — must become obsessed with the numerous XML applications that we mention here (and the worlds of detail that underlie each such application). But unless you plan to join their ranks, as a Web services consumer, all you need to know is how to use the discovery process.

Regardless of how deeply you dig into the details of Web services, the discovery process enables you, and every other Web user out there, to find Web Services providers with which you can conduct business. After that, you also have to satisfy their requirements that you can prove your identity as well as your ability to pay for their information and/or services before you get anything out of them. Of course free Web Services will be out there for the using (Yahoo! Mail and Hotmail are examples of some that are already available, albeit in more primitive trappings). However, with Web services, the old saw, "You get what you pay for," applies to them as much as it does to other things in life.

If you really want to play with the technologies that facilitate Web services, here are some Web sites of interest:

✔ **Software AG:** Software AG offers a sample UDDI repository with which you can interact at

```
www.softwareag.com/corporat/news/august2001/UDDI.htm
```

(Note that Software AG requires downloading and installing local software.)

✔ **CapeStudio:** CapeStudio offers a UDDI browser that you can use to interrogate a sample repository that it has assembled:

```
www.capeclear.com/products/capestudio/uddi_browser.shtml
```

✔ **XMethods:** Tony Hong of XMethods (and an occasional contributor to XMLhack) has a UDDI browser with a sample repository ready for immediate access at

```
www.soapclient.com/uddisearch.html
```

✔ **WebServices.org:** WebServices.org offers a download implementation of a UDDI registry for inspection and illustration at

```
www.webservices.org/article.php?sid=212
```

Search for *UDDI repository* in your favorite search engine, and you can probably come up with even more such options and opportunities by the time you read this.

We honestly believe that Web services will remake the computing landscape in the next five to ten years. For the time being, this world has not yet achieved a significant lift-off, but we expect that to occur in the next year or two. After that, the way we interact with computers, software, and data is going to change dramatically and radically.

Chapter 22

XML on the Spot!

* *

* *

XML is much more than just a pretty way of packaging or representing information. Properly applied, XML applications can drive the engines of business (large and small) and can help savvy companies and organizations make the most of data they might otherwise drown in (or spend the least on dealing with that data).

In this chapter, we explain what kinds of roles that XML can play when it comes to delivering information for everything from documents to databases to the metadata that keeps Web sites ticking and document repositories humming. We take a look at some brief case studies from corporate America, where XML boosts productivity and controls costs. We also explore cases where XML is unusually well suited for business applications, and then conclude with a scintillating survey of especially interesting real-world uses for XML.

When XML Data Meets the Web

Although you can use Cascading Style Sheets (CSS) — and to some extent, XSL Formatting Objects (XSLFO) — to display XML documents on the Web, in actual practice you won't really encounter native XML on the Web very often. That's because Web browsers — especially those that are older, with less up-to-date software — have problems digesting XML to some extent. Likewise, different browsers tend to treat the same CSS markup somewhat differently (take a peek at the cheat sheet in the front of this book for more information on what browsers support what technologies). A sad consequence of this state of affairs is that, although workable, the combination of XML and CSS is neither as predictable nor as usable as many Web professionals would like.

This helps to explain why, even when you visit Web sites belonging to XML zealots, such as `xml.org`, `xml.com`, `zvon.org`, `oasis-open.org`, and so on, you seldom see URLs pop up in your browser that end in `.xml`. At `zvon.org`, for example, you can choose a file format for display by clicking a menu selection near the top of the page. Although Figures 22-1 and 22-2 show the same document from `zvon.org`, Figure 22-1 shows its "HTML with CSS" version and Figure 22-2 shows its "XML with CSS" version. You can see the difference without too much more explanation.

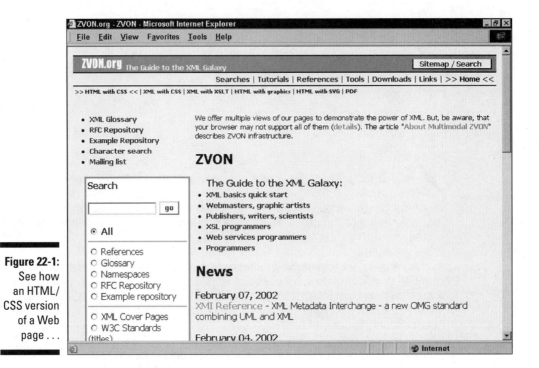

Figure 22-1:
See how an HTML/ CSS version of a Web page . . .

Because of the viewability issue, an increasing number of Web sites may store their data in XML form, but they deliver that data in HTML form. `zvon.org` uses a popular Web page processing engine called *PHP*. (The initials come from the earliest version of the program, which was called *Personal Home Page Tools*.) Basically, when a user requests a particular page view, PHP reads the data from the server's storage or cache and turns it into HTML before delivering any data to that user.

Because PHP reads and handles the page before turning it over to the Web server for user delivery, it's called a *preprocessor*; because both the "before" and "after" documents tend to be hypertext . . . well, you get the idea.

Thus, PHP is an alternative to eXtensible Stylesheet Language Transformations (XSLT) In fact, numerous other kinds of server-side technologies can manipulate data between the time that a user requests a page view and the time that the Web server responds. Some such technologies include Microsoft Active Server Pages (ASP), JavaServer Pages (JSP) and corresponding server-side programs called *servlets*, and so on.

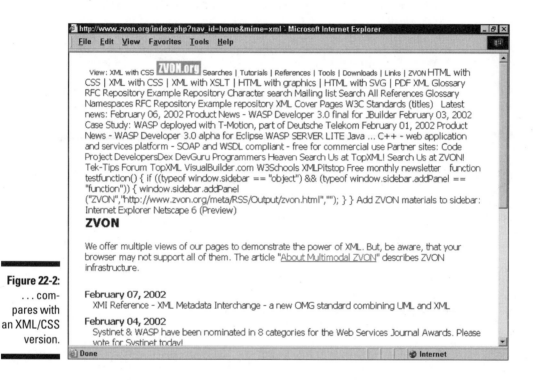

Figure 22-2:
. . . com-
pares with
an XML/CSS
version.

XML to the Rescue!

The discussions in this chapter show you how businesses use XML to describe documents and data-streamlining processes, improve productivity, eliminate paper, save time, and help get more products to more consumers more quickly.

In fact, using XML to capture and manage data or documents can be extremely helpful, especially when any of the following conditions hold true:

✔ A set of data or documents must be available to multiple applications. See our discussion of NDS in the section "Novell, Inc."

✔ Capturing complex document or data structures is a must. You can already find XML applications for everything from patient medical records to chemical formulas to family trees, and these examples are among hundreds of other complex cases and uses.

✔ Data has to be exchanged or modified over time. XML-based data or documents can be transformed into just about any format.

Putting XML to Work: Case Studies

When companies or organizations make the switch to creating and using XML-based documents and data, they must also decide how to access and transform those documents into a universally usable Web format. While they're at it, these same outfits often decide to adopt multiple transforms for output of XML-based data and documents, such as the Adobe Portable Document Format (PDF) and Rich Text Format (RTF) or plain-vanilla ASCII text.

In the following sections, we provide abbreviated reports about several major corporations' use of XML. Our goal here is to describe how these companies have used XML to solve real-world problems and achieve real-world productivity gains and cost reductions at the same time.

Please forgive us for skimping on the down-and-dirty details. Believe us; we could have written a book about nearly every report provided here. If you're interested in all kinds of e-commerce technology solutions, check out *E-Commerce For Dummies,* written by Don Jones, Mark D. Scott, and Richard Villars and published by your friends at Hungry Minds, Inc. It's chock full of case studies and offers some big-picture advice for building an e-based infrastructure.

Novell, Inc.

As in many other corporations, Novell's use of XML technology extends far beyond its impressive online efforts. In fact, Novell was an early and enthusiastic user of Standard Generalized Markup Language (SGML) technology for its online and documentation efforts before it began a systematic switch to XML in the mid-1990s. In many ways, Novell continues to push the envelope on what XML can do.

We interviewed Don Morrison, the Novell Director of Information Services and Technologies (IS&T) organization. Among other things, Don is in charge of the Novell corporate information architecture, including its data centers, help desk, and database administration functions. He's also been a vocal and forceful proponent of using XML to solve a variety of information-handling problems.

To accommodate new employees who come to work at Novell (the company employs over 4,000 people in various locations around the world), as well as employees who routinely move from one office to another, Novell turned to XML to formulate an interesting application called DirXML to support an initiative the company called Zero Day Start (ZDS).

This initiative helps Novell's Information Systems and Technology staff to set up system and network access for new employees to enable easy management of staff ID information, security badges, telephone assignments, and so on — all without a lot of hassle, time, or effort. Likewise, when employees move, ZDS makes changing address and telephone information simple and straightforward.

The cornerstone of ZDS is based on Novell Directory Services (NDS), which is a network service that manages employee identity information, system access, photos, location, telephone assignments, and even personnel records — all within a single system.

The XML technology extracts data from NDS and delivers it to other systems (combinations of hardware and software). The target systems that XML transforms from NDS service include

- ✔ PeopleSoft (a purchased and customized HR system) for personnel records
- ✔ A recruiting system that tracks applicant résumés, application form data, interview records, job offers, offer letters, and so on
- ✔ A facilities management database, which includes a security badge system (issuance, access rights, and usage monitoring)
- ✔ Novell's internal private branch exchange (PBX) phone system
- ✔ Novell's help desk system, which handles system and network account set-up and management, and maintains profiles on users' desktops, access rights, and so on

Although NDS acts as the primary repository for a single, coherent employee record, XML provides the technology that supports data interchange among all the various pieces involved. Employee data enters this elaborate system either through the recruiting system for new employees or through the PeopleSoft system for records on existing employees.

The facilities management, telephone, and help desk systems key off NDS data that describes the nitty gritty of the back end of the business.

The benefits of the ZDS for Don Morrison's Information Systems and Technology organization are pretty dramatic. For example, the system changes telephone connections for new employees and employee transfers entirely through software, eliminating set-up costs and reducing the need for a large technical support staff; the company has saved more than $100 per employee, — or, according to Morrison, over $1.5 million — since ZDS went into use.

Because the DirXML system supports so much of the detailed system access and information transfer work, Morrison has been able to manage data flow with fewer resources, giving the organization the opportunity to redirect both financial and highly-trained technical resources to other key projects. We think this speaks eloquently to the real value of XML applications — they're good for your bottom line.

IBM Corporation

In a company as huge and diverse as IBM, any recitation of uses for XML is bound to fall short of covering the full spectrum of activities and uses underway. One such application is the use of XML within the IBM Global Procurement organization, the group within IBM that's responsible for managing the supply chain for the company's computer and other manufacturing operations. The group works with IBM suppliers to order and manage products' component pieces and parts and with IBM contractors who put the pieces together according to customers' specifications.

IBM operates what's called a *production procurement supply chain*. This complex concept covers the procurement, shipping, tracking, and payments for components used in the company's just-in-time manufacturing operations.

Just-in-time operations streamline processes that specify, design, order, ship, and manage payments for parts for an enormous list of partners involved at each of these steps along this chain. Just-in-time processes also enable IBM to keep its stock low, only ordering components when necessary instead of in bulk. (They also keep the paperwork to a minimum because everything's done electronically.)

IBM's manufacturing partners are such a large and diverse lot that the company operates three types of systems to support its varying technical capabilities and sophistication:

- ✔ For the simplest and least sophisticated companies, IBM provides a Web-based interface, Forms Exchange, which permits any partner with Internet access and a Web browser (and the right account names and passwords) to interact with a series of screen-based forms related for various procurement management activities.

- ✔ For some suppliers with whom it has long-standing relationships, IBM supports an Electronic Data Interchange (EDI) environment to manage its procurement from those suppliers. EDI is actually a legacy operation that's becoming extinct; the company expects to accommodate few new EDI-based suppliers in the future.

EDI is a system that is currently in common use in business. It's rapidly being replaced by XML-based technologies.

✔ IBM's biggest impetus is an XML procurement management application called RosettaNet (see www.rosettanet.org), which is an open XML standard that's been widely adopted by high-tech manufacturing organizations around the world.

Unlike EDI, which provides only a mechanism for data exchange (something else at which XML excels), RosettaNet creates a transaction-handling model that includes *metadata* about specific types of information exchange (transactions, in other words). For example, using RosettaNet, when a purchase order is transmitted from IBM buyer to a supplier, that exchange is part of a transaction that also requires the supplier to provide a series of very specific responses to such paperwork, including

✔ Line-by-line checkoffs, denials, or postponements of specific order items

✔ Timing requirements on acknowledgement of receipt of the order

✔ Timing requirements on specific replies related to order, shipment, delivery, and so on

RosettaNet not only manages the data exchange, but also keeps track of the status and completion of all transactions of which data exchange is only a small part. It shouldn't be a big surprise that tracking status and completion used to be the most labor-intensive (and expensive) part of the manufacturing process.

We interviewed Craig Cornell, IBM RosettaNet Program Manager, to obtain this information. We discovered that IBM has been a key player in defining and maintaining the RosettaNet standard and in promoting its use in high-tech manufacturing.

One of Cornell's closing remarks sums this situation up nicely: "We think of XML and RosettaNet as absolute business imperatives." Given the complexity that RosettaNet manages so cost-efficiently, we can see why.

John Wiley & Sons, Inc.

As you'd expect in one of the world's foremost publishing companies, XML plays a major role in this organization's document handling strategies. The company is developing its XML technology, but XML is already playing a crucial role in the Wiley core businesses — publishing college-level textbooks, professional journals, and trade books, such as those in the *For Dummies* series.

Wiley actually started its markup adventures with SGML in the late 1980s, when CD-ROM and other forms of electronic publishing began to register on the radar.

The company's earliest e-publishing efforts began with SGML on the back end (it was used to describe its various publications and to capture document contents that adhered to such descriptions), but Wiley switched to transforming its output to HTML as soon as the power and popularity of the Web increased.

Because of its use of SGML, Wiley's document architecture and delivery model predicted the roles that XML and HTML play today. Wiley has maintained its SGML heritage but has retrofitted it to fit XML's less complex and more efficient model.

By 1996, the production and manufacturing division of Science, Technical, and Medical division (STM) started using XML for its high-dollar, high-content professional journals, converting the journals into a Web-compatible format.It has had good luck selling its journals in electronic format — they're available sooner, and Wiley can supplement content for its journals with lots of added information delivered electronically while supporting easy text searches of the XML-based documents.

Wiley has also created an application that maps data from an ONIX (Online Information Exchange) database to an XML-based system. The XML technology in turn enables the company to share book listings, descriptions, cover copy, and pricing data with partners such as Amazon.com, Borders.com, and other Web-based publishing retail organizations, making sure that its products make it to market as quickly — and through as many channels — as possible.

A Super Sampler of XML Applications

You can find hundreds of well-publicized standard or open XML-based applications documented at Web sites such as www.w3.org (the W3C Web site), XML.org (www.xml.org), and at Robin Cover's outstanding "XML Cover Pages" (www.oasis-open.org/cover). In addition, probably thousands of private or proprietary XML applications are in use in organizations and businesses around the world.

Here's a survey of XML applications that we don't mention elsewhere in this book:

- **Election Markup Language (EML):** Given some of the hoopla that surrounded the presidential election of 2000, it should come as no surprise that several XML-based ballot handling initiatives are underway. With XML on the case, we hope that the infamous hanging chad reverts entirely to trivia question status in the future. For more information, please visit:

```
xml.coverpages.org/eml.html
```

- **Extensible Log Format Initiative (XLF):** With a gradual switchover of Web servers from HTML- to XML-based documents already underway, server log formats are being expressed using XML markup. XML-based server logs are the rule now, which makes them easy to exchange and read on any platform; See

  ```
  www.docuverse.com/xlf
  ```

  for more details.

- **Gene Expression Markup Language (GEML):** GEML is just one of over a dozen, genome- and genetics-related XML initiatives underway. In particular, GEML aims to provide a standard way to express and exchange DNA microarray and gene expression data for biotech research. For the full story on this fascinating project, visit

  ```
  www.geml.org
  ```

- **Global Document Annotation Initiative (GDA):** GDA supplies a way to provide annotations for Web documents and to assist computers in interpreting meaning and value of documents. This XML application provides a way to enhance relevance of documents returned in response to concept and keyword queries and could enable a new generation of semantically aware search engines. Find more about GDA at

  ```
  www.i-content.org/GDA
  ```

- **Interactive Financial Exchange (IFX):** IFX is designed to provide an online financial services standard that enables the creation of a global, open, interoperable financial services e-marketplace. The IFX Forum, a nonprofit organization whose members include financial services companies, service providers, information technology companies, and customers for all such outfits, supervises this monumental effort. Invest some time at

  ```
  www.ifxforum.org
  ```

- **Open Content Syndication (OCS):** OCS is designed to make sharing information through *channels* (that is, technologies that provide portals and other sources with the technologies to offer continuously updated entertainment, music, news, or other content on the Web). OCS is based on peer-to-peer technology that makes distributing and locating information of all kinds a snap. If you're looking for an open channel, visit

  ```
  internetalchemy.org/ocs/index.html
  ```

- **Project Gutenberg:** Project Gutenberg is a source of an astonishingly large set of public domain electronic books and documents, including a wide range of novels, references, and other information. Project Gutenberg uses XML to store documents and transform them on demand in a variety of formats. Read more into this fascinating project at

  ```
  www.gutenberg.net
  ```

✔ **Species Analyst Project:** Species Analyst is an ongoing research project for developing standards and software to access natural history collections and observation databases worldwide. This project is working to replace an existing Web interface with a more powerful, flexible XML alternative. Collect further data at

```
tsadev.speciesanalyst.net
```

✔ **U.S. Congress: XML for Legislative Documents:** By law, Congress must make the text for all pending and enacted legislation public. What better venue than the Web can Congress choose? And what better way to capture necessary documents for delivery on the Web and other formats than XML? To lay down the law on this laudable initiative, please visit

```
xml.house.gov
```

✔ **U.S. Patent and Trademark Office Electronic Filing System:** In a high-tech age, the U.S. Patent and Trademark Office handles an enormous number of filings. What's better than paper filings? E-filings of course, and XML is well suited for capturing patent and trademark applications. Apply to this site for more information:

```
www.uspto.gov/ebc/index.html
```

✔ **Weather Observation Markup Format (OMF):** OMF helps to standardize a body of documents that are currently in a bunch of different formats. OMF defines and transforms differing formats to a single underlying standard format; it also extracts trend and historical data across a series of otherwise unrelated reports. OMF preserves original data but adds the kinds of annotations necessary to identify and aggregate such information. Could this lead to more reliable forecasts? See for yourself at

```
xml.coverpages.org/OMF-desc01-980522.html
```

Part VII
The Part of Tens

The 5th Wave   By Rich Tennant

"You might want to adjust the value in your 'Nudge' element."

In this part . . .

This is the revered and traditional closing for all *For Dummies* books. With tongue planted firmly in cheek, this part of the book summarizes, epitomizes, and concentrates the most important content that appears in this book. Chapter 23 describes the ten most widely used XML applications on today's Web sites. And Chapter 24 closes out this fiesta with the top ten resources for XML. We can't help it: We give this part a solid 10 rating! We hope you will, too.

Chapter 23

Ten Top XML Applications

. . . .

. . . .

*B*y itself, any XML document contains nothing but plain, simple text. But when you look at XML the right way, or when you use various XML-based technologies together, its benefits can't be overstated. XML applications provide powerful tools to display and work with your XML documents.

Industry requirements drive most XML developments. That's the reason so many XML applications inevitably embody industry initiatives. Many applications are already available — for free! In this chapter, we highlight a few of the most interesting XML applications designed for specific uses.

This is a chapter on XML applications, yes, but that doesn't mean the applications listed here are the only ones worth investigating. To see a fairly exhaustive list, visit www.oasis-open.org/cover/xml.html#applications or www.xml.com. With a little elbow grease, you may find an application that's perfect for your needs!

XHTML = XML + HTML

As we've mentioned elsewhere in this book (particularly in Chapter 2), XHTML takes easy, familiar HTML markup and rationalizes it within a more rigorous and regular XML framework. Don't let that stop you from using this excellent tool, though — in most respects, it's enough like HTML that even older browsers can't tell the difference as long as you follow safe formatting rules (see Chapter 2 for more on these rules).

Thinking about upgrading your HTML markup to its XHTML equivalent? Dave Raggett's wonderful HTML-Tidy tool is built into Chami.com's outstanding HTML-Kit utility, and does most of the conversion work for you automatically. Just don't forget to validate the results (which HTML-Kit also does for you).

XML Style Is a Matter of Application

The richest, most powerful ways to manage how XML data and documents are delivered to a Web browser involve the use of XML applications designed to read, organize, transform, and format XML into a variety of looks, feels, and formats. Possible forms of output include Rich Text Format (RTF), Adobe Acrobat's Portable Document format (PDF), HTML or XHTML, plain text, and many more formats. To pull off this kind of magic, though, you need to find out about numerous XML applications, including:

- The eXtensible Stylesheet Language (XSL), and its relatives, XSL Transformations (XSLT) and XSL Formatting Objects (XSL-FO).
- XML-based linking languages, especially XLink, XPath, and XPointer.
- And of course, you also need to understand how to grab XML content and reshape it into the exact form required to match your target format. For simple formats, such as plain text or XHTML/HTML, this is pretty easy; for more complex formats, such as PDF or RTF, you probably need help from special-purpose software tools.

Wireless Markup Language (WML)

As the name is meant to suggest, WML aims to support applications for wireless communications networks. It's part of an effort sponsored by leading telecommunications companies including Ericsson, Motorola, Nokia, and the wireless communications specialist, Unwired planet. In essence, WML is designed to make it easier to use handheld, wireless communications devices of all kinds to access the Internet.

WML is an XML application designed specifically to meet constraints inherent in wireless devices. These constraints include a small display area with limited user input capabilities (as on a cell phone), limited bandwidth (19.2 Kbps is typical for most handheld wireless devices), and limited CPU power and memory space. You might say that WML is a markup language designed with the phrase "small is beautiful" foremost in mind!

Read more about WML at `www1.wapforum.org/tech/documents/WAP-238-WML-20010626-p.pdf`. This specification is an effort staged by the Wireless Application Protocol (WAP) Forum; for general information on WAP, check `www.wapforum.com`.

DocBook, Anyone?

DocBook is a standard SGML DTD designed to capture computer documentation and other types of lengthy, complex documents (as we write this book, an XML Schema-based version is nearing completion as well). DocBook already enjoys worldwide use in hundreds of organizations that manage millions of pages of documentation in a variety of print and online formats.

Visit Robin Cover's site at `www.oasis-open.org/docbook/` for more information on this subject. Also visit `www.oasis-open.org/committees/docbook/xmlschema/index.shtml` to find out the latest status of the XML Schema-based version of DocBook.

Mathematical Markup Language (MathML)

Based on years of hard labor, the most recent version of the MathML 2.0 specification appeared on February 21, 2001. Before MathML came along, it was tricky to express mathematical equations inside Web pages. As an XML application, MathML supports mathematical and scientific markup for use on the Web. But it doesn't end there: You can also use MathML for computer algebra systems, mathematical typesetting, and voice synthesis.

Read more about MathML at its W3C home at `www.w3.org/Math/`. Robin Cover's site also offers a wealth of information on this application. Visit `www.oasis-open.org/cover/xml.html#xml-mml` for more information.

Scalable Vector Graphics (SVG)

Scalable Vector Graphics (SVG) is a language for describing two-dimensional graphics in XML. SVG 1.0 is a recommended W3C standard, which means that it's ready for production use.

SVG allows for three basic types of objects: vector graphic shapes (paths consisting of straight lines and curves), images, and text. The drive behind SVG is to develop a standard for the Web-based display of such objects.

Graphical objects can be grouped, styled, and added to previously rendered objects. What's more exciting is that these objects can be dynamic and interactive! The Document Object Model (DOM) for SVG, which includes the full XML DOM, allows authors to use scripting to create straightforward and efficient vector graphics animation for any SVG graphical object.

We wish we could outline all the fun ways to create graphics using SVG, but that would require its own book. To read more about SVG, visit the W3C at `www.w3.org/TR/SVG/`.

Resource Description Framework (RDF)

The Resource Description Framework (RDF) is a framework for metadata. RDF assures interoperability between applications that exchange application- or platform-specific information — you know, metadata — across the Web.

Why might this concern you? Because RDF helps increase the relevance of searches conducted in your XML documents. That fact alone gets us excited and might be a boon to you, too. (Okay, we admit, we're really into the metasearch thing. Anything to keep from wading through countless documents only to find irrelevant information on a two-headed reptile from New Guinea is okay in our book!) Briefly put, RDF provides a basis for generic tools for authoring, manipulating, and searching machine-readable data on the Web.

The RDF specification resides at `www.w3.org/TR/REC-rdf-syntax/`. To read more about RDF, visit Dave Beckett's excellent site on this subject at `www.ilrt.bris.ac.uk/discovery/rdf/resources/`.

Synchronized Multimedia Integration Language (SMIL)

We talked a little about graphics in the section on SVG, so now we turn your attention to multimedia. Ever since desktop computer systems started to include loudspeakers, multimedia has played a significant role on more than a few Web sites. If multimedia's your bag, you may want to keep up with the Synchronized Multimedia Integration Language (SMIL, pronounced, happily enough, "smile").

SMIL enables you to integrate a set of independent multimedia objects into a synchronized multimedia presentation. As stated by the W3C, you can use SMIL to

✔ Describe the temporal behavior (or sequential behavior, such as the sequence presented in an animation) of the presentation

✔ Describe the layout of the presentation on a screen

✔ Associate hyperlinks with media objects

The bottom line is that SMIL enables authors to create television-like content for the Web, and still avoid the limitations of traditional television. And, you don't have to worry about lowering the bandwidth requirements to transmit such content across the Internet. Yes, we mean that movies on the Web, without worrying about bandwidth, are theoretically possible, because producing audio-visual content is easy with SMIL. The best part is that using SMIL doesn't require that you learn a programming language; you can create it with a simple text editor.

To keep track of SMIL progress, stay tuned to `www.w3.org/TR/REC-smil/`.

Servin' Up Web Services

An interlocking collection of XML applications is under development to support so-called Web services (which we cover in more detail in Chapter 21). A *Web service* is a tool or capability that you use your Web browser to access; it doesn't reside locally on your own desktop, and it isn't saved on your hard drive. Web services permit users with just about any kind of computer (using any operating system) to run the same database access programs, read or send faxes, manage bank accounts or financial portfolios, and so on, without a care in the world. We shudder to think of all the possibilities.

The Web services infrastructure includes a bunch of pieces and parts designed to make it easier for service providers to create and advertise such services, and for would-be end users to identify and access such services. These pieces and parts include the following elements:

✔ **Simple Object Access Protocol (SOAP):** An XML-based technology designed to permit senders and receivers to easily exchange self-describing XML-based messages. SOAP enables arbitrary service providers and service consumers to communicate. For a super collection of SOAP resources, visit

```
http://xml.coverpages.org/soap.html
```

✔ **Universal Description, Discovery, and Integration (UDDI):** An XML-based technology designed to permit service providers to describe the services they offer, to permit those services to be discovered by those seeking same, and to establish how providers and consumers can inter-act with each other should a consumer decide to request services from a provider. Think of it as a kind of Yellow Pages that also brokers direct connections between those who list themselves therein (providers) and those who use them (consumers) to locate potential providers. A good place to start further investigations regarding UDDI is Robin Cover's pointers at

```
http://xml.coverpages.org/uddi.html
```

✔ **Web Services Description Language (WSDL):** An XML-based technology that permits Web services — and the message formats and contents nec-essary to interact with them — to be formally described and advertised. Those message formats are turn based on SOAP. Thus, WSDL provides the ways to integrate providers and consumers that UDDI brokers. For more information on WSDL, see Robin Cover's Web site at

```
http://xml.coverpages.org/wsdl.html
```

XML-Data

A highly collaborative effort produced the XML-Data specification, which provides a mechanism to reference binary data within XML documents. We include XML-Data in our application list because of its unique implications for XML. The XML-Data specification proposes that XML document types be described using an XML document itself, rather than through SGML-based DTD syntax.

XML-Data represents an XML element set that allows you to precisely describe text structures, relational schemas, and more. Simply put, at the center of XML-Data is a DTD for describing DTDs. But wait, we don't want to confuse anyone here. XML-Data does not replace a DTD; it's just an alternative expression for that DTD. The beauty of XML-Data is that it can specify so much more than an ordinary DTD.

To read more about XML-Data, and understand its powers, visit `www.w3.org/TR/1998/NOTE-XML-data/`. To be fair, you should also read the W3C's XML Schema work at `www.w3.org/XML/Schema`.

Create XML Applications with Zope

Although this chapter focuses on applications used with XML, we'd like to also point you to software that enables you to create your own XML applications. Zope 2.1.1 is a free, open-source application server that does just that. Created by Digital Creations, Zope runs on both Windows and UNIX platforms.

Zope works in an *object-oriented* environment. More plainly, Zope views a Web application in terms of objects, which define not only types of data, but also the kinds of operations (called *methods* in object-oriented programming lingo) that may be performed on those objects.

Zope enables you to combine objects to create powerful and flexible ways to acquire, manage, and manipulate all kinds of data. As you'd expect, these object collections can respond to Web requests dynamically, making building interactive Web-based applications a relative breeze. The result is dynamic content and a happy content creator (that would be you).

If you can't find the right XML application for your needs, you might want to create one yourself using Zope. Read more about this open-source treasure at `www.zope.org`.

Chapter 24

Ten Ultimate XML Resources

*Y*ou can find information on just about any XML topic online, in addition to other more "real" (or at least, less virtual) locations. If we had to boil this entire chapter down to a single tip it would have to be: "When looking for XML information, search the Web first and foremost." Chances are eXtreMeLy good that you can find what you seek!

XML's Many and Marvelous Specs

```
www.w3.org
```

For XML itself, and for standard XML applications, the place to start your search for descriptions, metadata, and other details is the World Wide Web Consortium (W3C) site. Check the left-hand column listing for the acronym you seek. In most cases, you can find it there. And when you visit the home page for your average XML application at the W3C's site, you find a plethora of pointers to other resources on the same subject, so it's a good place from which to mount broader searches as well.

An XML Nonpareil

`www.oasis-open.org/cover/`

Nonpareil isn't a chocolate candy covered with sprinkles. No, the XML nonpareil (which is just a fancy-schmancy word for unparalleled) on the Web is Robin Cover's XML Pages. At this site, you not only find pointers to relevant specifications and other related documents, but also see brief descriptions of the markup or application itself, as well as pointers to numerous other useful resources. If you're into XML, you may want to add this one to your bookmarks or favorites. *Note:* Robin's last name rhymes with "over" or "clover."

Top XML Tutorial Sites

We dare you to type *application* **tutorial**, (substituting the name or acronym of your favorite application, of course) in your favorite search engine. Go ahead. See? Your search produced a plethora of results. Nevertheless, we've found the following sites to be unusually useful when seeking sources for XML tutorials:

- ✔ `www.zvon.org:` A crazy, quirky, but incredibly competent Czech XML collective, Zvon offers some of the best XML tutorials we've seen anywhere. Check them out (pun intended)! Also, be sure to look up the original meaning of the term "zvon" in Czech; you'll never think of these guys as anything other than humble forever afterward. (Note for those of you too busy to look it up; it means "bell" or "ding-dong.")

- ✔ `www.xml.com:` An O'Reilly & Associates Web site devoted to covering XML news, applications, tools, and technologies, this site also offers a plethora of tutorials on everything from namespaces to SOAP (389 tutorials total during our last visit there, in fact).

- ✔ `www.w3schools.com/xml/:` World Wide Web Schools has its own XML School, which you can enter here. Check it out for a well-organized collection of information about basic XML, and important XML applications.

Try them; we think you'll like them!

XML in the Mail

Although mailing lists on the Internet are neither terribly interactive nor do they always address your questions without some effort on your part, they can be wonderful sources of information — and they provide a superb way for you to seek answers to particular, detailed questions that may not be addressed elsewhere on the Internet (at least, not so far as you can tell).

```
www.oasis-open.org/cover/lists.html
```

Once again, XML master and maven Robin Cover scores big with a massive collection of SGML- and XML-related mailing lists (nearly 100 in all). Visit his site to see what we mean; don't overlook the annotated listings on each list.

Excellent XML Examples

```
www.zvon.org
```

Although assiduous digging and careful reading of XML-related specifications can produce examples galore, example collections created specifically to instruct and demonstrate XML applications are quite worthwhile. Clever searches turn up lots of potential sources, but we've found those crafty Czechs at www.zvon.org to be a peachy source for well-organized and explained XML examples.

For a great collection of XML examples, please visit Zvon's Example Respository at www.zvon.org/HowTo/Output/index.html.

XML News and Information

Numerous trade publications are available in print and online. We've looked at most of them, but have found the following to be especially interesting, useful, or informative. In many cases, you can read them online and if you like what you see, qualify for free delivery of the printed versions.

```
www.xml.com
```

The O'Reilly Web site covers the topic pretty darn well and is usually worth reading. XML.com is not only a good source of information on topics you want to research, but it's also a good bellwether for topics you didn't know existed!

```
www.xml-zone.com/
```

Fawcette Publications' DevX includes an "XML Zone" that's chock-full of late-breaking XML news, information, tutorials, how-tos, and more.

```
www.fawcette.com/xmlmag/
```

Fawcette also publishes XML Magazine, which operates online. The XML Magazine is also worth regular visits.

```
www.oasis-open.org/cover/sgmlnew.html
```

Robin Cover — who else? — also provides regular news updates and information. This Web page is more newsy and less technical or how-to than the other items mentioned here, but it's still worth following.

```
www.ibiblio.org/xml/
```

Elliotte Rusty Harold's Café Con Leche XML News and Resources isn't just a great source for XML news and musings, it's also a wonderful XML resource in its own right (and you see his name later on in the "Building a Bodacious XML Bookshelf" section in this chapter; he's a real XML star, too). Visit the Café Con Leche XML News and Resources site and see for yourself!

```
comp.text.xml
```

In the Usenet newsgroup hierarchy, this newsgroup is a great source of XML news and discussion, although you sometimes have to blow a lot of chaff off the wheat.

XML Training Offerings

When it comes to training offerings, you find as much on XML online as you do in various classrooms in the real world. If you're interested in XML training, try to find offerings that best fit your learning style — and although it's undoubtedly cheaper to learn through self-study, computer-based training, or Web classes, sometimes the opportunity to interact with a real, live instructor in a real classroom is worth the extra time and expense.

The following training companies, among many others, offer classroom training on XML:

- ✔ **Global Knowledge:** www.globalknowledge.com
- ✔ **Software Skills Training:** www.software-skills-training.com
- ✔ **SkillBuilders:** www.skillbuilders.com
- ✔ **Zveno:** www.zveno.com/courses

Also, don't overlook offerings from local community colleges, colleges, and universities, many of which also offer classroom XML training.

When it comes to XML training via computer-based training (CBT) or online, check with your favorite online training company for more information — many, if not most of them, now offer online introductory and advanced XML classes. Everybody from DigitalThink to SmartForce has jumped on this bandwagon!

Commercial classroom training normally costs upwards of $250 per person per day (sometimes $500 or more); computer- or Web-based training seldom costs more than $700-800 per class (and prices at half that amount or lower are common). Be sure to pick XML training offerings that meet your education needs, but that also stay within your training budget!

Building a Bodacious XML Bookshelf

A quick hop to Amazon.com or your favorite online bookstore and typing **XML** as a title element or keyword choice produces hundreds of hits (323 hits in Amazon as we write this, in fact). XML has no shortage of reference, tutorial, introductory, or advanced material. If reading helps you learn, or you're like us and enjoy the heft and easy access to information that a good reference book can provide, you'll probably find it worthwhile to amass at least a small collection of XML books.

To begin with, we urge you to look for competitive reviews (like the customer reviews posted on Amazon and at other online bookstores, or published book reviews that you can find in abundance on the Web) and let them guide you to prospective purchases. At the bookstore, be sure to use your own judgment before buying anything; if you purchase online (and you can get some fabulous deals if you do) be sure you can get your money back if you return a book you decide you don't like later on.

All that said, here is our Top five list of XML books, any or all of which are well worth their purchase price:

  ✔ Elliotte Rusty Harold: *XML: Extensible Markup Language,* Hungry Minds, Indianapolis, IN, 1998. ISBN: 0-7645-3199-9. List Price: $39.99. The best technical introduction to XML around, period.

  ✔ Elliotte Rusty Harold: *XML Bible,* Hungry Minds, Indianapolis, IN, 1999. ISBN: 0-7645-3236-7. List Price: $49.99. A great general reference and how-to book, chock full of useful examples.

  ✔ Elliotte Rusty Harold and W. Scott Means: *XML In a Nutshell,* O'Reilly & Associates, Sebastopol, CA, 2001. ISBN: 0-596-00058-8. List Price: $29.95. The best compact all-around reference on XML and key applications available in print.

- Steven Holzner: *Inside XML,* New Riders, Indianapolis, IN, 2001. ISBN: 0-7357-1020-1. List Price: $49.99. A great all-around reference on XML and key applications, leavened not only with great examples, but also with implementation considerations and details.

- Erik T. Ray and Christopher R. Maden: *Learning XML,* O'Reilly & Associates, Sebastopol, CA, 2001. ISBN: 0-596-00046-4. List Price: $34.95. An excellent step-by-step guide to learning and using XML for building basic documents.

Notice that Elliotte Rusty Harold's name keeps popping up in our short list of XML Great Books? Coincidence? No way!

Studying XML for Certification

For further proof that XML is making the big time, numerous groups and organizations are starting to offer exams to warrant the knowledge and skills of those with the moxie to take and pass such tests. Although this particular market is still in its infancy — by which we mean we've not begun to see the total range of XML certifications by any means just yet — already, you can choose from a surprising number of options to demonstrate your knowledge, skills, and expertise.

Here's a list of organizations that offer XML certification at present (at least, ones that we can find), with pointers to more information about their programs and credentials:

- IBM's Certified Developer program includes an XML specialization. For more information, visit

  ```
  www-1.ibm.com/certify/certs/xm_index.shtml
  ```

- Active Education offers the Certified XML Expert (CXE) program to warrant an individual's knowledge of vendor-neutral XML standards, applications, and content development skills. Check out the CXE program at

  ```
  www.certifyxml.com
  ```

- Global Knowledge has created an XML Developer Certification that combines training in basic XML terms, concepts, markup, and applications with coverage of ASP or Java programming to warrant individuals who can build XML-based systems and solutions. For more information, point your browser to

  ```
  www.globalknowledge.com/training/certification_listing.asp?PageID=12&certid
          =215&country=United+States
  ```

✔ Learning Tree International has yet another XML Development Certified Professional program that covers a broad range of topics, skills, and XML applications, supported by a collection of 3 core courses and 10 elective course topics. One of the more comprehensive XML certification programs currently available; read more about it at

```
www.learningtree.com/us/cert/progs/7062.htm
```

✔ U2test, a Pakistani-based skills and competency testing outfit, has an XML exam (and certificate) available. To find out more, visit

```
www.u2test.com/avtestn.asp
```

✔ BrainBench offers exams on XML and XSL that are warranted by the International Webmaster's Association (a Web-oriented professionals' association). For more information, check out their exam offerings under the general heading of "Web Design and Development" at

```
www.brainbench.com/xml/bb/homepage.xml
```

By the time you read this book, more XML certifications may be offered. To find out about certifications not in the previous list, check out general certification resources online, such as `www.gocertify.com` or `www.itcertinfo.com`.

Serious Searches Lead to Success

What we've presented in this chapter is only the merest suggestion of the enormity of resources, publications, news, information, examples, tutorials, and other useful XML resources available to you. Don't forget that the power of the Web when viewed through your favorite search engine — be that engine Yahoo!, AskJeeves, Google, AltaVista, or whatever — can lead you to just about any XML-related information. The sooner you start searching, the sooner you start finding what you need. Good luck!

Appendix A

About the CD

*W*ell, the moment you've been waiting for has arrived — you finally get to see all the great stuff we packed into the *XML For Dummies,* 3rd Edition CD. From browsers to text editors (and more) it's all about you — and your XML needs.

The CD does not have a customized user interface. Instead, we built the contents around XHTML files that you can open with any Web browser. Look for a file named readme.txt and use its index to search most of the content of the CD. The only stuff not accessible through the Web browser interface is a collection of folders containing software for your evaluation and use. This material is documented in this appendix in the section entitled "What You Find."

You find the following goodies — and more — on the CD:

- ✔ The W3C's amazing, XML-capable Web browser, Amaya
- ✔ ArborText's excellent Epic Editor (another XML editing tool)
- ✔ XML Spy's swiss-army-knife-like XML Spy that not only edits XML, but also works with XSLT and XML Schema, too

System Requirements

Make sure your computer meets these minimum system requirements. Otherwise, you might have problems using the contents of the CD. And we don't like problems!

✔ A PC with a Pentium II or faster processor or a Mac OS computer with a G4 iMac 800 MHz or faster processor.

✔ Microsoft Windows Me or later or Mac OS system software 9.0 or later (Mac OS X is preferable).

✔ For best performance, we recommend that Windows Me-equipped PCs (or newer) and Mac OS computers with PowerPC processors have at least 128 MB of RAM installed.

✔ At least 250MB of hard drive space available to install all the software from the CD. (You need less space if you don't install every program.)

✔ A CD-ROM drive — sixteen speed (16x) or faster.

✔ A sound card for PCs. (Mac OS computers have built-in sound support.)

✔ A monitor capable of displaying at least 16-bit color or grayscale.

✔ A modem with a speed of at least 57,600 (56K) bps. (We're so sorry if you still have this speed.)

If you need more information on the basics, check out the following books:

✔ *PCs For Dummies,* 8th Edition, by Dan Gookin

✔ *Macs For Dummies,* 7th Edition, by David Pogue

✔ *Windows 98 For Dummies*

✔ *Windows NT Workstation 4 For Dummies*

✔ *Windows 2000 Professional For Dummies*

✔ *Microsoft Windows Me Millennium Edition For Dummies*

✔ *Windows XP For Dummies*

The last five books are all by Andy Rathbone, and the Workstation and Professional titles include contributions from Sharon Crawford and the Microsoft Corporation. All are published by Hungry Minds, Inc.

Using the CD with Microsoft Windows

If you're running Windows 98, NT, .Net, 2000, or Me, follow these steps to get to the software items on the CD:

1. **Insert the CD into your computer's CD-ROM drive.**

   Give your computer a moment to take a look at the CD.

2. **When the light on your CD-ROM drive goes out, double-click the My Computer icon. (It's probably in the top-left corner of your desktop.)**

This action opens the My Computer window, which shows you all the drives attached to your computer as well as the Control Panel and a few other handy things.

3. **Double-click the icon for your CD-ROM drive.**

Another window opens, showing you all the folders and files on the CD.

4. **Double-click the file called** License.txt.

This file contains the end-user license that you agree to by using the CD. When you've finished reading the license, close the program (most likely Notepad) that displayed the file.

5. **Double-click the file called** Readme.txt.

This file contains instructions about installing the software from this CD. It might be helpful to leave this text file open while you're using the CD.

6. **Double-click the folder for the software you're interested in.**

Be sure to read the descriptions of the programs in the next section of this appendix (much of this information also shows up in the Readme file). These descriptions give you more precise information about the programs' folder names and about finding and running the installer program.

7. **Find the file called** Setup.exe, Install.exe, **or something similar (the name varies depending on the software), and double-click that file.**

The program's installer walks you through the process of setting up your new software.

Using the CD with the Mac OS

To install the items from the CD to your hard drive, follow these steps:

1. **Insert the CD into your computer's CD-ROM drive.**

In a moment, an icon representing the CD you just inserted appears on your Mac desktop. Chances are, the icon looks like a CD-ROM.

2. **Double-click the CD icon to show the CD's contents.**

3. **Double-click the Read Me First icon.**

This text file contains information about the CD's programs and any last-minute instructions not covered here.

4. **To install most programs, just drag the program's folder from the CD window and drop it on your hard drive icon.**

5. **Some programs come with installer programs; with those, you simply open the program's folder on the CD and double-click the Install or Installer icon.**

After you've installed the programs you want, you can eject the CD. Carefully place it back in the plastic jacket of the book for safekeeping.

If you're using the Mac OS X, you can use the nifty Unix-based tools on this CD.

Using the CD with Linux

To install the items from the CD to your hard drive, follow these steps:

1. **Log in as root.**

2. **Insert the CD into your computer's CD-ROM drive.**

3. **If your computer has Auto-Mount enabled, wait for the CD to mount.**

   Otherwise, follow these steps:

   a. **If you're using the command line interface, at the command prompt type**

   ```
   mount /dev/cdrom /mnt/cdrom
   ```

   The `cdrom` device mounts to the mnt/cdrom directory. If your device has a different name, then exchange `cdrom` with that device name — for instance, `cdrom1`.

   b. **If you have a graphical interface, right click on the CD-ROM icon on the desktop and choose Mount CD-ROM.**

   The CD-ROM mounts.

4. **Browse the CD and follow the individual installation instructions for the products listed.**

To remove the CD from your CD-ROM drive, follow these steps:

1. **If you're using the command line interface, at the command prompt type**

   ```
   umount /mnt/cdrom
   ```

   The CD-ROM dismounts. You can safely remove it from the CD-ROM drive.

2. **If you're using a graphical interface, right click on the CD-ROM icon on the desktop and choose UMount CD-ROM.**

   Your CD-ROM dismounts. You can safely remove it from the CD-ROM drive.

What You Find

Table A-1 provides a summary of the software on the CD arranged in alphabetical order by package name. The product names correspond to the folders that appear on the CD, so they should be easy to find!

For more information about these products, check out Chapter 20.

Table A-1		Software Found on the CD	
Name	**Tool Type**	**URL**	**The Deal**
Ælfred v1.2a	Nonvalidating parser	www.opentext.com/ services/content_ management_services/ xml_sgml_solutions. html#aelfred_and_sax	Freeware
Amaya	Browser	www.w3.org/amaya/	Freeware
Epic Editor LE	Authoring	www.arbortext.com/ html/epic_editor _overview.html	Commercial Product
Expat	Nonvalidating parser	www.jclark.com/ xml/expat.html	GNU Software
Jumbo	Browser	www.vsms.nottingham. ac.uk/vsms/java/ jumbo/	Freeware
LARK	Nonvalidating parser	www.textuality. com/Lark/	Freeware
Mozilla	Browser	www.mozilla.org/	Open Source
SP	Validating parser	www.jclark.com/ sp/index.html	Freeware
XMetaL 2.1	Authoring	www.softquad.com	Evaluation
XML Pro v2.01	Authoring	www.vervet.com	Demo
XML Spy 4.2	Authoring	www.xmlspy.com/	30 Day Evaluation Version

(continued)

Table A-1 *(continued)*

Name	Tool Type	URL	The Deal
XML4J Parser 3.2.1	Validating parser	www.alphaworks.ibm.com/tech/xml4j	GNU Software
XSBROWSER	XML Schema Browser	www.xsbrowser.org/	Freeware
XSL Lint	XSL error checker	http://nwalsh.com/xsl/xslint/xslint.html	Freeware
XT	Parser	www.jclark.com/xml/xt.html	Freeware

Book-related CD Content

In addition to the many software packages mentioned in the previous sections, the CD also contains lots of information based on content that appears in the pages of the book itself.

The `xmlfd3e` folder contains the majority of the files, most of which are XHTML documents. Here are the details:

- ✔ `default.htm`: The home page for the entire collection (start your exploration of the folder here).

   The CD contains several files called `default.htm`; this home-page file is at the root of the xmlfd3e folder, at the same level as all the subfolders.

- ✔ `copy.htm`: Important copyright information. The `xmlfd3e/contents` directory contains lists of the book's contents by chapter. To access the files

   1. **Open the `default.htm` file and choose Chapter Contents.**

      You see a hyperlinked listing of all chapter titles.

   2. **Click a chapter title to see a list of what that chapter covers.**

      You can go straight to a chapter by clicking the appropriate file-name (the files are named `chnncont.htm`, where *nn* is the chapter number). You might find that this is a faster way to access a chapter's specific information.

   3. **To return to the list of contents, click the Chapter Contents button on the bottom image map or text-navigation menu.**

The steps for accessing files in the other directories listed in this section are very similar. Always start in the `default.htm` folder, and always click subfolders to see contents. You can always return to the main list by clicking a related button at the bottom of the screen.

Here's a list of other directories:

- ✔ `xmlfd3e/examples`: This directory contains example XML markup that appears in the book, sorted by chapter. To return to the list of chapter titles, click the Chapter Examples button on the bottom image map or text-navigation menu.

    Or you can go straight to a chapter by clicking on the appropriate filename (the files are named `chnncont.htm`, where *nn* is the two-digit chapter number) to see the examples from that chapter.

- ✔ `xmlfd3e/extras`: This directory contains information about XML online resources and applications, and includes a copy of all the DTDs that are used anywhere in the book. To return to the list of titles in the Extras section, click the Extras button on the bottom image map or text-navigation menu.

- ✔ `xmlfd3e/urls`: This directory includes a hotlist of all URLs mentioned in the book.

If You Have Problems of the CD Kind

We tried our best to compile programs that work on most computers with the minimum system requirements. Alas, your computer might differ, and some programs might not work properly for some reason.

The two likeliest problems are that your system doesn't have enough memory (RAM) for the programs you want to use, or other programs are affecting the installation or running of a program. If you get error messages such as `Not enough memory` or `Setup cannot continue`, try one or more of the following methods and then try using the software again:

- ✔ **Turn off any antivirus software that you have on your computer.** Installers sometimes mimic virus activity and might make your computer incorrectly believe that a virus is infecting it.

- ✔ **Close all running programs.** The more programs you're running, the less memory is available to other programs. Installers also typically update files and programs. So if you keep other programs running, installation might not work properly.

✔ **Have your local computer store add more RAM to your computer.** This is, admittedly, a drastic and somewhat expensive step. However, if you have a Windows 95 PC or newer or a Mac OS computer with a PowerPC chip or newer, adding more memory can help the speed of your computer and allow more programs to run at the same time.

If you still have trouble with the CD, please call the Customer Care phone number: (800) 762-2974. Outside the United States, call 1 (317) 572-3994. You can also contact Customer Service by e-mail at techsupdum@wiley.com. Wiley Publishing, Inc. will provide technical support only for installation and other general quality control items; for technical support on the applications themselves, consult the program's vendor or author.

Appendix B

Glossary

● ●

ASCII (American Standard Code for Information Interchange): A coding method to translate characters, such as numbers, text, and symbols, into digital form. ASCII includes only 127 characters, and is only useful for English (okay, and Latin, but nothing else really).

attribute: In XML, a property associated with an XML element that is a named characteristic of the element. An attribute also provides additional data about an element.

attribute declaration: In XML Schema and DTDs, an attribute declaration is markup that defines the name of an attribute and its properties.

attribute-list declaration: In DTDs, a declaration that defines the name, datatype, and default value (if any) of each attribute associated with an element.

CDF (Channel Definition Format): An XML-based file format, developed by Microsoft.

CGI (Common Gateway Interface): A standard that allows external programs of various types to interact with Web servers, usually to provide interactive responses or services related to user input from a browser.

channel: Information about organized content on an intranet or the Internet. Channels enable Web developers to categorize and describe Web site content and make that data available to users on demand.

character entity: A string of characters that represents other characters; for example, `&lt;` and `&Egrave;` show a string of characters (`lt` and `Egrave`) that stand for other characters (< and È).

character set: When referring to script, a collection of values that maps to some specific symbol set or alphabet.

child element: A document element that occurs within some parent element, and is therefore part of that parent's content model.

choice group: In XML Schema, a method that allows you to make either/or choices between two elements, in addition to choices between several elements.

closing tag: XML elements that contain content must begin with an opening tag and end with a closing tag. XML syntax for a closing tag is `</element-name>`, where `element-name` is a placeholder for the element's name.

CML (Chemical Markup Language): An XML language with specific extensions for describing molecules and compounds.

comment: An SGML markup construct that permits authors to insert documentation, notes, and remarks into documents that are ignored when an XML document is parsed or processed. Comments begin with the markup string `<!--` and end with the markup string `-->`.

complex type definition: In XML Schema, a definition of an element that can contain other elements and/or can contain attribute declarations.

compositor element: In XML Schema, a container for references to other element declarations.

content identifier: A token that can be used to uniquely identify any piece of data or content.

content model: Defines the order in which components (usually, child elements but also datatypes such as `#PCDATA` or `#CDATA`) may or must appear within an XML document.

CSS (Cascading Style Sheets): A method of markup that allows Web developers to define how certain HTML, DHTML, or XML structural elements, such as paragraphs and headings, should be displayed using style rules instead of additional markup. The versions of CSS are CSS1, CSS2, and CSS3, with CSS2 being the most recent recommendation and CSS3 under development (as of February 2002).

data intensive: Describes text content that includes many additional constraints, such as patterns of content.

datatype declaration: In XML Schema, markup that tells the processor the valid format for the content of an XML Schema element or attribute.

declaration: In programming languages (and metalanguages such as SGML DTDs and XML Schema documents), a declaration is a way to identify some kind of variable or data structure, and to associate a specific name with one or more specific attributes to indicate what kind of value or values should be associated with that name. In DTDs, the `ELEMENT` declaration is associated with a specific name, and other characteristics, to identify and describe valid document components.

DocBook: A heavy-duty DTD designed and implemented by HaL Computer Systems and O'Reilly & Associates. DocBook is used for authoring books, articles, and manuals, particularly those of a technical nature.

document element: See *root element.*

document prolog: The portion of an XML document or DTD that occurs at its very beginning, and defines the document's content, and may reference external and/or internal DTDs, XML Schemas, style sheets, namespaces, and other sources for context or definitions for content.

document type declaration: A declaration that tells the processor where a DTD is located that may also contain additional new or custom declarations for the particular document in which it appears. Also known as a DOCTYPE declaration.

DOM (Document Object Model): A platform- and language-neutral programming interface that allows programs and scripts to access and update the content, structure, and style of documents in a standard way.

DOS (Disk Operating System): The original PC operating system, first introduced in 1982. DOS has been largely supplanted by Microsoft Windows on most desktops.

DSSSL (Document Style Semantics and Specification Language): A superset of XSL. DSSSL is a document style language used primarily with SGML files.

DTD (Document Type Definition): A statement of rules that specifies which elements (that define markup tags) and attributes (that define values associated with specific tags) are allowed in your documents.

e-commerce (electronic commerce): The exchange of money for goods and services between businesses, or between businesses and consumers, across the Internet or another public network.

EDI (Electronic Data Interchange): A standard for the electronic exchange of basic business information.

element: A named section of a document that may be either the document root or some child element that is normally defined by start- and end-tags that enclose document content, or an empty tag that includes no content. In the bean burrito DTD and Schema, `Recipes` is the root element and `Recipe` is the element within which individual recipes may be defined.

element content model: A way to include a specification regarding children in element declarations. For example, you can specify that an element may contain only child elements.

element declaration: In XML Schema and DTDs, markup that defines the name of an element and its properties, including what child elements the element may include.

element type: A specific — or named — element defined within an SGML DTD or an XML Schema, such as Recipe or Title.

element type declaration: Provides a description of an element type and its content within the DTD.

empty element: An element used in markup languages that does not require a separate closing tag. In XML, an empty element is identified with a slash (/) before the closing greater than sign (>), as in the <br/> element used in HTML and XHTML. When expressed as markup, an empty element may also be called an empty tag.

entity: A named object in an SGML DTD that represents a string of characters; thus the entity &Addr; could stand for "2207 Klattenhoff Drive, Austin, TX, 78728-5480". Entities provide useful shorthand when they're used to represent strings (like the preceding address) that appear in multiple or numerous locations in a document.

entity declaration: Defines a named set of text information that can be referenced by its name within a document or DTD. As the document or DTD is processed, every time the entity name is encountered, it's replaced by the set of information associated with that name. Thus, it provides useful shorthand for text that appears repeatedly in a document or DTD.

external parameter entity references: A string of characters that refers to information that appears in a separate file from the DTD or document prolog in which it appears.

external subset: A portion of a DTD that's stored in an external file. Also called an *external DTD* or an *external DTD subset*. Not all DTDs have external subsets, but any XML document or DTD that references another DTD does have an external subset.

FAQ (Frequently Asked Questions): A collection of questions and answers related to a specific topic. FAQs are most commonly found on Internet newsgroups.

formatting object: In XSL, a piece of a document (which may be a single document element, or a parent element and its various children) to which some particular formatting operation is applied. Thus, the children elements of the CookingInstructions element, Cinst, might be associated with a formatting object that produced a numbered or bulleted list when processed.

freeware: Software available for use at no charge.

FTP (File Transfer Protocol): An Internet file-transfer service based on TCP/IP protocols. FTP provides a way to copy files to and from FTP servers elsewhere on a network.

GedML (Genealogical Markup Language): An XML language used to describe genealogical data.

general entity: An entity created in a DTD but used in an XML document; this differs from an internal entity, which is defined in a DTD and used only in that DTD (not in documents based on that DTD).

GUI (Graphical User Interface): As opposed to the plain text of a DOS command line, a computer interface designed for users to use a mouse (or trackball) to interact with (by clicking) graphics, windows, and menus to get information.

HTML (HyperText Markup Language): One of the document-description markup languages used to create Web pages.

hypertext: A way of linking document locations, so that clicking a particular hypertext element takes the user's browser from one document to another document.

inheritance: The result of an element (a child or sibling) having taken on the characteristics assigned to a higher level element (parent).

inline style: A style rule that appears within the same XML document that contains the element to which the rule applies. This might involve writing XSLT instructions or CSS directives in a document prolog as a separate text block.

internal entity: In DTDs, an entity that contains the definition for its content (or substitution value) directly within the declaration itself, instead of referring to such content within some other, external file.

internal subset: The portion of the DTD that appears within the document. Also called an *internal DTD subset* or *internal DTD*. Not all DTDs include an internal subset; those that refer only to external DTDs may properly be said to contain no internal subset.

intranet: A private network within a company or organization that uses the same protocols as the Internet, but that can't be accessed by Internet users.

ISO (International Organization for Standardization): The most popular computing- and communication-standards organization. It is comprised of standards bodies, such as ANSI, IEEE, EIA/TIA, CCITT, and so forth, from all over the world.

ISO-Latin-1: Also known as ISO 8859-1 (the numeric equivalent), ISO-Latin-1 is the default character set for HTML and XHTML; modern XML implementations are more likely to use the ISO 10646 character set, also known as Unicode, but can also use ISO-Latin-1 (where Web browsers may be involved, this can help avoid potential display difficulties).

Java: An object-oriented programming language used for Web application development. It was created by Sun Microsystems.

JavaScript: An inline scripting language often used with HTML or XHTML (and only infrequently with XML) to add dynamic behaviors or interactive capabilities to Web pages and related documents.

linking element: An element that contains a hyperlink. In HTML `img` and `a` elements are examples of linking elements. In XLink, `simple` elements are examples of linking elements.

locator: Data that identifies a resource to which a link may be made using some kind of linking elements; such resources may include documents, special display formats (such as Adobe's Portable Document Format, or PDF), or binary files (graphical images, executable files, and so forth).

macro: A text or code script that performs an action when called, usually used to automate repetitive activities, such as combinations of keystrokes, a series of mouse-click sequences, or both.

MathML (Mathematical Markup Language): An XML language that provides a way of representing mathematical and scientific content on the Web, especially where complex formulas or arcane notation are used.

metadata: Within a document, specially defined data elements that describe the document's structure, content, or rendering, or that use external references to describe these features of the document. (Metadata literally means data about data.)

metalanguage: A language used to communicate information about language itself; many experts consider both SGML and XML to be metalanguages because they are used to define other markup languages, such as HTML and XSL.

MIME (Multipurpose Internet Mail Extension): Extensions that allow e-mail messages to carry multiple types of data (such as binary, audio, video, and graphics) as attachments. MIME types are also used to identify document types during transfers over the Internet. XML documents are `text/xml` or `application/xml`.

mixed content: A type of content model that permits XML elements or child elements to contain character data.

MSXML (Microsoft XML): The Microsoft Internet Explorer XML parser.

multimedia presentation: A presentation that involves two or more forms of media (text, audio, and video, for example).

namespace: See *XML namespace*.

node: Used in XML to denote a piece of a document's tree structure, as generated when the document is parsed or processed (as according to the Document Object Model [DOM] or some other processing model).

notation declaration: Associates a notation name with information that can help find an interpreter of information described by the notation. Thus, to permit an external program to handle some kind of multimedia format in an XML file, a notation could be defined to associate the file extension .mov with some kind of multimedia player.

numeric entity: A string of numbers that represents a character. These are identified by an ampersand followed by a pound sign (#). For example, < and È show a string of numbers (60 and 200) that stand for characters (< and È). More commonly called *character entities*.

object: A unit of meaning or value in a programming or markup language, where objects have names and associated values called properties or attributes. Objects are like maps or descriptions of specific sets of values, called object instances, in that they define a name and structure for information, but don't define specific sets of values that follow such definitions. Only object instances contain actual values, and have some correspondence to "real data." Objects are also associated with specific operations or transformations called methods that create, manipulate, or destroy specific object instances.

object-oriented programming: A method of programming in which data is defined in terms of objects, and where objects may be acted upon by operations called methods. In contrast to other programming techniques (such as procedural programming, where code acts directly upon data values and variables), objects are much more self-describing in terms of their attributes or properties and in terms of the methods that apply to them. In many ways, XML is an object-oriented markup technology.

occurrence indicator: A symbol, such as ?, *, and +, that's included in a DTD element declaration to further provide structural guidance about how elements are to be applied within a document. For example, an occurrence indicator may say how many times a portion of a content model may appear within a document.

OFX (Open Financial Exchange): A specification that provides a standard way of describing financial data and transactions in a way that banks, Web protocols, and your personal financial software can understand.

operating system: The underlying program that enables computer-system hardware to run other applications. Macintosh, Windows, UNIX, and DOS are common operating systems.

Packaging/Extensions layer: In Web services, a data management or handling layer primarily concerned with establishing, managing, securing, and packaging information for exchange between service consumers and producers. See Chapter 21 for more information about the Web services model.

parameter entity: An entity created and used within a DTD, where the value associated with that entity occurs in an external file or definition in a way that's easy to change. The value of this entity may then be used to alter or guide the processing of the document, so that one value might cause the document to be processed for print output, and another value might the document to be displayed on a screen.

parent: In a content model, an element that contains one or more other elements is called a parent or parent element; the contained elements are called children or child elements.

parsed character data: Also called PCDATA, this is text that the document processor actually looks at.

PDF (Portable Document Format): A graphics file format created by Adobe Acrobat. To view a PDF file, you must download Adobe Acrobat Reader or have access to another Adobe application, such as PageMaker or PhotoShop.

POST method: A means by which users return information to a Web server using an HTML form. Posted data returns to the server as directed by a CGI script. Often, such data is analyzed or processed in some way by an application that then returns a new Web page, often generated on-the-fly, to the user's browser.

processing instruction: Similar to the prolog, a special directive in an XML document that provides a way to send instructions to computer programs or applications, not humans.

processor (also XML processor): A special software program that knows how to read, interpret, and internalize the structure and contents of an XML document. Any time that a program reads and handles an XML document, an XML processor is involved in that activity.

property: A named value associated with a data object; for XML elements, attributes play the same role that properties play for objects.

pull technology: Technology that enables users to retrieve information from a Web server (using a Web browser); servers that offer news or entertainment channels may be accessed by configuring Web browsers to read and update information at regular intervals ("pulling" those updates from the server). Client initiation of activity represents pull technology; server initiation of activity is what represents push technology, as noted in the following definition.

push technology: Technology that initiates delivery of material from a server to a properly equipped client (Web browser). Some kinds of software update services (such as Windows Update as implemented in Microsoft Windows XP Professional) automatically deliver updates to registered clients as soon as they become available. Also called *push publishing*.

resource: Any resource that can be retrieved over the Internet; for example, a document, image, sound file, or even a list generated automatically in response to a query.

restriction constraint: In XML Schema, a limit applied to a built-in datatype that can be narrowed as needed.

root element: In XML, a single top-level tag; a created element that is the equivalent of the `html` element in HTML. Also called a *document element*.

schema: In general, a pattern that represents the data's model and defines the elements (or objects), their attributes, and the relationships between the different elements. A schema can also be a language written in XML that defines the rules for the structure and the content of an XML document.

scripting: A simple method for including programming or processing instructions within a Web page, usually to facilitate user interaction or changing displays or behavior. See *JavaScript*.

scripting language: A specialized language used to create sequences of simple instructions that, when inserted into a Web page, control various elements of the page, such as the user interface, styles, and HTML markup. JavaScript and VBScript are the primary scripting languages.

selector: In CSS, the part of a style rule that identifies the element (or elements) to which that rule applies.

semantics: The science of describing what words mean; it's the opposite of syntax. In XML, semantics are conveyed in various ways: through element names, content models, and through value restrictions and occurrence indicators.

SGML (Standard Generalized Markup Language): A metalanguage used to construct markup languages, such as HTML and XML.

SGML declaration: A declaration that acts separately from a DTD to provide specific instructions to an SGML parser.

SGML parser: A text-handling program that interprets SGML markup in a document and builds a model of the document's structure and contents. Normally, an SGML parser then passes that model to some other program for further action, so that it may be edited, displayed, or archived.

sibling (also **sibling element**): Two document elements that are both child elements of the same parent element are sibling elements to one another. Thus, in our recipe markup language, `CookingInstructions` and `ServingInstructions` are siblings, and share the same parent, `Recipe`.

simple type definition: In XML Schema, a definition of an element that can contain only text; by contrast, complex type definitions can contain simple types, fixed values, and even parameters.

SMIL (Synchronized Multimedia Integration Language): An XML language that allows the integration of a collection of multimedia objects that follow a schedule, which is laid out by the developer.

SQL: Either of two database-management programming languages from Sybase and Microsoft.

SQL server: A database server that uses the Structured Query Language (SQL) to accept requests for data access.

style rule: A rule in an XML document that identifies a style pattern specifies an action that must be applied when the pattern is found. Such rules can result from the application of CSS, or by the application of XSL.

style sheet: A file that holds the layout settings for a certain category of a document. Style sheets, like templates, contain settings for formatting features such as headers and footers, tabs, margins, fonts, columns, and more.

substitution group: In XML Schema, this is a technique that allows you to define one element that may be substituted for one or more other elements of the same type (or derived from the same type).

syntax: The rules that govern the construction of intelligible markup language documents or markup fragments, similar to the grammar rules used in spoken languages, such as English.

tag: In markup languages, the term tag refers to the ways in which document elements appear within documents. They generally take one or two of the following forms: `<element-name/>` (a single form for empty elements), or `<element-name>` and `</element-name>` (opening and closing forms for elements that contain content).

TCP/IP (Transmission Control Protocol/Internet Protocol): The family of formal rules and formats for networked communications, called protocols, used on the Internet. This family of protocols (also known as a protocol suite) takes its name from two of its most important members: the Internet Protocol (IP) used to carry individuals packages of data from a sender to a receiver, and the Transmission Control Protocol (TCP) used to provide reliable transport of messages between a sender and a receiver.

template: The instructions in an XSLT style sheet that control how an element and its content should be converted. A template identifies which element in a document should be changed and then specifies how the element should be changed.

text intensive: Content that does not need to be in any specific format other than text strings.

Transport layer: In Web services, a layer that acts like the highway that carries messages from senders to receivers across the Internet. For Web services, the most commonly used protocol to provide this capability is the HyperText Transfer Protocol (HTTP).

traversal: The result of clicking a link. By clicking a link, a Web browser *traverses* from one resource to another.

tree: A diagram of an XML document that is constructed as the document is processed with a structure that corresponds to the order of and relationships among the elements that the XML document contains. The general name for such diagrams is a *parse tree;* for XML documents, that name may be used, or it may also be called the *document tree*. This diagram may be queried, navigated, or manipulated as a way of acting upon the contents and structure of the related document to which the diagram corresponds.

Unicode character set: A 16-bit character encoding scheme, defined in ISO/IED 10646, which encompasses standard Roman and Greek alphabets, plus mathematical symbols, special punctuation, and non-Roman alphabets including Hebrew, Chinese, Arabic, Hangul, and other ideographic character sets.

UNIX: One of the most powerful multiuser operating systems around; designed by a hacker in 1969 as an interactive time-sharing operating system to play games on.

URI (Uniform Resource Identifier): A character string that identifies the type and location of an Internet resource.

valid: When an XML document adheres to a DTD or schema.

validating parser: A software utility that compares an XML document with a declared DTD or XML Schema; if the document includes no violations of the rules that a document description states, that document is said to be valid. But if errors or violations are detected, that document is said to be invalid.

W3C (World Wide Web Consortium): An organization that develops standards for the Web (and the Internet), including markup languages, communication protocols, and XML applications too numerous to mention.

Web service: A tool or capability that can be accessed through the Web, rather than being run locally on a desktop. Such services may not even require a Web browser (but rather, may draw on services access capabilities inherent to other programs).

well-formed document: An XML document that adheres to XML's syntax rules.

white space: The areas in a document where text or graphics don't appear; the blank part of a page.

WIDL (Web Interface Definition Language): An object-oriented, SGML-based markup language that helps designers create powerful, intuitive, Web-based user interfaces.

WYSIWYG (What You See Is What You Get) interface: Any interface or application that allows users to enter and see information as it will appear in the final document, as opposed to an interface or application that shows markup or other content obscuring a document's appearance.

XHTML (eXtensible HyperText Markup Language): The reformulation of HTML 4.0 as an application of XML 1.0.

XLink (XML Linking Language): An XML language that provides a simple set of instructions to describe the links among objects.

XML (eXtensible Markup Language): A system for defining, validating, and sharing document formats so that they are well formed.

XML declaration: The markup at the very beginning of an XML document that specifies which version of XML the document is written in as well as other information. (As of this writing, declarations must refer to XML 1.0 because that's the only version available.)

XML entity: A string of characters that lets a text viewer (such as a browser) display a symbol, but prevents the viewer from interpreting the symbol as markup. An entity often enables a viewer to represent a larger range of characters than might otherwise be possible, yet keep character sets small.

XML namespace: A unique identifier (attached through a prefix) that links an XML markup element to a specific DTD or schema. For example, in XML Schema, you add the prefix xsd or xs to an XML Schema element to indicate that it belongs to that namespace: `<xsd:element name="Recipes">`.

XML notation: A form of XML markup designed to accomplish some specific objective; examples include the mathematical and chemical notations supported by MathML and CML (both of which are XML applications), respectively.

XML Schema: A W3C language that defines the rules for the structure and the content of an XML document. The resulting document specifies the overall structure of an XML document and identifies all the components of the XML document, as well as how they can be validly used.

XML Schema document: A document written in the XML Schema language, according to rules defined by the Worldwide Web Consortium (W3C).

XPath: An XML language that describes directions for how to get from one place in an XML document to another. XPath is used by XSLT and XPointer.

XPointer: An XML application that provides a method for accessing specific locations within a document, even though you may not have edit privileges for that document.

XSL (eXtensible Stylesheet Language): An XML language that defines the specification for an XML document's presentation and appearance.

XSL-FO (XSL formatting objects): Defines how XML documents should be displayed or converted into various forms of output, such as the Adobe Acrobat portable document format (PDF).

XSLT (XSL Transformations): An XSL conversion tool that provides a set of rules to convert documents described by one set of elements to documents described by another set of elements.

Index